The Free Economy and the Strong State

The Politics of Thatcherism

Andrew Gamble

D0096851

Duke University Press
Durham 1988

First published 1988

Published in the U.S.A. by
DUKE UNIVERSITY PRESS
Durham, N. Carolina
and in Great Britain by
MACMILLAN EDUCATION LTD
Houndmills, Basingstoke, Hampshire RG21 2XS

Printed in Great Britain

Library of Congress Cataloging-in-Publication Data
Gamble Andrew,
The free economy and the strong state.
Bibliography: p.
Includes index
1. Great Britain—Politics and government—1979—
2. Great Britain—Economic policy—1945–
I. Title.
JN231.G35   1988   320.941   88–11828
ISBN 0–8223–0865–7
ISBN 0–8223–0890—8 (pbk.)

'The part played in history by individuals, which was overemphasised by Carlyle, and is still exaggerated in our day by his reactionary disciples, tends, on the other hand, to be unduly minimised by those who believe themselves to have discovered the laws of sociological change. I do not believe that, if Bismarck had died in infancy, the history of Europe during the past seventy years would have been at all closely similar to what it has been.' — **Bertrand Russell** (1934)

'The Old Testament prophets did not say "Brothers I want a consensus". They said: "This is my faith, this is what I passionately believe. If you believe it too, then come with me."' — **Margaret Thatcher** (1979)

'I don't at all mind having enemies. But not too many at the same time please.' — **Margaret Thatcher** (1981)

Contents

vii

Preface

This book is a continuation of a study of postwar Conservatism which began with *The Conservative Nation* published in 1974. Its more immediate origins lie in an article entitled 'The Free Economy and the Strong State' which appeared in *Socialist Register* in 1979. It also draws freely on the articles I have contributed to a number of journals in recent years, particularly *Marxism Today*, in which I have attempted to analyse Thatcherism and the policies of the Thatcher Government. Re-reading those articles and some of the confident judgements and assertions contained within them, and comparing them with what has happened since, has made me aware that there are few things more difficult than trying to make sense of contemporary political events and the direction in which they are moving. It is a belief that the attempt still needs to be made that is the primary motivation for this more extended study.

The book is organised in the following way. Chapter 1 analyses the new politics which emerged in the 1970s in response to the world recession, the exhaustion of Fordism as a regime of accumulation, and the breakdown of American hegemony. Thatcherism was one expression of this new politics, but acquired its distinctive characteristics through the exceptional and deep-seated crisis of state authority that developed in Britain in the mid-1970s. Different aspects of Thatcherism as a new hegemonic project are then explored in subsequent chapters.

The Thatcherite project seeks to promote a free economy and a strong state, and the meaning of these terms is explored in Chapter 2, through an examination of the ideas and doctrines of the New Right, and its two main strands – identified here simply as the conservative New Right and the liberal New Right.

Chapter 3 seeks to place the rise of Thatcherism in the context of postwar British politics, and highlights a number of episodes and issues which are significant for understanding the context in which Margaret Thatcher became Leader of the Conservative party and how Thatcherism first began to emerge during her period as Leader of the Opposition.

Chapter 4 reviews the record of the Thatcher Government, the main events, policies, and achievements of its first eight years. It asks how radical and successful the Thatcher Government has proved in the light of its own manifesto commitments in 1979.

Chapter 5 examines the debates on the legitimacy of Thatcherism as a representative of the Conservative tradition, and probes the question: Is Thatcherism Conservatism? Its character as statecraft rather than ideology is strongly emphasised.

Chapter 6 analyses the debates on Thatcherism as a hegemonic project, by discussing the thesis of authoritarian populism and the criticisms that have been made of this from class politics, feminist, and state policy perspectives.

Chapter 7 provides a summary of the main points and the themes of the book, and an analysis of Thatcherism in terms of its success in managing the different requirements of the politics of support and the politics of power. It discusses the new policy agenda which the Thatcher Government has created and whether the Government has succeeded in its primary objective, to turn Britain round and reverse the long decline.

I have incurred many debts in writing this book. I should particularly like to thank Martin Jacques for the exceptional intellectual and editorial stimulus he has provided during the last eight years; Ralph Miliband for commissioning and commenting on the original article that suggested the theme of this book; Steven Kennedy, Gillian Peele and a Macmillan reviewer for reading and criticising a first draft; friends, colleagues and students at Sheffield, with whom I have discussed the themes of this book. Special thanks for their help and stimulus in different ways and at different times are due to Henry Drucker, Patrick Dunleavy, Henk Overbeek, Stuart Hall, Bill Schwarz, Bob Jessop, Teddy Brett, Colin Leys, David Baker, Ruth Levitas, David Marquand, Bea Campbell, Zig Layton-Henry, John Ross, Chris Rodway, David Coates, Anthony Arblaster, Steve Ludlam, John Solomos, Bill Jordan, Tessa ten Tusscher, Chusichi Tsusuki, Stuart Walkland, Jack Grainger, Paul Ginsborg, Neil Lyndon, Hugo Radice, Hans Kastendiek, Raymond Plant, Mick Cox and TSC.

ANDREW GAMBLE

Spring 1988

1
A crisis of hegemony

The new politics

During the 1980s a new politics became established in the West. There were different national variants but many common themes. In the 1980s its most celebrated exponents were the governments of Margaret Thatcher in Britain and Ronald Reagan in the United States. The new politics came to be thought of primarily as a new conservative politics.

It was not, however, confined to the Right. The opportunity and the necessity for new policies, new projects, new purposes and new doctrines were created by the breakdown of hegemony at both international and national levels during the 1970s. At the international level the breakdown occurred when the undisputed economic supremacy which the United States had enjoyed since the 1940s disappeared, and the world economy was plunged once more into recession. At the national level it occurred when the policies and institutions of postwar social democracy began to be discredited. The authority of the social democratic state in the fields of citizenship, representation and economic management was undermined.

The loss of hegemony did not occur suddenly. It was a long-drawn-out process. Hegemony exists when the political leadership of a group or a nation is exercised with minimal dispute and resistance. Constant work and struggle is required to achieve and to maintain it, for no hegemony is ever complete, and many attempts to establish hegemony are never realised. That is why hegemonic projects are encountered much more frequently than hegemony itself.

1

The radical right programmes of both Thatcher and Reagan were responses to the breakdown of authority and stability in the world system and in national politics. From the outset they offered to restore strong national and international leadership on a new basis. They planned to restore the vigour of British and American capitalism through a new accumulation strategy; they planned to rebuild the system of alliances and defences of the West; they planned to change the balance between state and society and reinvigorate their national cultures.

These were new hegemonic projects which openly repudiated the older hegemonic projects of British social democracy and American welfarism. Both were seen as having failed. They were rejected as sets of institutions and policies for managing advanced industrial societies and also as models of the kind of good society political activity should be seeking to create.

The breakdown of hegemony forced a new policy agenda on governments. As policies began to change so new political doctrines emerged to justify the new measures and to suggest how they might be extended. But the changes in political institutions and modes of political organisation that the new policies often required occurred much more slowly. The new doctrines and political rhetoric ran far in advance of them.

The new politics developed in response to the events and crises of the 1970s. It did not have a single focus or a single driving force. The various crises of state authority on which it fastened had developed separately and although there were some interrelationships there was at no time a single problem to which all the others could be reduced. As structures of authority weakened so the task of governing became more intractable. But at the same time it created new space for more active and creative political leadership, the forging of new coalitions of voters and interests, the framing of new policies, the articulation of new ideologies and doctrines, in short the construction of new hegemonic projects.

The opportunity for challenging the policies enshrined in the 'Great Society' programme of the United States or Britain's welfare state arose out of events during the 1970s that changed the parameters and assumptions of national politics. The relative political stability and prosperity of the advanced capitalist world that had been painfully established after the years of world war and postwar reconstruction gave way to renewed turbulence, domestic conflict and international tensions.

What all states faced in the 1970s was a growth in the number of problems that did not seem capable of being solved by ordinary political means. The space for asserting national sovereignty was shrinking; economic management was increasingly unsuccessful; the structures for mobilising consent for national policies were no longer adequate; and the bases of social order and national identity were under threat. The inability of governments to find solutions weakened political authority and generated a deep malaise and pessimism about the possibility of rational management of public policy. Governments appeared weak and indecisive.

None of these problems were new. All had figured in domestic political argument from at least the mid-1960s onwards. But what changed in the 1970s was appreciation of their scale. The trigger for this was the collapse of fixed exchange rates in 1971/2 followed by the quadrupling of the oil price in 1973 and the generalised world recession which then ensued. The collapse of currency stability and the rise in oil prices did not cause the recession but such events drew attention to the increasingly precarious foundations of western prosperity, since cheap energy and stable money had been two of the key factors in postwar expansion. The long boom was now definitely over and a period of much slower growth lay ahead. Following the acceleration of inflation after 1971 and the steep rise in unemployment after 1973 it was recognised that managing the economy successfully was going to be much more difficult than in the previous two decades.

The slowdown in growth and the breakdown of fixed exchange rates undermined the policy regimes that had developed in the period of prosperity. Controlling inflation assumed a higher priority than maintaining full employment; public expenditure programmes no longer seemed affordable and were reined back; and strict curbs on wages and internal demand were applied.

All governments in the mid-1970s were forced to adopt

similar crisis packages to deal with the problem of inflation and the disappearance of growth. At first the disappearance of growth was regarded as temporary and an early resumption was anticipated. But it soon became clear that the shocks of the early 1970s were not accidents but signalled deep and permanent changes in the political and economic organisation of the world economy. Waiting for the storm to pass was no longer enough. The world outside was never going to be quite the same again.

The world system

The single most important reason for the development of a new politics was the shift in the political and economic balance of the world system. This had two main features: the exhaustion of the old regime of accumulation known as Fordism, and the decline in the position of the United States. The emergence of an increasingly interdependent world economy over a period of several centuries has brought an unprecedented enlargement of production, population, trade and communications. But political authority within this relatively unified world economy has remained fragmented between a large (and increasing) number of states. This modern world economy has never experienced rule from a single centre, and has owed its dynamism to the permanent competition and occasional armed conflict between states as they seek to promote particular national interests within the framework of international cooperation.[1]

The world system follows no fixed cycle or pattern of development. Every succeeding phase brings new possibilities and novel features. Periods of relative stability within the world system have been associated firstly with the establishment and diffusion of a major new technology capable of revolutionising all the major branches of production, and secondly with the emergence of one state which enjoys such undisputed industrial, commercial, and financial supremacy that it can exercise hegemony. For a time it can act as though it were a world state, a central authority laying down rules and providing services for the world economy.

Both these conditions were realised during the period of exceptional stability and prosperity experienced during the 1950s and 1960s: the diffusion of technologies based on electric motors into new sectors, particularly consumer goods, and the undisputed hegemonic position of the United States.[2]

During the years of prosperity and rapid expansion of national economies the foreign economic policy of the leading capitalist powers settled into a pattern. The intense debates during the postwar reconstruction period gave way at the end of the 1950s to a (belated) acceptance of the agreements made at Bretton Woods. Currencies were made convertible, trade became multilateral, exchange rates were fixed, and progress towards reduction of tariffs through successive rounds of negotiation through the General Agreement on Tariffs and Trade (GATT) were endorsed. The International Monetary Fund (IMF) and the World Bank were confirmed as the principal international agencies charged with policing and lubricating the system.[3]

Fordism

The ultimate acceptance of a regime of multilateral trade and payments was made possible by the huge expansion of output and markets based on the full development of the technologies and methods of industrial organisation known as Fordism.[4] The Fordist regime of accumulation was based on assembly-line mass production, and the gradual elimination of skilled workers through the systematic incorporation of their skills into the production process using the techniques of scientific management.

Mass production entailed mass consumption which had to be achieved either through exports or through the enlargement of the domestic market. The latter was achieved through new measures of national economic management designed to maintain high and stable levels of demand, and through the emergence of collective bargaining arrangements which ensured that wages were high in the leading sectors and that wage increases matched increases in productivity and prices.

There was nothing inevitable about the establishment of

such a regime of accumulation. The political conditions for it had first to be created. The internal political battles for the acceptance of interventionist state policies were prolonged, and the trade unions' ability to win a strong bargaining position in the mass production industries was not conceded without a struggle.

There was inevitably a wide variation in how far and when these conditions were realised in different countries. But as the industrial methods of Fordism became established, they helped the emergence of social democratic regimes. Social democracy, in its different national variants, subsequently allowed the full logic of Fordism to unfold. Organised labour was successfully incorporated as a support for the modern industrial order and there followed an era of exceptional growth in output, living standards and the public sector, throughout the advanced capitalist countries.

The world recession

As the world system has developed, states have often experienced difficulty in maintaining their autonomy in the face of changing patterns in world trade and production and in political, military and economic competition from other states. This is particularly acute when a period of relative political stability and economic prosperity gives way to a period of political conflict and economic uncertainty.

The breakdown of international hegemony and the emergence of a crisis of accumulation in the world economy forces all national governments to reconsider the role of their countries within the world system. They must rethink what their essential national interests are and adapt policies accordingly. The adequacy of national accumulation strategies in respect of foreign economic policy, stabilisation policy and industrial policy has to be reassessed in the light of changing world circumstances. Such rethinking can provoke lively internal debate and major social and political conflicts. The merits of greater autonomy versus greater dependence, of protectionism against free trade, of currency blocs against freely convertible currencies, of controlling inflation against maintaining employment, of markets against planning, as well as questions of military and diplomatic alliances all come under examination.

This was the context of the new politics of the 1970s. The breakdown of the hegemony exercised by the United States and the relative exhaustion of profitable investment opportunities threw the Fordist regime of accumulation into turmoil. The abrupt slowing down of economic growth in the mid-1970s reopened numerous questions that had been thought settled. The foundations of postwar prosperity were put in doubt. The increase in interdependence since 1945 had initially increased rather than diminished the authority of governments because of the growth in the pool of resources available to be distributed through market and political mechanisms. When the pool stopped growing, and even began contracting, national governments struggled to retain their authority.

The advent of the recession was triggered by the deflationary measures which many countries adopted to contain the upsurge in inflation in 1973/4 and to reduce their non-oil imports so as to protect their balance of payments.[5] The check to demand and confidence dramatically exposed the obsolescence of many established industries. Investment opportunities in many fields had become exhausted because markets were saturated and in many industries it was difficult to make any further gains in productivity with the existing technology. A huge shake-out of labour began plunging national economies into the kind of mass unemployment that had not been experienced since the 1930s.

It soon became clear that a major restructuring of the world economy would have to be carried through, involving the liquidation of a huge amount of capacity, the disappearance of a large part of existing employment, and the introduction of new technological systems. The deployment of new technology was aimed at preserving the competitiveness of some parts of national and international capital. It was not itself the direct cause of the unemployment but what it underlined was that previous levels of employment in those industries would never return. New levels of productivity and new standards of competition had been established which all companies and industries in the future would have to match.

Right at the centre of the new politics has been the question of how this process of restructuring which has been forced upon every national economy is to be handled. Who is to bear the costs of change? What elements of the old institutions and programmes can be rescued? What can be adapted to meet the new circumstances? For many national economies faced with the closure of steel industries, coal-mines, and car plants the process of restructuring has often appeared as a process of de-industrialisation, the disappearance of their principal industries amidst growing penetration of the home markets by foreign imports, the inexorable increase in their dole queues and pressure on their public finances.[6] The growth of new technologies such as microelectronics has promoted very rapid growth in a few new sectors and fundamental reorganisation in all others. A new regime of accumulation based on flexible specialisation in patterns of employment and corporate organisation, has begun to emerge.[7]

All this would be hard enough to handle within a single political system. But its management is enormously complicated by the fact that the redistribution of labour between skills and occupation is taking place not only within national economies but between them. The restructuring involves some major shifts in the international division of labour. The division of labour that became established in the 1950s involved exchange of manufactures and primary products between advanced capitalist states and third-world countries, and an increasing exchange of manufactures between the developed states themselves. In the 1970s new patterns in the world division of labour began to emerge, spurred on by the rapid development of certain third-world states, and by the impact of the oil revenues that now accrued to the oil producing states.[8]

The impact of the recession has been very uneven both within states and across the world economy. Just as there are regions and industries within national economies such as the Sunbelt of the United States and the South East of England which have continued to grow throughout the recession, so there are regions of the world economy whose growth has not been constrained by what has been happening elsewhere. The worst effects of the slow-down have been borne by the older industrial heartlands of Western Europe and the North-East of the United States and by many areas of the third world, particularly those dependent on the export of particular commodities. The beneficiaries are those regions and economies bordering the Pacific. This looks set to be the centre of world accumulation in the next phase of expansion.

The decline of the United States

Alongside the disruption of Fordism as a viable regime of accumulation a second crucial change which has shaped the new politics is the weakened position of the United States. The inability of the United States in the 1970s to exercise undisputed leadership was a result of the long-term decline in its relative economic strength. This change influenced the calculations made by all states.

The period of undisputed American hegemony over the world system was relatively short – 1945 to 1973. So successful was the reconstruction of the economies of Germany and Japan and so rapid the pace of expansion in the 1950s and 1960s that the productivity gap between Japan, the European Community and the United States had narrowed and in some cases disappeared by 1970. The costs of overseas investment by American firms and the world-wide military forces which America maintained after 1941 could initially be funded with ease in a world hungry for dollars, but in time they created a chronic balance of payments deficit which undermined the dollar and with it the stability of the international monetary system. The collapse of the gold exchange standard in 1971 brought an end to the system of fixed exchange rates and removed an important barrier to rapid inflation. No new means of restoring long-term stability to the currency markets was devised in the 1970s or the 1980s, nor was much progress made towards the solution of common problems such as co-ordinating policies of national economic management or reducing third-world debt.[9]

Yet despite the pressure towards a fissuring of the world economy into protectionist blocs, as had happened in the

1930s, the openness of the western economy was largely preserved, and a plunge into depression was avoided during the 1970s and early 1980s, although at times the possibility came dangerously close. The reorganised political and economic system of western capitalism demonstrated enormous resilience and after the initial series of shocks confidence began to recover. This owed something to the new politics also. Many on both left and right welcomed the new political space which the recession created, as well as the possibilities for refashioning institutions and redesigning policies in radical ways.

The recessions after 1973 sharpened political conflict within and between states but did not shatter the commitment of national governing classes to the preservation of the system of economic interdependence and military alliances that had become so firmly established after 1945. The military position of the United States remained supreme. It was its hegemony in the economic field that had disappeared. The political fragmentation of the European Community and the unwillingness of Japan to exercise a political role commensurate to her new economic importance meant that there was no alternative to continued United States leadership, yet in many fields the United States refused to compromise in the pursuit of its national interests, and lacked the authority any longer to exercise leadership for the whole world system.

The economic divisions in the western bloc in the 1970s were overshadowed by the deterioration in relationships between the superpowers, and the beginning of the new cold war. But even here, as events during the Reagan presidency demonstrated, it was no longer always possible to mobilise the western powers behind a common foreign policy forged in Washington. The differences in interests and perceptions of the Soviet Union were now marked and subjected the Alliance to considerable strains.

With growing pressures towards isolationism in the United States itself the future of an Atlanticist foreign policy was thrown into doubt. The possibility of a more equal trilateral arrangement between the three main centres of the western world was canvassed, as was the possibility of neutrality and isolationism. After a period in which all these questions had seemed to be settled, the political agenda suddenly opened up. Politicians could dream again.

The crisis of social democracy

The crisis in the regime of accumulation and the shifts in the political organisation of the world system which took place in the 1970s were the fundamental changes which made a new politics possible and necessary. But the content of this new politics was often provided by local concerns, specific to the institutions and circumstances of particular countries. Nevertheless here too certain common themes can be seen. The institutions and policies of social democracy came under attack almost everywhere. The challenges were made through ideological debate as well as by new political programmes and movements. Many of these challenges began before the appearance of the global crisis of accumulation and hegemony. But they became much stronger once the political and economic foundations of the postwar order had been undermined.

Social democracy as a form of political regime has many variants but a common feature in postwar Europe was the existence of a democratic constitution under which all citizens enjoyed certain civil, political and social rights. Political participation was not restricted by property, birth, race or gender. Enfranchising the whole citizenry and allowing freedom of speech, association and assembly created powerful pressures for further extensions of rights and the remedying of abuses and disadvantages through government action.

This had been foreseen by those liberals and conservatives who had opposed extending the franchise. They had feared that at worst a democratic regime would allow the rich to be despoiled of all their possessions by the poor and at best that it would create steady pressure towards collectivism in public policy through increases in public spending programmes and general taxation. Whether or not socialist parties were elected into office all governments would be obliged under the pressure of a democratic electorate to adopt collectivist measures.[10]

Liberal democracies would be ineluctably transformed into social democracies.

The programmes most associated with social democratic regimes are programmes to combat unemployment and programmes to guarantee welfare by ensuring minimum standards of support for all citizens. Social democracy has been associated with a progressive enlargement of the public sector, whether measured by assets, spending, taxes or employment. The range of public responsibilities has been steadily expanded. The impulse behind such policies has been to mitigate the pressures towards inequality stemming from the way markets operate, although how far social democratic regimes have succeeded in practice in remedying inequality has been a matter of debate.[11]

What the existence of a social democratic regime ensures is not progress towards socialism or even greater equality in the final distribution of resources, but rather the mobilisation of pressure from below for state policies and programmes to correct extreme inequalities and disadvantage. Such pressures often coincided with pressures from above for state intervention to meet particular needs for the system as a whole which private initiative was unable or unwilling to supply.

The growing support for collectivism during the twentieth century, across the whole political spectrum, allowed accommodation to be reached eventually between established dominant interests and the interests of the new popular movements. In some countries social democratic regimes emerged out of the strength of the organised working class. In others they developed despite the weakness or absence of such movements. But in almost all cases they represented some form of accommodation between the demands for political and economic democracy from below and the needs of capital.

In this way stable political regimes, many of them explicitly social democratic, emerged in most advanced western capitalist states. A regime of accumulation based on Fordist principles of mass production and mass consumption only reached its full potential when political mechanisms to ensure a high and constant level of demand and to transfer many of the social costs of accumulation to public agencies were established. In many states governments also explicitly accepted responsibility for maintaining the legitimacy of the entire social order. Recognition on both left and right that such extensions in the range of responsibilities for government had become desirable and necessary greatly smoothed the path of internal accommodation and allowed a durable policy consensus over a wide range to be consolidated.

In many European countries the popular forces most identified with social democratic programmes were the parties and trade unions of the organised industrial working class. But collectivist measures in economic and social policy were also sponsored by many other political agencies. In states where the industrial working class was less strong and less organised many of the programmes and policies which elsewhere would be termed social democratic were still introduced.

One of the consequences of a social democratic regime has been the raising of expectations about entitlements and rights. The claiming of new rights and the defence of existing rights become an essential part of politics. Those groups denied rights or discriminated against have the opportunity to organise and mobilise to demand them. The ideal of universal participation makes it difficult to defend the exclusion of such groups.[12] Nevertheless powerful forces can mobilise to prevent it. The full development of social democracy is heavily constrained by the existence of divisions of race, gender and religion.

The extent to which the goals of social democracy were achieved varied greatly between states, but most social democrats continued to believe that the drift of policy was in their direction. This was all changed by the events of the 1970s, which saw the emergence of a pervasive crisis of social democracy. The authority of national governments was rapidly eroded, and the institutions and assumptions of social democracy came under sustained assault from both right and left. The impact was uneven. The states that were hit hardest were those whose economies were relatively weak.

The crisis of social democracy as a hegemonic project was precipitated by the exhaustion of the Fordist regime of accumulation and the new instabilities in the world system. The global crisis reinforced the challenges to the authority of the state that were already under way in three main areas; citizenship rights, representation and economic management.

Citizenship

The challenge to the social democratic concept of citizenship took the form of attempts to block the extension of equal civil, political, and social rights to all citizens. This attacked one of the fundamental ideas of the social democratic state. Demands for equal rights encountered resistance because they threatened some of the most entrenched relationships of power in society. The reason why such demands came to be raised was partly the working-out of the logic of social democracy and partly the impact on national economies of the global Fordism of the 1950s. The need for supplies of new labour led to large-scale migration from third-world to metropolitan countries and a major expansion in the employment of women. At the same time a capitalism based upon mass consumption facilitated the development of new leisure interests and life-styles, many of them incompatible with the maintenance of a traditional family structure and traditional sexual division of labour.[13]

The cultural explosion that took place in the 1960s created a powerful feminist challenge to the patriarchal family and to the continued subordination of women throughout society. It brought into question for the first time one of the assumptions of the postwar order – the nature of the family structure. This posed unwelcome questions for many social democrats in all parties, since to take the claims of the women's movement seriously would involve radical reform of both state and civil society.

Faced by this challenge most social democratic parties moved very slowly indeed, but the mere threat that they might act was sufficient to galvanise a movement in defence of the patriarchal family, focusing upon permissiveness, crime and education. The family was presented as under threat and its authority breaking down as a result of social democratic doctrines and policies which were undermining standards in schools and destroying the ethic of hard work, personal responsibility and abstinence.

Racial divisions have also contributed to the erosion of the social democratic hegemonic project in several countries. The large movement of migrant labour which played such an important part in the postwar boom introduced permanent ethnic minorities into a number of countries. Some, such as the United Kingdom, had previously had few ethnic divisions. A key political issue became the citizenship status of these workers and their dependants, whether they possessed full citizenship or were only 'guest workers' and therefore what rights they could claim when they encountered discrimination. Their demands were fiercely contested by anti-immigrant groups within the dominant white communities.

The threat to the patriarchal family and the white nation in the 1960s seemed to be expressed most openly once women's groups and black groups became active in pressing their demands for equal rights. The real threat came from processes central to the Fordist regime of accumulation. The conservative wing of the New Right, however, was not disposed to make the world economy a scapegoat. Social democracy was a far more tempting target. Social democratic politicians might not actively encourage the aspirations of either feminists or immigrants, but they were seen to be tolerant towards them. They conceded the case in principle, pleading expediency as the reason why faster progress could not be made. Many on the right concluded that the social democratic state now offered no protection against the forces that were attacking the patriarchal family and the white nation; indeed often its agencies seemed in alliance with those very forces.

In several countries the attack on social democracy first took shape through an emphasis on the politics of gender, race, national identity, and social and public order. The failure of social democratic administrations to keep order in the schools, to control immigration, to halt the rise in crime, and to protect the family fuelled growing discontent among vocal minorities.[14]

This erosion of the consensus on citizenship occurred before the dislocation in the world economy had damaged the engine of postwar prosperity and had discredited the techniques and many of the institutions and policies by means of which western capitalist societies had been managed. Once this occurred then the politics of race and the politics of gender took on further significance.

The extent of the world crisis of accumulation meant

that all governments needed to achieve a major internal redistribution of resources. Those with least political power were most vulnerable. Within the working class the groups that stood to lose most were women and blacks and particular regional communities. The costs of restructuring the economy, however, could be loaded much more easily onto such groups if the political credibility of their case for equal rights had first been destroyed. Conversely, if social democratic arguments retained their dominant place in public debate on welfare provision, it would be less easy to ignore the claims of blacks and women and other disadvantaged groups to assistance and subsidy from the state.

The advent of recession therefore has made the onslaught on social democracy more rather than less necessary for the new Conservatism. A central goal has been to discredit the social democratic concept of universal citizenship rights, guaranteed and enforced through public agencies, and to replace it with a concept of citizenship rights achieved through property ownership and participation in markets. In this way a class of sub-citizens is created, consisting of those who, being unable to participate in markets, are forced to remain dependent upon the state. Such dependency becomes a stigma, and allows the demands of these groups to be disregarded.[15]

Representation

The second challenge to social democracy arose over the representation of interests and the determination of the public interest. One of the permanent problems for any state is how to mobilise consent. During the 1970s the characteristic social democratic modes of representation began to appear inadequate for the task of legitimating the complex ensemble of agencies, institutions, powers and responsibilities which make up the modern state. As the size of the state sector has expanded so the need has grown to find ways of ensuring that all powerful interests and bodies of opinion are given appropriate channels of representation, so that the legitimacy of the state is maintained and the implementation of policy decisions made as effective as possible.

The traditional route for achieving this has been through elected legislatures or parliaments. By choosing representatives the people can exert control over the laws that are passed and make the executive accountable for its actions. The complexity of modern government business, however, makes scrutiny of the executive by elected representatives exceptionally difficult to perform, while the rise of party has severely limited the scope for independent judgement. In Britain, for example, it has transformed MPs into supporters of the executive rather than representatives of their constituents.

The deficiencies of party government either as an effective check upon increasingly powerful executives or as a reliable representative of volatile electorates have been frequently rehearsed.[16] Reform of parliaments and of electoral systems are often canvassed but everyone is aware that the root of the problem is the relative power of executives and legislatures, which executives are little disposed to change. The imbalance that has developed renders most of the traditional accounts of democratic government inoperative.

A second form of representation is the system known as corporatism. Instead of attempting to aggregate the opinions and votes of all individual electors representation of interests is performed through organised interests and their direct contact with government agencies. By discussing in detail the content of new legislation with the groups most directly concerned governments can hope to ensure successful implementation of their policies.[17]

In this mode of representation accountability to the people is indirect but more effective. It mostly takes place, however, in secret and works through continual compromises and the achievement of a consensus on the limits of acceptable policy, for which politicians must then achieve support in their parties and among voters through the use of modern media methods of persuasion. Parliamentary elections and parties become auxiliaries to the great engine of corporate power, and the compromises worked out between the representatives of labour, capital and the central bureaucracy.

Systems of corporate representation grew up or were installed in most social democratic regimes. They eased the problem of governing but they never completely solved the problem of legitimacy. They were also required to deliver more and more. At the extreme, as in Britain, the strain became too great and corporatist structures collapsed.

The only alternatives to legitimating policies through the endorsement of organised interests and the media are either to return to endorsing them through party and parliament, or to institute a presidency above both legislators and special interests. The charismatic president speaks to and on behalf of the people directly.

Corporatist modes of representation were held responsible for many of the failures of economic management in the 1970s. They had given vetos on policy to special interests and were too inflexible in coping with the demands of adjustment to the changes in the world economy.[18] Conservative critics of corporatism argued that it produced weak government. They wanted a new strong state, which did not need to bargain with organised interests. They wished to assert a national interest beyond the sectional interests of the pressure groups and lobbyists. Restoring the authority of the state was a priority. The way to achieve it was through strong and decisive political leadership, an end to compromises and concessions.

Economic management

The most direct challenge to social democracy came over the conduct of economic policy. If there had been one boast of postwar social democrats it was that mass unemployment had been eliminated and that the kind of problems that had plagued capitalist economies were things of the past. The discovery of the secret of perpetual growth was thought to make possible a long-term strategy for redistributing resources and making equality of opportunity a reality.[19]

The policy of full employment and the major new welfare programmes were regarded as major reforms which had permanently altered the character of capitalism. The enlargement of the public sector, the safeguarding of the private sector, the extension of public ownership and social security, the widening of public responsibilities and powers, the guaranteeing of political, civil, and social rights for all citizens – this provided a domestic package which social democrats and many politicians from all parties thought secure against attack from either left or right.

What was ignored was how dependent the edifice of social democracy was on continued good performance by the world economy and how that good performance of the 1950s and 1960s was much less dependent on Keynesian techniques of economic management than many supposed.[20] The ability of Keynesian measures to maintain full employment depended crucially on the political strength of social democratic institutions. When the strength was available, during the 1940s and 1950s, a Keynesian programme for unemployment was not needed. When it was needed, social democracy was no longer strong enough to deliver it.

The Keynesian approach to economic management was assailed by the new doctrine of monetarism. Monetarists argued that the Keynesians not only had an incorrect model of how the economy worked but also that their policies were leading to a progressive acceleration of inflation.[21] The question of inflation and the inability of social democratic regimes to control it was taken as symptomatic of the policy stance of social democratic governments. They were presiding over an erosion of market disciplines and institutions such as sound money. The failure to control inflation by means of demand management in the late 1960s and early 1970s led many governments to experiment with increasingly severe controls on prices and incomes, often trying to use corporatist structures in a bid to win consent for the policies and to make them work.

During the 1970s full employment was formally subordinated to the control of inflation as a policy priority, and this victory of the new politics over the old was reinforced by the major restructuring of public sectors that accompanied it, with spending on many programmes being drastically reduced, and attempts made to end universal entitlements and the provision of services on any basis other than ability to pay. The failure to maintain full employment and the principle of an expanding public sector greatly damaged confidence in social democratic governments and cast doubt on whether social democracy as an ideal was any longer either achievable or desirable. In the 1970s there were many prepared to argue it was neither.

Thatcherism

This book is largely devoted to an analysis of Thatcherism, the policies, events, and ideas associated with the British Conservatives under the leadership of Margaret Thatcher in opposition between 1975 and 1979 and in government between 1979 and 1987. Thatcherism is the most striking Conservative expression of the new politics, and the character of the 'Thatcher experiment' or 'Thatcher Revolution' has received much international attention. But it is important to place Thatcherism in the perspective of the events and changes described in this chapter. Thatcherism has its own local peculiarities, but it cannot be properly understood except in the context of what is happening to the world economy. The crisis of accumulation and the crisis of social democracy are world phenomena, and Thatcherism is one particular national response.

Discussion of Thatcherism has come to dominate British politics. On a superficial level it is not hard to see why. A third consecutive general election victory in June 1987 ensured that Margaret Thatcher would become the longest-serving British Prime Minister this century. There was even speculation that she intended to see out the century as Prime Minister. Rarely has any British politician so dominated a period as Margaret Thatcher dominated the 1980s. The term 'Thatcherism' is one sign of it. It has come to stand for the distinctive ideology, political style and programme of policies with which the British Conservative party has been identified since Margaret Thatcher became their Leader.

Analysis of this new political phenomenon has not been lacking. A flood of writing has poured out. Few aspects of Margaret Thatcher's policy, ideology and personality have not been dissected and assessed. Many different interpretations have appeared explaining the significance of Thatcherism and its impact on British politics. The term has been taken up by academics, journalists and politicians. Even the Prime Minister has started using it occasionally.

Yet despite its ubiquity the usefulness of the term remains controversial. This is because it has come to be used in so many ways. Thatcherism has no single unambiguous meaning. Critics of the concept argue that it is misleading firstly because it directs attention to what is trivial and relatively unimportant, and secondly because it attributes to the actions and ideas of the Thatcher Government a degree of coherence and purpose that does not exist.

The first type of criticism is often encountered on the Left. Tony Benn, for example, has objected to the use of the term because it implies that the most important problem is Thatcher and Thatcherism, and therefore suggests an anti-Thatcher Government rather than a socialist Government is what Britain needs.[22] For such critics the term Thatcherism is a diversion from understanding the real developments in British politics, because Thatcherism is in principle no different from other and earlier forms of Conservatism. The Conservative party changes its ideology and its leaders to suit the circum- stances of each period. Its basic objective, the defence of its class interests, remains the same. Thatcherism as a programme of policy is therefore quite separate from Margaret Thatcher herself. Her disappearance would not mean the end of the policies with which she has come to be identified. To term the programme which the Conservatives adopted in the 1970s 'Thatcherism' is to personalise it, and in doing so to distort its character, by directing attention to what is least important about it – the peculiarities of style and belief that are associated with one particular leader.

The second type of criticism is found among some Conserva- tive sceptics, but also among many journalists, such as Peter Riddell.[23] They are sceptical about Thatcherism as a concept, because they doubt that the Thatcher Government set out to pursue clear and consistent ideological objectives, and they think that even if it had it would never have achieved them. They note that, as with all previous Governments, there is an enormous gulf between rhetoric and achievement, and they conclude that the actual impact of Thatcherism is far less than is claimed by supporters and opponents alike.

Some of the points made against the concept of Thatcherism are sound, but they hardly constitute a case for dispensing with the term. All labels simplify complex political phenomena, but it would be very hard to do without terms like Stalinism, Butskellism, and Powellism. These terms are not explanations in themselves but phenomena that are clearly identifiable and coherent enough to warrant further investigation. Thatcher is one of a very few British political leaders whose name has been used to denote the particular ideology, political style and programme for government with which she has become associated. No other British Prime Minister this century has had his name used in quite the way that Thatcher has. This alone would warrant further investigation of why the term has come to be used so widely.

Critics of the concept of Thatcherism are often reacting to their own construction of what the term signifies. But after only a short immersion in the writing on Thatcherism it should be apparent that there is no one uncontested meaning. The term denotes a phenomenon for investigation, not a known entity. This investigation can proceed on a number of levels. Limiting the concept of Thatcherism to one particular aspect of the phenomenon, such as the personal style of the Leader or a particular ideology, will not explain much.

Nevertheless this aspect of Thatcherism should not be ignored. Thatcherism cannot be reduced to the personal project of a single individual because it was not created by one person and is much more than just a style of leadership. But it is called Thatcherism because the personal contribution of Thatcher has been extremely important. A different Conservative Leader elected in 1975 would still have had to contend with 'Thatcherism' in the party, in business, and in the media, but might have reacted very differently.[24]

What makes the term Thatcherism appropriate to describe what happened to the Conservative party after 1975 is that Thatcher identified herself with the ideas and the causes of the New Right and used her position as Leader to promote the spread of these ideas in a manner that was highly unusual for a Conservative Leader.

Thatcher is therefore important to Thatcherism. But an analysis of Thatcherism that only concentrated on Thatcher would be seriously inadequate. Thatcherism is used to refer not only to a style of leadership but also to a set of doctrines and a programme of policies. None of these exists in isolation. Thatcherism arises within a particular context and set of constraints. To understand Thatcherism requires knowledge of how interests and opinion are represented in Britain through parties, pressure groups and parliament; how the state and the policy-making process is constituted; how the economy is organised and how it is integrated into the world economic and political order.

This makes Thatcherism, like every other complex political phenomenon, highly contradictory. Whatever coherence it possesses has had to be constantly reasserted and re-forged. Its unity does not depend on simple pronouncements and declarations of will by Margaret Thatcher. In analysing Thatcherism the key problem is to decide what gives it coherence. Is it simply the position of Margaret Thatcher, as Leader of the Conservative party since 1975 and Prime Minister since 1979? Most writers on the phenomenon of Thatcherism have thought that there was more to it than that. But they have disagreed on what the correct interpretation should be. Three broad themes may be distinguished; Thatcherism as a hegemonic project; Thatcherism as a class or accumulation strategy; and Thatcherism as statecraft.

The interpretation of Thatcherism as a coherent hegemonic project has sometimes been misrepresented as concentrating exclusively upon ideology. It came to be associated with the journal *Marxism Today*, under the editorship of Martin Jacques. But the notion of hegemony always involved class strategies and political calculation as well as ideology. In an influential article in 1979[25] Jacques argued that Thatcherism was a response to the convergence of three trends: (i) the long-term structural decline of the British economy and the advent of the world recession; (ii) the collapse of the third postwar Labour Government and the consequent weakening of the social democratic consensus; and (iii) the resumption of the Cold War.

These developments created the space and the opportunity for a new hegemonic project on the right. This sought to rebuild the political dominance of the Conservatives, firstly by assembling a large enough coalition of voters and interest groups; secondly by projecting a new conception of the public interest and a vision of the ideal social and political order; and thirdly by defining policy priorities, developing a credible programme of policies, in part tailored to the specific fears and demands of voters and organised interests, but also addressed to the main problems of government, particularly economic policy and external relations.

Several hegemonic projects may exist at one time, and compete against one another. The establishment of a durable hegemony requires the emergence of a consensus both on the desirable shape of the society and on the policy priorities for government. True hegemony comes about when there is no longer serious conflict over the fundamentals of social organisation. Thatcherism has been widely interpreted as a hegemonic project, aiming at the replacement of the discredited social democratic consensus of the postwar period with a new consensus for the 1990s. At first it signified especially an intense ideological struggle, but it also involved from the first political calculation aimed at winning and maintaining support, as well as a programme of policies for reorganising the state, improving economic performance and reversing British decline.

The second theme in the interpretation of Thatcherism finds its coherence to lie in this last feature; in its policies for restoring the conditions for profitable capital accumulation. Thatcherism is interpreted as class politics, finding means by which the long relative decline of the British economy can be reversed, and British capitalism restored to international competitiveness. The theorists of hegemony see an accumulation strategy as part of the hegemonic project; for theorists of class politics it is by far the most important part. Electoral politics and ideological debate are sometimes regarded as no more than smokescreens for the class strategy that underlies them.

The third theme seeks coherence for Thatcherism in statecraft. The focus here is not the hegemony of an entire class but the survival and success of a particular political organisation, in this case the Conservative party. The policy decisions of the Thatcher Government reflect the Conservative political interest. The legitimacy of Thatcherism as an expression of the Conservative tradition of statecraft has been a major focus for debate about Thatcherism within the Conservative party itself.

A variant of this theme analyses Thatcherism in the context of the constraints and pressures of the policy-making process itself, arguing that it is the way in which the state is organised which is much more important for understanding how policies are formulated and implemented than ideology or class interest.

The argument of this book is that the most appropriate framework for explaining Thatcherism and charting its development is that of hegemony, because this alone allows proper weight to be given to ideology, economics and politics. The different insights that have emerged from the various perspectives can be utilised to show the complex character and the limits of Thatcherism as a hegemonic project.

Studying Thatcherism as a struggle for hegemony suggests analysis at a number of different levels; as a set of intellectual doctrines; as a popular political movement; as a style of leadership; as a bloc of interests; and as a programme of policy. All these pose different questions, and only in seeking to find answers to them can the full complexity of Thatcherism and the tensions within it be explored. The questions include:

(i) on the politics of support:
– how popular is Thatcherism?
– who votes for Thatcher and why?
– has Thatcherism succeeded in creating a new dominant party system?
– how has the Thatcher Government succeeded in overcoming so much internal and external opposition?
– which classes and groups does Thatcherism represent?
– how has Thatcherism been shaped by the doctrines of the New Right?
– what is the relationship of Thatcherism to Conservatism?
– what tensions exist in the doctrine of the free economy and the strong state?
(ii) on the politics of power:
– does the Thatcher Government possess a viable accumula-

tion strategy capable of reversing British decline?
- how far has the Thatcher Government centralised the British state and increased its repressive powers?
- in what ways has the Thatcher Government restructured the state?
- how radical were the policies of the Thatcher Government and how successful has the Government been in implementing them?

These questions can all be subsumed under one central question – does Thatcherism represent a coherent hegemonic project, capable of founding a new consensus? For many of these questions there are as yet no firm answers. What evidence and argument there is will be explored in the chapters of this book – through surveys of the main events, actions, and policies of the Thatcher years (Chapters 3 and 4); discussion of the chief interpretations of Thatcherism on right and left (Chapters 5 and 6); and a summary of the main conclusions (Chapter 7). But the first task (in Chapter 2) is to explore the doctrines of the New Right, since it was this intellectual movement which played an important role in shaping the Thatcherite project, even if many on the New Right have long since despaired of the radicalism of the Thatcher Government.

2
The New Right

Surely it is high time for us to cry from the rooftops that
the intellectual foundations of socialism have all collapsed.
[F. A. Hayek]

The origins of the New Right

The new politics of the 1970s spawned many new political
movements and political programmes across the whole political spectrum. The most powerful and influential of these new
forces has been labelled the New Right, although many
question whether it is new and a few who find themselves
labelled 'New Right' question if it is right. What the term
certainly does not signify is either a unified movement or a
coherent doctrine. A wide range of groups and ideas make up
the New Right, and there are many internal divisions and
conflicts.[1] The most important division, which is explored in
this chapter, is between a liberal and a conservative tendency.

   What all strands within the New Right share, however, is
the rejection of many of the ideas, practices and institutions
which have been characteristic of social democratic regimes
in Europe and of the New Deal and the Great Society
programmes in the United States. The New Right is radical
because it seeks to undo much that has been constructed in
the last sixty years. New Right thinkers question many of the
assumptions which had become accepted for the conduct of
public policy while New Right politicians have sought to build

electoral and policy coalitions which challenge key institutions and key policies.

As a political programme the New Right is identified with opposition to state involvement in the economy. They are fierce critics of Keynesian policies of economic management, and high public expenditure on welfare. But New Right politicians are also renowned as advocates of national discipline and strong defence. They argue that the programmes of both social democrats and socialists have been discredited by experience. Social democratic policies led to the morass of inflation, mass unemployment, excessive taxation and a swollen public sector. As the state became more and more interventionist so the authority of governments became progressively weaker in the face of powerful trade unions and other sectional interests.

The operation of social democracy itself therefore created a climate in which the foundations of social and public order were rapidly undermined and the prospects increased of their restoration through authoritarian means. But if authoritarian government was instituted by the left it would only create another inefficient, overmanned centrally-controlled economy of the Soviet type.[2]

To preserve a free society and a free economy the authority of the state has to be restored. Apart from its libertarian wing all strands of New Right opinion see this as essential. This is why the phrase which best summarises the doctrine of the New Right and the hegemonic project which it has inspired is 'free economy/strong state'. Different meanings are attached to these two terms and they are given different weight by liberal and conservative tendencies within the New Right, but if the New Right has a unity and if it deserves to be distinguished from previous 'rights' what sets it apart is the combination of a traditional liberal defence of the free economy with a traditional conservative defence of state authority.[3]

The idea of a free economy and a strong state involves a paradox. The state is to be simultaneously rolled back and rolled forward. Non-interventionist and decentralised in some areas, the state is to be highly interventionist and centralised in others. The New Right can appear by turns libertarian and authoritarian, populist and elitist. This ambiguity is not an accident. It derives in part from the fact that the New Right has two major strands; a liberal tendency which argues the case for a freer, more open, and more competitive economy, and a conservative tendency which is more interested in restoring social and political authority throughout society. What makes matters more confusing is that not only do those within the New Right regard the importance of these tendencies differently, but those who have written on the New Right often concentrate upon one of them to the exclusion of the other.[4]

This in part reflects the different meaning the term has come to have in different countries. In the United States the New Right is identified with the network of single-issue groups which have mushroomed in the last fifteen years to campaign on issues like abortion, bussing, and positive discrimination.[5] In Britain the New Right has been used to denote monetarist and free market economics. But it has also been used to refer to the new politics of race, gender and culture that has been developing since the 1960s.[6]

It is important to avoid the New Right becoming an omnibus term for every political development on the right. But a fairly broad definition is probably inescapable. The rich array of doctrines and the wide variety of political programmes and movements which can be justifiably included as part of the New Right mean that attempts to confine the term to a narrowly defined set of policy positions or doctrines are likely to confuse.

One reason for this is that the New Right should not be regarded primarily as an ideological phenomenon, although the specific ideologies associated with it have naturally attracted a good deal of attention. The aspect of the New Right which is of greatest interest and importance for the analysis of a political phenomenon like Thatcherism is its existence as a political movement which unites diverse ideological strands with the organisation of interests and the formulation of programmes of policy through to the establishment of distinctive governments. This focuses on the novelty and creativity of New Right political leadership and the extent to which the practical assault on the institutions and policies of social democracy has been successful, and therefore on the degree to which the New Right has succeeded in determining the political agenda for the 1980s and 1990s.

What is new in ideological terms about the New Right is that it is now rare to find politicians who support order and authority who are also protectionists and collectivists. The Social Imperialist wing of modern Conservatism has retreated to the margins of right-wing politics; the only substantial remaining manifestations of it are the Fascist parties. Conservatives have appropriated the liberal ideas of a market order and a free economy although their significance within a conservative discourse has been transformed. There are many liberals and libertarians associated with the New Right, and many of the New Right's most distinctive ideas have been contributed by them.[7] But as a political phenomenon the New Right has been predominantly a Conservative movement, to the embarrassment of some of the intellectuals who contributed to its early development.

The liberal conception of a free economy denoted a spontaneous harmony of interests generated through the voluntary exchanges of free autonomous individuals within a framework of agreed rules. To safeguard the order which the market spontaneously generated a state was needed, but a state minimal in its functions and limited in its powers. Although the state was to be limited, however, it needed to be strong in carrying out its functions. Policing the market order required vigilance and firm action to enforce laws impartially so that competition might be fair, exchange voluntary, and the fruits of enterprise secure. Liberals wanted a state that was both limited and strong. 'Limited' is not the first word that suggests itself to describe the arms spending of the United States. Yet the call for a minimal state today is made by some of the strongest supporters of unlimited defence budgets and permanent military preparedness against the threat posed by the Soviet Union.

Many nineteenth-century liberals like Cobden were as strongly opposed to excessive arms and defence expenditure as they were to any other form of public expenditure. All were regarded as wasteful and an abuse of the state's powers. The strong state they wanted to see had nothing in common with the strong state of the old imperial states of Europe dominated by their landowning classes and inspired by dreams of military conquest and territorial aggrandisement.

Liberals saw the spread of the principles and practice of the free economy and the establishment of economic interdependence throughout the world as the means of breaking down national boundaries and national rivalries and securing peace. In this century, however, many supporters of the free economy have become supporters of large and permanent defence sectors. The division of the world economy into rival blocs and the increasing interdependence of the capitalist world led to a decisive shift of Conservative opinion in all countries away from national protection towards military and economic co-operation under United States leadership after 1945.

The advent of the New Right in the 1970s marked a further stage in this development. For many British Conservatives the free economy means not merely the domestic economy but the international economy as well, and its defence is indissolubly tied up with preserving the leading role played by the United States and with maintaining strong military forces against the threat of Soviet aggression.

The free economy and the strong state

The call for a free economy and a strong state is therefore capable of several different interpretations. A state may be considered strong because of the means of repression at its disposal and its willingness to use them. But more durable strength depends on the institutions and policies of the state, including the occasional use of force, being accepted as legitimate. The use of the coercive power of the state is justified when it is employed to defeat and contain those interests, organisations and individuals which threaten the survival of the free economy either by flouting its rules or resisting the outcomes which flow from market exchanges.

If the state makes the protection of the free economy its priority then it creates the basis for its own legitimacy. Once all illegitimate functions and responsibilities are stripped from it the state is no longer the weak state of social democracy, overburdened by ever-widening responsibilities and infested by special interests which seek to use the political process to portray their sectional interest as the public interest. It can concentrate on defending what is the true public interest – upholding impartially the rules of the market order.

The difficulty for the New Right is that while they are quite clear about the correct balance between the strong state and the free economy in their ideal world, they face the difficulty of how that ideal is to be realised in the world they actually inhabit. The New Right would like to be conservative but they are forced to be radicals. They have to struggle against the forces which have gravely undermined the market order and which, if left unchecked, will destroy it. The New Right has needed to identify how the existing state can be reformed in order to permit the restoration of the rules, the institutions and the culture of the free economy. Since the New Right diagnosis of the condition of the interventionist, high-spending state of social democracy is so severe, radical measures have to be prescribed for recovery. But here there is a problem. The New Right must obtain a mandate for reform and implement it through the political institutions which, according to New Right analysis, have been responsible for the destruction of the market order.

The New Right has to believe simultaneously in the malign and perverse effects of democratic politics on the free economy, and in the possibility of using that same democratic politics and that same interventionist state to reverse the process of creeping socialism.[8] This creates considerable tensions in New Right practice and still more in the practice of New Right Governments. They can be seen in the different arguments which have been advanced to justify a strong state.

The state must be strong firstly to unwind the coils of social democracy and welfarism which have fastened around the free economy; secondly to police the market order; thirdly to make the economy more productive; and fourthly to uphold social and political authority. The first argument commands agreement throughout the New Right. To restore a free economy firm and decisive action is necessary to cut public spending programmes and taxes, to privatise public assets and public services, and to abolish interventionist and regulatory agencies. The idea of a radical rupture in public policy and therefore the need to be prepared to deal with resistance, whether from the central bureaucracy or from organised interests, were central themes in New Right deliberation during the 1970s. There was talk in Britain in Margaret Thatcher's circle of advisers of the need for the next Conservative Government to 'prepare for a confrontation with the trade union Left'.[9]

Implementing a radical programme is seen to require a power struggle. The state must be prepared to take firm measures to reduce state spending and state subsidies, and then be determined enough to resist challenges to its authority that come from those who are disadvantaged by the changes. The political calculations involved in fighting a major strike like the British coal strike in 1984/5 were complex, but all variants of New Right opinion were agreed that this was the kind of struggle that had to be won if there was to be any chance of implementing other New Right policies.

This need to clear a space for the implementation of radical policies is met again and again in New Right writing. The state must be strong in order to reverse the trend towards collectivism which has become established and to break the resistance of all special interests, including the new class of public sector professionals who are likely to oppose the radical policies of a New Right Government. Trials of strength with major interests and entrenched lobbies are welcomed as providing opportunities to assert the authority of the Government and to signal its intentions.

Reducing the size of the state and the range of its responsibilities commands assent from all parts of the New Right, and it is hard to see how this could be accomplished without the use of strong government. But the other justifications for a strong state are more controversial even within the New Right.

Policing the market order means maintaining a central authority strong enough to maintain formal exchange equality between all economic agents. At minimum this requires the enforcement of laws that protect property and persons and enforce property rights. But more controversially it also legitimates action by the state to suppress private coercion, monopoly and discrimination. If formal exchange equality does not arise spontaneously – if, for example, there is persistent discrimination against individuals on the basis of gender, race or religion, does this justify the state intervening to ensure that free and equal exchanges can take place? Few on the New Right will so argue. Economic liberals who might be expected to be most sympathetic wish to protect existing property rights, whatever their origin, but they are much more wary about the use of state power to extend rights.[10] Their suspicion of the state generally overcomes their desire to see the basis of the market order extended. Conservatives have fewer problems. There is no good reason in their view why claims of abstract rights should be allowed to undermine important social and political institutions.[11]

A further difficulty is the extent to which the state should become involved in policing the market order. There is a conflict between protecting the private sector from state interference and ensuring that market rules are properly enforced within the private sector. The degree of regulation which the latter implies can be considerable. The Thatcher Government faced the criticism that, in denationalising some public sector companies, such as telephones and gas, it was creating new private sector monopolies. The reluctance of the Thatcher Government to report mergers to the Monopoly Commission, and to introduce statutory regulation of the activities of the City of London, also indicated that the Government was less interested in policing the market order than in enlarging the private sector and giving companies free rein within it. A liberal state that is weak in regulating private capital and in enforcing the rights of market agents may lose legitimacy. Its ability to protect the public interest will be questioned if in practice it adopts a policy of *laissez-faire* towards whatever is done in the private sector.

The third justification for a strong state concerns efficiency. The rolling back of collectivism is not enough. What is also required is a forceful and imaginative state policy aimed at modernising the economy by speeding up the pace of change and making the whole society more competitive and enterprise-ing. According to this view markets are a valuable instrument of policy for forcing through change. They are not valued primarily because they guarantee individual rights but because they offer the best way of allocating resources, providing incentives, and stimulating growth. The overriding goals of economic policy become efficiency and modernisation. Other questions such as the size of enterprises or the rights of particular groups or whether government should be centralised or decentralised are subordinated to them. Reform of institutions such as the central bureaucracy and the education system become priorities.

This view is highly interventionist. It is not concerned merely with using state power to break resistance during a process of disengagement from the commitments of social democracy. It seeks to reshape the institutional framework of the free economy. The citizens have to be forced to be free and enterprising, otherwise there is no guarantee they will be so. By seeking to overhaul many existing institutions in radical ways, such views come into conflict with the conservative disposition to defend existing institutions and established privileges. This has produced some of the greatest conflicts inside the Thatcher Government. If the Government has proved *laissez-faire* in its attitude to the private sector, it has been far from *laissez-faire*, at least in its aspirations, towards state and public institutions. In this respect the New Right is a radical and a modernising force, capable of inspiring policies that are far removed from the popular conception of *laissez-faire*, and involve the Government in highly interventionist and centralist policies.

The fourth argument for a strong state is the conservative argument. A free economy is seen as a prop for a strong state instead of the other way round. The authority of the state is all-important and no principles or policy goals, such as the sanctity of individual rights or the need to maximise economic efficiency, can be allowed to override it. The task of the state is to ensure that authority is upheld throughout society because this is the basis on which its own authority rests. Private property is an important bulwark of social authority and it is for this reason that a free economy must be preserved. But there is disagreement over whether social institutions like the family comprise a private domain from which the state should be excluded or whether the incursions of collectivism have so weakened key institutions that an interventionist policy to restore traditional standards of morality and behaviour is justified.[12]

To sanction widespread social engineering, even in the cause of restoring authority and traditional standards throughout society, is not welcome to Conservatives. They hope it will not be necessary. As with the liberal New Right there is a naive optimism often encountered among New Right Conservatives. Despite the long night of collectivism in the twentieth century, many of them still believe that the character of the nation is still sound. If only the grip of collectivism and social democracy can be prised loose, the natural enterprise, patriotism and independence of the people will reassert themselves spontaneously. For pessimists in the Conservative ranks, the poison of dependence and alien doctrines cannot be expelled easily or swiftly. A long period of vigilance and struggle will be necessary – and the creation of a strong state prepared to act illiberally to stamp out undesirable behaviour and attitudes, to rebuild social and political authority, and to re-educate the people in the duties and values expected of them.

Despite their differences of emphasis and disagreements all strands of the New Right accept that one of the main reasons for seeking the restoration of state authority is the maintenance of a free economy. This linking of conservatism and liberalism in a common programme owes much to political changes that have come about through the development of the world economy. As economic interdependence through an international division of labour has become more pronounced so powerful domestic lobbies have developed in every country to preserve the international order and the openness of the world economy. The autonomy of national governments has decreased and the attractiveness and feasibility of autarky as an option for national policy has weakened.

The commitment to economic liberalism has been much stronger in the 1980s than it was in the 1930s. The breakdown of international capitalism in the 1930s destroyed faith in capitalism and gave a significant boost to collectivist doctrines of both right and left. In the current recession, however, it is these collectivist doctrines and institutions that are under attack. The new politics that has emerged has a double thrust – on the one side the upholding of the principle of the international economic order and co-operation, on the other the unceasing effort to modernise each national economy to make it more effective in international competition. Free economy/strong state not only expresses the strange partnership of liberalism and conservatism that has finally flowered at the present time, but also the core elements of state policy as it has developed during this period of slow growth and recession in the 1970s and 1980s.

Capitalism is the most dynamic and productive of all economic systems known to history. But it must still depend upon institutions which the market itself cannot generate spontaneously. This leaves a major role for government. Each national government is obliged to maintain relatively open markets but must be prepared to cope with the effects of openness on its domestic economy. These pressures become acute in a period of recession. It is not only protected economies that require strong states. Defending a position within the world market requires a commitment to openness to ensure prosperity and to intervention to ensure competitiveness.

The doctrines and the political movements that have been grouped under the label 'New Right' may have revived many old liberal and conservative ideas. But the New Right does not represent a simple return to a nineteenth-century politics of liberal political economy and Victorian values. It is an expression of the new politics of the 1970s. The quest for a free economy and a strong state is a response to the changed circumstances of the world economy and the internal disarray of social democracy. This is indeed how the New Right see it themselves. Their doctrines are not intended to recreate some lost golden age but to make the free economy the new Utopia which can guide the development of contemporary industrial societies.

The liberal New Right

The liberal tendency in the New Right is itself a broad spectrum. It embraces monetarists and supply siders, followers of the Austrian school and anarcho-capitalists, students of public choice and public welfare, apostles of privatisation and deregulation. The causes espoused in recent years by free market economists include strict money supply targets to reduce inflation, negative income tax, floating exchange rates, indexation, constitutional rules to enforce balanced budgets and limit government spending, abolition of trade union legal immunities, reduction of income tax and abolition of progressive tax rates, privatisation of all enterprises in state hands, introduction of education vouchers, private health insurance in place of state support, and many more.[13]

This writing represents a major revival of the themes and concerns of liberal political economy. The liberal New Right have developed theories of the way the capitalist economy functions, theories of the political system and the policy-making process, and theories of social institutions. On this basis they make very precise recommendations on which government policies are needed to sustain and develop the market economy and which policies injure it. They have developed a coherent and plausible accumulation strategy, which has become extremely influential if not universal, and has helped shape the economic policies of several Governments in responding to the recession and the restructuring of the world economy.

The central question is always what are the conditions under which markets function best. It is taken as axiomatic that markets are inherently superior to any other way of organising human societies. The problem is seen to be creating the conditions in which markets can function and removing whatever obstacles exist or may arise to their operation. The economies presided over by social democratic regimes are clearly market economies, but in the view of the New Right they are fettered and unable to realise their full potential and in danger of being transformed into something else entirely, the command economies of state socialism. To counter this the New Right have campaigned for sound money, a major reduction in taxation and public expenditure, and a programme of deregulation and privatisation.

Sound money

The call for the restoration of sound money has been central to the New Right's criticism of social democracy. It was the economic policy issue on which the New Right first made a major impact. The doctrine of monetarism which began to be advanced in the 1960s by Milton Friedman and others was a restatement of the quantity theory of money and a major challenge, both as theory and policy, to Keynesianism. The intellectual arguments about the way the economy works have not been settled; indeed the divisions between proponents of different macroeconomic theories have tended to widen[14] and much doubt has been thrown on the theoretical and empirical foundations of monetarism. But what gave monetarism its ascendancy was the marked deterioration in economic performance in the 1970s. Governments seemed unable any longer to manage economies successfully. The acceleration of inflation in the late 1960s was followed by a steep rise in unemployment after 1973 which undermined confidence in Keynesian methods and techniques. The monetarist critique was available and plausible. It was widely disseminated through academic and media channels and it began to be voiced by leading politicians.

What gave monetarism its practical importance, however, was not its coherence as a doctrine nor its academic credentials nor even its conquest of the financial press. What was decisive was the breakdown of the regime of fixed exchange rates in 1971/2. Keynesian economic management could be practised either within closed economies or in an international economy in which the degree of openness remained limited. One of the critical tests of openness was the exchange rate. If rates were fixed and the exchanges successfully policed by the central banks, then the limits within which demand could be managed in any domestic economy were tightly fixed. The money supply was necessarily under firm control. Overexpansion of the money supply would result in a balance of payments crisis and an exchange rate crisis. The agreement by governments to maintain fixed exchange rates and to devalue only in exceptional circumstances ensured relatively stable monetary conditions throughout the western economy during the period of the long boom (1951–67).

Once the system of fixed exchange rates became unsustainable owing to the financial weakness of the United States, the major external constraint on domestic financial prudence was removed. The opportunity was created for an unlimited inflation, as countries sought to expand domestic demand in order to sustain employment and prosperity, while allowing their currencies to depreciate to keep their costs in line with those of their competitors. Such a situation did begin to unfold in 1973, a year of very rapid growth throughout the western economy, fuelled by large injections of domestic demand and increases in money supply. Prices in certain sectors began to rise rapidly.

At the end of that year oil prices were quadrupled by the Organization of Petroleum Exporting Countries (OPEC), which punctured the bubble of speculation and optimism and triggered a recession. Output began to fall but the inflationary pressure which the monetary expansion had created was still increasing. The adoption of a new set of international monetary rules became a matter of urgency to prevent a plunge into depression and the collapse of the international economy. No return to fixed exchange rates was possible, given the political disunity of the leading western powers and the undermining of the United States' economic hegemony. But what did prove possible with the co-operation of national governments, often assisted by pressure from the IMF, was the adoption of monetarist policies to contain inflation and satisfy the international financial markets.[15]

Formal abandonment of expansionist demand management policies, the publishing of strict money supply targets, and the announcement of major cuts in public expenditure programmes became the tests which the financial markets applied to the policies of national governments. Maintaining the confidence of the financial markets was critical for maintaining the value of the national currency. The price of remaining within the international economy came to be acceptance of the sound money policies imposed by the financial markets, although the vulnerability of national economies to dictation by the markets varied, depending in part on the character and extent of their integration into the world economy and in part on the strength of corporatism within their domestic politics.

No one allotted the financial markets the role of makers and breakers of governments. It arose simply through the way these markets themselves worked in an era of recession and floating exchange rates. It was made possible by the huge volume of mobile liquid capital and by the ever-increasing sophistication and integration of the financial circuit.

The imposition of sound money policies on national governments in the mid-1970s gave an enormous boost to those domestic lobbies which were arguing for the adoption of monetarism. The international political and financial climate was no longer favourable to national Keynesianism and those countries, like France after 1981, which tried to practise it experienced a major flight of capital and an exchange crisis which were generally sufficient to return errant countries to the new orthodoxy.

It was convenient for monetarists that their campaign for a basic change in the methods of macroeconomic management should coincide with the external pressure for sound money imposed by the financial markets. But monetarists' belief in sound money was much more than just a technical case for how best to reduce inflation in a time of recession. Monetarists believed that the full employment objective of postwar stabilisation policy was fundamentally misconceived. Trying to achieve it was leading to accelerating inflation and the undermining of one of the essential requirements for a market order – the role of money as a stable medium of exchange and store of value.[16]

Monetarists argued that the control of inflation should become the top priority of any domestic stabilisation policy, regardless of any increase in unemployment that might be caused. In the years before the recession monetarists predicted that the unemployment that would be created by applying monetarist policies would be small and transitional, the unavoidable price that had to be paid to put the economy back on a sound footing. But some New Right economists were already recognising that a major restructuring of the world economy was in prospect and predicted that very high levels of unemployment might be experienced for a long period unless radical measures were taken, not merely to control inflation but also to tackle many of the distortions that had crept into the market economy.

The key political point that monetarists made against Keynesians was that maintaining the fundamentals of the market economy was far more important than trying to ensure particular market outcomes. No monetarist ever said that full employment was not desirable. But the pursuit of full employment could endanger the free economy if, for example, a government decided to introduce controls on wages and prices in a bid to suppress the inflationary effects of its management of demand. Unemployment was preferable if that was the price that had to be paid to prevent a creeping politicisation of the economy and the suspension of markets in the determination of wages and prices.

Kalecki had argued at the beginning of the Keynesian era that if full employment were accepted as a reform within capitalist societies it would tilt the balance of power significantly towards labour, since it would remove one of the main levers by which government policy was kept within parameters acceptable to the business community. Effective measures to reduce unemployment had always produced a crisis of confidence in the financial markets. Confidence was restored when the measures were dropped. Acceptance by the business community of measures to make full employment permanent meant dispensing with the discipline which unemployment, through periodic lay-offs, and the threat of unemployment, through dismissal, had helped to create in the workforce.[17]

Many economists have argued that it is mistaken to attribute the high levels of employment in the postwar period to Keynesianism. There would have been a low level of unemployment almost regardless of the stance of macroeconomic policy. The political and economic reconstruction of the western world which took place under American guidance in the 1940s saw the decisive defeat of those political forces which wished to extend social democracy and national Keynesianism. The regimes that emerged from this period represented compromises between the demands of organised labour and the needs of capital. Some advances were registered but the international order which was established ensured that these gains would be limited. How limited was only revealed in the 1970s when the return of mass unemployment was seen as signalling the end of Keynesianism rather than the occasion for its application. The traditional doctrine of sound finance in the new fashionable guise of monetarism reasserted itself. Keynesianism when it was tried was not needed and when it was needed was not tried.

The importance of sound money is acknowledged by all New Right economists. A stable medium of exchange and store of value is essential for markets to function. If the commodity that is used as money becomes unstable rational calculation becomes much more difficult and in many instances impossible, and exchange starts to break down, with all manner of distortions such as speculation and the search for hedges against inflation creeping in. Inflation makes market outcomes appear even more of a lottery than they in fact are, and this can have a corrosive effect on many of the values and attitudes such as trust and honesty which are essential for the smooth working of an exchange economy. Stable prices are therefore the foundation for prosperity. They do not guarantee prosperity but they make prosperity possible.

There is considerable dispute, however, within the New Right as to the means by which sound money is best achieved, and also the priority which should be given to it in relation to other New Right objectives. Three important debates have been carried on – firstly between monetarists and Austrians; secondly between advocates of the gold standard and floating exchange rates; and thirdly between monetarists and supply siders.

The protagonists in the first debate have been Milton Friedman and F. A. Hayek, two of the most influential New Right theorists and publicists.[18] Friedman quite early established himself as the leading exponent of monetarism, while Hayek is the most prominent representative of the Austrian school and is a veteran of ideological struggles stretching back to the 1930s. Hayek has never called himself a monetarist, and has important disagreements both with Friedman's methods of analysis and with his conclusions

Hayek attaches no less importance to the problem of

inflation than Friedman. He wrote trenchant accounts of the dangers it posed and of the follies of Keynesian demand management. But he was strongly critical of the gradualist methods proposed by many monetarists for squeezing inflation out of an economy. This method involved devising a financial strategy which would set targets for key monetary indicators. They would be reduced each year until inflation had disappeared. Hayek argued that such a strategy would take too long, and would allow hostile political forces time to organise to dilute or to overturn the policy. Spreading the unemployment associated with a return to financial discipline over several years would make any government in a democracy vulnerable to attack from the opposition parties. The better way, Hayek argued, would be to be bold from the outset, abolishing inflation at a stroke by introducing a complete reform of the currency as Germany did in 1923. The immediate level of unemployment would be severe because of the scale of bankruptcies. But the recovery, Hayek believed, would be extremely swift, and it would take place from the outset on the foundation of stable money.

A second controversy has centred on the rival merits of the gold standard and floating exchange rates.[19] Partisans of the former have always argued that the world economy can only enjoy lasting financial discipline if there is an objective foundation for the exchange of currencies which is not open to political manipulation. Former admirers of the gold standard, such as the long-serving Governor of the Bank of England, Montagu Norman, though that one of its main advantages was that it was politician-proof. It provided an automatic mechanism for ensuring that the domestic price level of each country participating in international trade remained relatively stable, and that deficits and surpluses on the balance of payments were rapidly corrected.

For supporters of the gold standard the postwar gold exchange standard, which linked currencies to the dollar and the dollar to gold, provided many of the advantages of the gold standard system, but did depend heavily on the ability of the United States to underwrite it. The breakdown of this system after sustained pressure on the dollar came when the dollar's convertibility into gold was suspended in 1971. This obliged all currencies to float against one another, and supporters of the gold standard freely prophesied that the removal of external constraint would produce a major inflation. They were not mistaken. The supporters of the gold standard, however, are very much in a minority in the New Right. Far more in evidence are the supporters of floating exchange rates. Economists, such as Milton Friedman, and politicians, such as Enoch Powell, were advocates of floating exchange rates in the early 1960s, and even some long-standing advocates of a gold standard, such as Hayek, have recently changed their minds.[20] The reason is that, desirable though a gold standard system might be for an international market order, few on the New Right believe that the political conditions for its reintroduction can be realised. The only feasible system would be a modified form of the gold exchange standard, but there is no single national currency which can form the lynchpin of this system as the dollar used to do, and besides many on the New Right feel that there are some major drawbacks also. It gives too much power to central banks and imposes a straightjacket on the world economy which may hinder its restructuring and development.[21]

The advantage of floating exchange rates is that they establish a market for currencies, and allow buyers and sellers to determine their price. Provided that governments adopt monetarist policies internally there will be no reason for continual currency depreciation or for inflation to accelerate. The system of floating exchange rates relies on internationalisation of monetary disciplines by national governments, but in any case the financial markets will operate to penalise severely any country which does not follow sound money policies.

Hayek has carried this argument still further by suggesting that the most effective way of ensuring internal financial discipline is not by entrusting it to some regulatory body like a Central Bank but by allowing a free market in all currencies. This would mean extending the reach of the international financial markets into every national economy by ending each national government's jealously guarded monopoly over the issue of the legal form of money. If all national currencies become legal tender, citizens would choose to hold their savings and even make their transactions in those currencies which they expected to keep their value best. The success of a Government's stabilisation policy would no longer be judged infrequently and haphazardly at the time of a general election. It would be subject to a daily plebiscite. The good money would drive out the bad.[22]

Supply-side economics

A third debate that has developed within the New Right concerns the rival merits of monetarism and supply side policies.[23] Supply siders do not dispute the importance of sound money, but they do claim that far too much attention has been paid to the task of restoring financial stability, and not enough to the problem of getting the economy moving again. They give priority to reawakening enterprise and restoring incentives rather than to rebuilding the monetary circuits that underpin exchange. They urge major reductions in public expenditure and taxation as the priority for economic policy, because they believe that it is the high taxes social democracy requires to finance its programmes that is stifling enterprise, depressing productivity, and leading to high inflation and high unemployment.

Supply siders argue that what is of real importance is creating a successful capitalist economy. Central to capitalism in their view is not money but enterprise and production. The task is to liberate energies by cutting taxes and deregulating economic activity. Then the budget will balance and prices will stabilise, if only production can be stimulated sufficiently. Monetarism is condemned for being deflationary and restrictionist, and for failing to break out of the vicious cycle of decline which has been the legacy of social democracy and big government. The Thatcher Government in its early years was criticised in precisely these terms by leading American supply siders.[24]

Yet, despite this difference of emphasis and the contrasting assessments of the implications of the huge American deficit that emerged after the partial implementation of supply side policies by the Reagan Administration, the gap between monetarists and supply siders is not vast. Milton Friedman is a firm believer in the need to cut taxes to very low levels (20 per cent is his target), and he has written extensively on the need for a major reduction in government spending programmes. The issue is what comes first, and whether a government is justified in taking risks with funding its budget and therefore with inflation and the value of its currency, so long as it has a clear grasp of what makes a successful accumulation strategy for reinvigorating capitalism.

The concentration by monetarists on the control of inflation, and their argument that this was a technical question of economic management, sometimes obscured the crucial political dimension of New Right thinking. The more politically sophisticated monetarists, as well as non-monetarists like Hayek, had no difficulty with the central propositions of monetarism: inflation is a monetary phenomenon; it has to be cured by monetary means; it is always caused by the supply of money expanding faster than the output of goods and services; governments are responsible for the money supply; therefore it is governments that are primarily responsible for inflation.

They pointed out, however, that this analysis suggested that governments acted as they did because they were either stupid or ignorant or the victims of poor advice. For Hayek the real issue was why governments felt obliged to expand the money supply. What were the political pressures which created a continual bias towards inflation? The technical reasons for inflation and how it might be halted were trivial beside this question.

New Right economics provides a comprehensive critique of state intervention in market processes. State intervention is criticised on three main grounds: because in practice it produces worse results than do market solutions; because administrative and bureaucratic methods are inherently inferior to markets as a means of allocating resources; and because it is objectionable on moral grounds. None of these arguments is new; all of them were deployed in the long intellectual struggle against socialism and collectivism in the 1920s and 1930s.[25] But at that time socialism and collectivism were relatively untried systems and doctrines. This was no longer true by the 1970s; the experience of collectivism in practice had by then revived the appeal of the free market.

At first this writing took the form of polemics against particular kinds of state intervention. Such arguments were often highly specific, related to particular policies and problems. The Hobart Papers of the Institute of Economic Affairs, for example, provided a series of case-studies in public policy, arguing that there were always market solutions available, and that they worked better than the established administrative solutions.

A particular target was controls of every kind, particularly price controls and rent controls. Controls were criticised because, while they might give short-term benefits, they produced long-term damage, and ended up making the situation worse than it was at the beginning. Controls worked by freezing or regulating prices and therefore preventing markets from functioning. If markets could not function some other method was needed for rationing resources, and this meant using either administrative rules or administrative discretion. The flaw in any system of rationing is that it tends to perpetuate the original shortage. It brings into play no mechanism by which the shortage itself might eventually be overcome. The great merit of markets for their protagonists is that the rationing is done through prices rather than administratively. High prices discriminate against those without money, but they also encourage the entry of new producers. Supply increases until both the high prices and the shortage which occasioned them are eliminated.

The detailed case against particular controls was used to build a general argument against intervention. The hallmark of New Right economic thinking is a distrust of all solutions to problems of public policy that do not involve markets. In those cases where the principle of state intervention is accepted, such as government control of the money supply, New Right economists argue strongly that policy-makers should apply general rules rather than use administrative discretion, because the former are likely to cause less long-term damage to markets. Yet, even here, the difficulty of ensuring adherence to general rules on the part of the policy-makers themselves leads some to prefer market solutions, such as Hayek's scheme for choice in currency discussed above.

Public expenditure

One of the most important areas where this approach has been applied by New Right economists lies in the field of public expenditure and taxation. The existence of a substantial sector where services are provided by public bodies means a large area where administrative rather than market criteria hold sway. New Right economists have endeavoured to show that market solutions would in every case be superior to the established public provision, and that there are very few goods which cannot be supplied through markets.[26] This claim has been made most controversially for health and education, but it extends to all services in the public sector, even defence. The argument is that good intentions and high ideals are not enough. Any service will be more efficiently provided if it is subject to competitive tender and free from administrative controls and political interference. Another crucial argument is that any system of administrative rationing necessarily confers privileges on those groups best able to lobby the bureaucracy. The most disadvantaged groups derive least benefit from the services set up to help them. If services were provided through markets then not only would there be less waste and inefficiency but there would also be greater choice.

The New Right criticises public welfare programmes not only because of their expense, but also because services provided collectively are regarded as inefficient in meeting the needs of the people they were designed to help. They destroy choice and they entrench dependency. The attack on the public sector draws on the traditional liberal preference for self-help and independence and financial prudence, but it also sets out to demonstrate that the poor would actually get a better deal if they had to rely for the provision of essential services on making discretionary decisions about how to spend their income, instead of being forced to rely on the discretionary decisions of administrators. These arguments were always controversial. But the fact that they were put at all indicated a new self-confidence and a new assertiveness by the advocates of free markets and competition. The universal welfare programmes, the extended public sectors, and the institutions and policies of corporatist economic management that had grown up piecemeal over many decades, became a major battleground.

The achievement of the New Right was to place the supporters of public provision and public services on the defensive. The New Right attacks on the grounds of cost and efficiency were predictable, but what was less expected was the New Right claim that they had a superior moral vision of what a free society should be like. Their concept of citizenship saw freedom and equality being achieved through the daily plebiscite in the market, not through the infrequent plebiscite in the political system. This combination of morality and efficiency proved irresistible to many Conservative politicians, who were instinctively hostile to high welfare spending. New Right economics supplied them with a well-developed set of principles for the discussion and analysis of all public policy questions. Liberal political economy became intellectually fashionable again in the 1970s. If anything its scope and potential were now enhanced, since its adherents were not afraid to develop it by extending their analysis to the public sector and the problems of public choice, the activities of politicians and bureaucrats, as well as the traditional focus on the behaviour of buyers and sellers in markets.[27]

Much of the confidence of the new breed of New Right ideologues who filled the research institutes and colonised parts of the financial press, as well as some university departments, derived from the rediscovery of the analytical properties of liberal political economy. The intellectual case for markets appeared overwhelming, much as the intellectual case for planning had appeared overwhelming to an earlier generation of intellectuals. It was the universal cast of liberal political economy that appealed – not the case for this market solution or that, but the case for markets in general.

Milton Friedman was a key figure in the debate that developed around monetarism and macroeconomic management, as well as being a key protagonist in the arguments about the superiority of market solutions to administrative solutions. But the case for the inherent superiority of markets over all other forms of social organisation was made by Hayek and the Austrian school, by the theorists of public choice, and by political philosophers like Robert Nozick.[28]

One of Hayek's major contributions has been his emphasis upon markets as a discovery process, the constant search for new methods, new needs and new sources of supply. All the Austrians put great emphasis upon the role of entrepreneurs as the creative force in a market economy. Hayek's market economy is not an economy of perfect equilibrium, perfect competition and perfect knowledge. Instead it is characterised by uncertainty and imperfect knowledge, constant shocks and adjustments. Hayek's argument against socialism and collectivism is not that markets offer a painless and frictionless method of allocating resources, but simply that markets are the method that works best because it utilises the dispersed and fragmented knowledge which is available only to individuals in their particular local circumstances.[29] The conclusion for policy from Hayek's deliberations on law and society is that instances of 'market failure' need to be tackled not by suspending markets by attempting to centralise knowledge and decision making in a planning agency, but by removing the obstacles that prevent markets from functioning and new entrepreneurs from emerging with new ideas on how to satisfy whatever needs exist.

The economics of politics

The public choice school has applied the methods of economic analysis to the behaviour of agents in the public sector. They have identified numerous shortcomings in the way in which political and administrative systems operate, comparing them unfavourably with the way in which economic markets operate. The chief defect of political and administrative systems lies in the way in which they aggregate preferences. Voters are allowed only one decision every few years, and then are unable to discriminate between different policies that are presented to them. Instead they must vote for a candidate or a party which presents a package of policies covering a wide spectrum. Voters are also fundamentally irresponsible. They lack the kind of budget constraint which all consumers, even armed with the magical properties of credit cards, have to face. As Milton Friedman has explained:

The fundamental defect of the political mechanism [is that] it is a system of highly weighted voting under which the special interests have great incentive to promote their own interests at the expense of the general public. The benefits are concentrated; the costs are diffused; and you have therefore a bias in the market place which leads to ever greater expansion in the scope of government and ultimately to control over the individual . . . In the economic market . . . each person gets what he pays for. There is a dollar-for-dollar relationship. Therefore, you have an incentive proportionate to the cost to examine what you are getting.[30]

The contribution of public choice as a new intellectual discipline to the development of the New Right was that it provided powerful theoretical arguments against any notion that public bodies were disinterested and enlightened, while private individuals and companies were self-interested and rapacious. Public choice theorists started with the assumption that politicians and bureaucrats had their own interests which they pursued with the utmost vigour. The difference between private and public bodies was not that one had a special relationship to the public interest denied the other, but that the pursuit of self-interest by private bodies was qualified by the existence of a framework of rules and by competition. These constraints did not exist for public bodies.[31]

The conclusions which many in the New Right drew from public choice was that markets were much superior to democracy in representing and aggregating individual choices. It was only a short step to arguing that democracy needed to be hedged around with restrictions to ensure that it did not permit encroachments upon the private sphere. A key theme of New Right writing is the necessary limits of democracy and how different areas of policy can be removed from democratic control. Much ingenuity has been spent on devising constitutions and entrenched bills of rights. Such reforms would remove from democratic governments the right of taking certain decisions and would require them to operate certain policies within prescribed limits. The idea that there should be a constitutional amendment to oblige the United States

Government to balance the budget is one of the more modest of these proposals.

Theoretical arguments which stress the creativity of markets and the defects of administrative systems have been further buttressed by the revival of moral arguments against equality. Robert Nozick's restatement of contract theory is the best known of these, but it by no means stands alone.[32] Hayek is also extremely keen to show that there is no moral basis for redistribution and that the pursuit of equality is a chimera which does untold damage to markets.[33]

A significant feature of these arguments is the abandonment of the claim that the pattern of rewards and incomes which is the outcome of markets is in any sense just. Hayek denies that the question has any relevance. The set of general rules that define the market order can be considered just but not the outcomes themselves, because these depend on luck, chance, accident, effort, skill, inherited wealth, inherited talents and many other factors. For Hayek and many of the New Right the market is a lottery. There is no necessary link between effort and reward. What should be important to every individual is not the justice of the outcomes but the range of outcomes and therefore of choice that the market makes possible. Any attempt to enforce a particular pattern of distribution must destroy many of the benefits that flow from an unhampered market.

Nozick adds the further twist that, provided all property holdings have been acquired without coercion, there is no moral basis for redistributing property against the owner's consent. American libertarians, such as Murray Rothbard, argue similarly that all redistribution, including all forms of taxation, becomes violation of individual rights and is therefore illegitimate. This requires the privatisation of all state functions, including the police, the courts, the bureacracy and the military.[34] Nozick himself is more circumspect. He defends the case for a minimal state, and therefore for some taxation. It is anything beyond the minimal state, including the 'extended' state of social democracy, that he wishes to rule out.

The conservative New Right

The second major tendency in the New Right is the conservative. As a doctrine Conservatism has always been characterised by its emphasis upon the conditions that are required for the establishment and maintenance of social order. These conditions include the need for authority, hierarchy and balance. Conservatives have generally been fierce critics of liberal doctrines of individualism which justify the removal of all restraints in the path of individual freedom. In Conservative eyes such ideas are dangerous since they can lead to the erosion of essential institutions that promote social order.

The hostility which Conservatives have always displayed towards liberal ideas of freedom made them at one time critics of capitalism and individualism. It was the progress of the new ideology of liberalism that first led to the articulation of Conservatism as a doctrine. But once collectivist forms of liberalism and socialism began to emerge, the basis for a convergence between some strands of liberalism and conservatism was created. What has made this convergence possible is the common respect of both traditions for property. Conservatives have always placed great emphasis upon property as one of the foundations of authority and order. Their suspicion of *laissez-faire* capitalism has not disappeared, but it has been moderated by the greater dangers which collectivism is seen to present.

Conservatives gradually began to acknowledge the contribution which capitalism as an economic system makes to the preservation of a good as well as a free society. Conservatives came to terms over a long period with capitalism and emerged in most countries as staunch defenders of the free enterprise system. For the New Right to include a conservative tendency is no accident because of the recognition by Conservatives that there are very different forms of liberalism, and that the advanced form known in Europe as social democracy constitutes a major threat to conservative values and institutions. Conservatives can make common cause with the liberal tendency in the New Right because they have a common enemy. Both see the destructive impact of social democracy upon the institutions that sustain capitalism.

Liberals may express this concern in terms of freedom of the individual, while Conservatives emphasise the erosion of authority. Both, however, regard the trends established by the growth of public sectors and the kind of government intervention practised since the 1940s as pernicious. Both focus on the rise of a 'new class' of public sector professional employees who come to staff the agencies of the public sector and who have a vested interest in its continued growth.[35]

For the conservative New Right no less than for their liberal counterparts the postwar compromise was a major mistake and has to be reversed. The special interests that infest government have to be confronted and their power reduced. The authority of the state itself and authority within all major social institutions has to be restored. Under the promptings of the new class the state has expanded into areas which should be left to other institutions. In usurping their role the state has overburdened itself and undermined precisely those institutions, particularly the family, on which it depends for its own support. Social democracy destroys the balance between state and society, threatening the creation of an atomised mass society, the rise of an authoritarian state, and the shrinking of the domain of private life.[36]

Conservative writing is often less systematic, certainly less voluminous than liberal writing. One of its hallmarks is its tendency to become a moral discourse, a discourse about the good society and the enemies that threaten it. These enemies are numerous and they come from within and from without the social order. Often the two are linked in the Conservative mind.

Enemies without

The origins of the conservative New Right lie in the reorientation of foreign policy in the years of postwar reconstruction following the defeat of Fascism. Foreign policy became dominated by the perception of a new threat – the Soviet Union and international communism. Conservatives had always regarded protection of their societies against external assault as one of their most important priorities. This made them the protagonists of strong defence. In the postwar context strong defence was not conceived in national but international terms. It was the whole western economy lying outside the Soviet sphere of influence that needed to be organised and defended. Countries could no longer stand on their own, so extensive alliances were concluded, and an era of unprecedented co-operation between states in the western sphere opened. At its core was the United States.

The establishment of NATO in 1949 marked the start of a major internal and external mobilisation against communism. For Conservatives the containment of communism rapidly became their overriding priority. Defence of the free world against totalitarianism involved a new recognition of the virtues of the free enterprise system and democratic politics. A substantial realignment of political forces took place, with a further splitting of left-wing parties and the coalescence of liberal and conservative forces. The terrain of domestic politics in the countries of the NATO alliance was founded on the exclusion of the communists from government office and the establishment of a consensus between right and left on the main lines of foreign policy – the necessity for whole-hearted participation in the Atlantic Alliance to guard against the Soviet threat.[37]

The consensus on foreign policy underpinned the accommo-dation on domestic policy that was reached in many states, but it also set limits to further moves towards collectivism. The ideological war against communism weakened the legiti-macy of all socialist ideas, placed socialists on the defensive, and created a climate of intolerance towards the Left which at times involved persecution of those with radical and liberal opinions.

There exists a clear continuity between the resurgence of right-wing influence in the 1950s and the subsequent emer-gence of the New Right. Some of those who were later to become leading figures in the New Right both in Britain and the United States broke from the Left during the early period of the Cold War.[38] The loss of their former faith in the Soviet Union and socialism was given as the main reason for changing their allegiance. A major stimulus to the emergence of the New Right in the 1970s was the renewed perception of a

Soviet threat following the breakdown of *détente* between the superpowers.[39]

The new ideological onslaught against Russia and international communism was fuelled by fears of a major shift in the strategic balance which, it was alleged, was giving the Soviet Union and military initiative. The loss of South Vietnam and the establishment of Soviet client states in Africa and the Middle East reawakened fears of Soviet domination and led to charges of appeasement and calls for increased military preparation. Conservative politicians like Ronald Reagan and Margaret Thatcher campaigned tirelessly for major increases in the arms budget and a much more aggressive stance towards the Soviet Union, not just to half any further expansion but to begin rolling back the tide of international communism.

Central to the Conservative New Right was this perception of renewed danger from the Soviet Union. It was accompanied by much writing on the theme of the weakness and decadence of the West. Conservatives argued that what was required was not merely a big increase in military rearmament but ideological and political rearmament as well. The disarray of the western Alliance had to be remedied and military and political unity restored. This was an urgent priority. But as important was the need to combat internal subversion. For the Conservative New Right the greatest threat to the survival of the free world lay in the erosion of national will and political authority which was the legacy of postwar social democracy.[40]

The new element in right-wing discourse in the 1970s is this linking of the external threat to the western democracies with the internal threat created by social democratic policies and institutions. In *The Road to Serfdom*, published in 1944, Hayek had argued that there was no half-way house between even the mildest socialist measures and full-blown totalitarianism.[41] The idea that social democracy was a Trojan Horse for communism had long been popular in right-wing rhetoric. Conservatives in the 1970s, however, took this one stage further by arguing that the dismantling of many aspects of social democracy was now necessary if a successful resistance to communism was to be mounted. Effective defence against enemies without meant first hunting down enemies within.

Enemies within

The decadence of democracy is a major theme for the conservative New Right. The permissiveness and tolerance promoted under liberal and social democratic regimes allows subversives and militants the space they require to attack the soft underbelly of western society. Enemies of the free society penetrate the universities, the schools, the media, the unions, the churches, the civil service, even the security forces. From these vantage-points they seek to stir up discontent and to undermine the institutions of a free society by challenging authority. The society is propelled towards chaos and as authority breaks down everywhere the scene is set for a take-over by the left and the imposition of an authoritarian state.[42]

The most urgent task which the Conservative New Right identified in the 1970s was to reverse the drift towards chaos and authoritarianism by restoring authority at all levels in society. This became first of all a call for tough government. The coercive power of the state should be used against the most visible agents of chaos and disorder – strikers, criminals, demonstrators and vandals. Public order and essential services should be maintained at all costs. The enemies of democracy should be shown that the government was strong enough and determined enough to use the power at its disposal. The government had to demonstrate that it could not be coerced by any direct challenge to its authority.

As important, however, was the need to combat the forces which sapped the will of democratic governments to resist challenges to their authority. It was necessary to change the climate of ideas which shaped the political agenda and the assumptions that governed the formulation and implementation of policy. The main threat here was posed by the growth of the 'new class', the army of public sector professionals and ideologues whose tentacles reached into every corner of the modern state and who exerted enormous influence on the way the politically practicable and the politically desirable were defined. The attack on the new class was spearheaded by the group of American intellectuals who have been dubbed the 'neo-conservatives'.[43] They criticise the assumptions and the ambitions of postwar social and economic policy. They argue that too much of modern planning by public agencies failed to observe the limits which are inherent in human action, limits both of understanding and of knowledge. They are sceptical also of the optimistic expectations held by so many of the new class about the ability of government to change both the nature of human beings and of society.

The attack on the new class continues the critique of rationalism and the enlightenment which has long been a key theme of Conservative thought. Much of this writing is pessimistic and reflects unhappiness at the nature of contemporary society and the forces which are moulding it. Capitalism is not endorsed with any great enthusiasm. But it is endorsed. An influential essay by one of the leading American neo-conservatives, Irving Kristol, was entitled 'Two Cheers for Capitalism'.[44] Capitalism is defended as the best available economic system which, despite its flaws and its inability to inspire allegiance, must be preserved. Capitalist institutions, in particular private property, are regarded as a vital line of defence in the protection of individual freedom and the private domain.

But there are other Conservatives who feel no such pessimism. For them there is nothing 'unheroic' about capitalist civilisation. On the contrary they marvel at its achievements and its dynamism. For them it is the most remarkable economic and cultural system known to history. The working of capitalism itself generates a moral and political system whose watchwords are individual responsibility, freedom and democracy.[45]

Whether they are pessimistic or optimistic, however, all parts of the conservative New Right are agreed that what is most important are the institutions that sustain capitalist economic activity. This places them closer to Hayek than to Friedman. Markets and free competition are not ends in themselves for New Right Conservatives but only means to those ends. Roger Scruton ridicules the idea advanced by Nozick and other New Right libertarians that taxation is necessarily coercive and therefore in almost all cases unjust and an abuse of power.[46] Conservatives argue that, important though it is to protect the private domain from arbitrary power, the authority of the state is as important a principle as the rights of individuals. The proper level of taxation cannot be decided by abstract *a priori* reasoning about the rights of the individual, but can only be decided in relation to the actual circumstances of government.

For Conservatives the crucial need is to restore the balance between the different parts of the social order and to prevent the undermining of authority. The causes they have taken up and the campaigns they have helped launch reflect this. Capitalism in the sense of the free enterprise system and competitive markets is only a part of their good society. As important are the institutions that underpin the workings of markets. This explains why New Right Conservatives, in contrast to most New Right liberals and libertarians, are preoccupied with the problems of civil society and political culture. They place great stress on the problems of the family and the erosion of patriarchy; on the schools, and the standards and content of education; on the multiplying threats to public order; on the problems of racial and sectarian divisions; on the churches and the threat to public and personal morality; and on the limits of democracy.[47]

These two strands of the New Right helped create the intellectual ferment which was part of the context in which Thatcherism emerged, and played a major part in shaping its concerns and objectives. It supplied ideas for challenging the dominant ideas within British politics and the Conservative party. It suggested a novel political strategy for the Conservatives which broke from the assumptions and limitations of the 1940s settlement; and it offered a new strategy for accumulation and reversing economic decline. In the hands of a major political leader plans for making the economy free once more and the state strong were to be welded into a powerful political programme, capable of reversing the decline in Conservative electoral fortunes and seizing the new agenda of British politics for the Right.

3
From Butler to Thatcher

The greatest task of the statesman . . . is to offer his people
good myths and to save them from harmful myths.

Enoch Powell

Much of the novelty and shock of Thatcherism in the 1970s
was due to the contrast with the style and the policies of
postwar Conservatism. Some Conservatives, such as Sir Ian
Gilmour, argued that the Thatcherite wing of the party
was repudiating the British Conservative tradition of non-
ideological politics and pragmatic statecraft that stretched
back to Disraeli.[1] But the particular quarrel of the Thatcherites
was with the attitudes, assumptions and policies to which
Conservatives had become committed in the 1940s and 1950s.[2]
It was the acquiescence by Conservatives in the social democratic compromise in domestic policy which they most wished
to challenge. They always claimed that they were the true
Tories, restoring the party to its traditional principles. To
understand why Thatcherism was so controversial in the
1970s, it is important to place it in the context of developments
in British politics, and in particular in the Conservative party,
since 1945.

Postwar reconstruction

The 1940s mark an important watershed in British politics,
both because of the war and because of the election in 1945
of the first majority Labour Government. The failure of the

61

policy of appeasement in the 1930s was not only a serious defeat in foreign policy; it was also a serious reverse for Conservative domestic policy. The successful prosecution of the war demanded a coalition government, and although the majority of its supporters in the House of Commons remained Conservatives, the Leadership of the Coalition passed to elements that were hostile to many of the assumptions of pre-war policy. The opponents of appeasement also tended to be opponents of balanced budgets and sound finance. They were receptive to the ideas of Keynes and Beveridge for radical changes in the orientation of economic and social policy after the war.

The political momentum behind reconstruction was powerful. Labour ministers tended to see it in terms of an explicit bargain between the working class and the British state. But many Conservatives also accepted the desirability and the inevitability of a major extension of government responsibility surviving into peace-time. Some, like Harold Macmillan, had already been strong critics of the negative and passive stance of Government policy before 1939. Others, like R. A. Butler, recognised the new circumstances the war had created, and became enthusiastic reformers.[3]

The existence of a progressive element within the Conservative leadership and among their MPs in 1945 did not mean, however, that they formed a majority. What completed the education of the party was the substantial defeat it suffered in 1945. At the previous general election held in 1935 the Conservatives had polled 11.8 million votes, which represented 53.7 per cent of the total vote, and had elected 432 MPs. In 1945 they polled only 9.9 million votes, 39.4 per cent of the vote, and elected only 213 MPs.

The loss of more than half the parliamentary party in the election and the size of the Labour majority made the defeat appear more overwhelming than it actually was. The demoralisation of the Conservatives was certainly profound, in part because of the widespread expectation before the poll that with Churchill at their head the Conservatives were certain to win. What the defeat did was to strengthen the hand of those elements in the party who wanted to see a major change in the party's policy. They were quite content to accept the reconstruction plans prepared by the Coalition Government, which the new Labour Government began to carry into effect, as a new permanent framework for domestic policy.

The major changes in domestic policy to which the Conservatives became reconciled in the 1940s were firstly the changed position of the trade unions, which was achieved partly through the repeal of the 1927 Trade Disputes Act and partly through their greater involvement in national policy making; and secondly the enlargement of the public sector through the new measures of nationalisation, the improvement of welfare and education programmes, and the setting up of the National Health Service.

The rise of the New Conservatism and the ascendancy of the progressive wing of the party was made easier because the limited domestic accommodation with organised Labour became combined with a new bipartisan foreign policy consensus in the late 1940s. The commitment to the Atlantic Alliance and the fight against international communism reinforced the need for domestic peace. Though the political rhetoric of the 1940s, particularly Churchill's, was extreme, portraying all social democratic governments including the British Labour Government as half-way stages to communism, there was no programme for rolling back socialism. There was no need for one. All the Conservatives desired was that they and not Labour should be administering the new swollen state sector. Once they had achieved that aim, their ambitions to 'Set the People free', proclaimed in the 1951 election, rapidly subsided.

The contribution of the New Conservatism of Butler and Macmillan to policy was slight. It was never a coherent doctrine. But it gave the leadership legitimacy and provided time for the essential work of party reorganisation. The rebuilding of Conservative electoral strength and the re-emergence of the party as a strong contender for government was aided by the demonstrated readiness of its leaders to accept much of the programme that Labour had implemented.

Labour politicians found it hard to believe, and predicted the return of mass unemployment and the wholesale dismantling of welfare services. The electorate was not convinced. The Labour vote held but the Conservative vote recovered strongly in 1950 and 1951. In the second election, despite running second to Labour in terms of votes, the collapse of the Liberal vote gave the Conservatives a clear parliamentary majority.

Returning to government only six years after having suffered so major a defeat testified to the great powers of recuperation of the Conservative party and its ability to subordinate all other considerations to the pursuit of office. The New Conservatism perfectly fitted the need of the party in the 1940s. A reactionary Conservative programme could have been suicidal for the party. Instead its new leaders saw clearly that the party needed to adjust its perspectives to win back lost electoral ground and to present itself as the party best suited to manage the enlarged public sector.

The party succeeded to an extraordinary degree, winning three elections in a row and increasing its parliamentary majority each time (although its share of the vote rose only marginally). Macmillan and Butler, two of the principal architects of the New Conservatism when in opposition, now emerged as the dominant figures in the Government. They advanced a generation of younger politicians like Macleod, Maudling, Powell and Heath. They presided over an economy that was enjoying the benefit from the great surge of growth in the world economy that began in the 1950s and was based on the generalisation of the production methods of Fordism throughout the capitalist world.

Very little that was inherited from Labour was dismantled by the new Conservative Government. Ministers had to be pressed to proceed with even the limited measures of denationalisation to which they were committed in their manifesto.[1] While they wanted commercial disciplines encouraged in the new nationalised industries they felt there was no danger or special problem with retaining these industries within the public sector now that Conservatives were back in charge of the government. There was no crusading zeal to roll back the frontiers of the state and revive enterprise. The level of taxation and the level of public expenditure were little altered.

What did stop was the momentum for further state control and ownership. The Conservative Government, while it did not disturb the fundamentals of the new social democratic order, believed at first in consolidation rather than in any further extension of the logic of the new system. It experimented with market policies, most notably by placing much greater reliance on monetary rather than fiscal policy and by easing rent controls. The new role and enhanced position of trade unions was accepted. No proposals for any new legislation on trade unions made any headway during the thirteen years the Conservatives were in power. Unemployment and inflation were both miniscule by later standards. In eight out of the thirteen years unemployment was below 500 000 and it never went above one million. The rate of inflation never reached five per cent and in most years it was below three per cent. The growth of the economy, although interrupted by balance of payments crises and by periodic deflations of demand to protect sterling, was still substantial. It was not spectacular by comparison with many other economies but it still allowed Butler when he was Chancellor of the Exchequer to predict in 1955 that the standard of living in Britain would double in twenty-five years.

Ministers could be forgiven for feeling increasingly complacent about domestic politics as the decade wore on. Certainly they felt no pressure from their Right on domestic issues. The 1950s saw the establishment of the Institute of Economic Affairs and the harrying of the Conservative Government by Edward Martell's Freedom League.[5] But despite the threatened revolt of the middle orders of society, hard pressed by the grinding levels of socialist taxation, it obstinately refused to happen. The confidence of the New Conservatives can be judged from Butler's remark in his 1953 budget speech: 'Those who talk about creating pools of unemployment should be thrown into them and made to swim' and Harold Macmillan's judgement after the 1959 election: 'The class war is over and we have won it'.[6]

Amidst this relative domestic tranquillity the Government was preoccupied with the consequences of Britain's decline as a world power: the disengagement from Empire, the halting steps towards closer involvement with Europe, and the continuing contest between the superpowers. The extent of British overseas responsibilities remained substantial in the 1950s; Britain was still a major military power with a network of bases and colonies around the world. At least until the traumatic Suez invasion in 1956 British governments had a clear conception of a British sphere of influence, and could still contemplate acting alone in defence of what were defined as British interests. Britain was a welfare state in the 1950s but also a warfare state. The burden of maintaining overseas military bases was heavy for the British economy because of their cost in foreign exchange and therefore their impact on the balance of payments and the strength of the pound.

The old politics of Empire began to come apart in the 1950s, but the Conservative leadership had some consolation in having found a new politics of the nation which allowed them to claim the mantle of prosperity and to appear before the people as the protectors of welfare and social rights, and the providers of growth. The years of the long boom were also those of the final stage of the British Empire. The success of the new domestic accumulation strategy, which was producing unparalleled prosperity, made the winding down of the external support to the British economy which the Empire had provided seem no longer important. The existence of the Empire and Britain's world position had greatly assisted the constitutional advance of the Labour movement. But through the establishment of a Fordist regime of accumulation and the 1940s settlement in domestic politics, a durable accommodation between capital and labour appeared to have been reached, and the basis for a stable hegemony created. The Conservatives had once again emerged as its chief political agent.

Despite the problems of foreign policy the Conservatives achieved remarkable success in the 1950s. The political problem which had seemed so momentous in the 1920s – how the political and social claims of the rising Labour movement were to be met – had been solved and in a way which appeared to allow the Conservatives to retain their traditional leading political role. Ever since the advent in the 1880s of mass democracy, which most Conservatives had instinctively opposed, the leadership of the party had been uneasily aware of the frail base of support on which the Conservative party rested. In a population already predominantly urban and industrial no secure pre-industrial or traditional social base for a mass Conservative party existed. The Conservatives had to become a party of the industrial proletariat or it had to face being marginalised. The winning of the working-class votes it needs to be able to form governments has been preoccupying Conservative leaders ever since.[7]

The ferment of the 1960s

The domestic calm did not last. As the withdrawal from Empire gathered pace so the precarious foundations of British prosperity were exposed. The relative decline of the British economy became a focus for concern once more. Britain had long lost any pretension to being the world's leading industrial power but it was a new experience to find its economic performance so easily outclassed by states with similar resources and populations. British governments had committed themselves to an accumulation strategy based on encouraging the spread of the production methods and consumption patterns of Fordism throughout the economy, while maintaining and gradually increasing the openness of the economy to trade and capital flows. But the performance of Fordist industries in Britain in most cases never began to match the performance of similar industries elsewhere.[8]

The unease that began to grip political and administrative circles in the late 1950s about Britain's stuttering economic progress (rapid though it was by historical standards), gave rise to a wide-ranging debate on how British society and the British economy could be modernised.[9] To become modern implied rejection of traditional attitudes and established institutions. This was an uncomfortable position for Conservatives to take up, but it was a task which many of the leadership accepted with enthusiasm.

The first major programme of measures to modernise Britain and reverse its economic decline was launched by the Macmillan Government in the late 1960s. At the end of his career Macmillan found an opportunity to follow the *dirigiste* instincts which had been so evident in his writings in the 1930s. The New Conservatives as a group had no inhibitions about extending state involvement and state responsibilities where they thought it necessary and desirable. Most of the available models of modern high-performance economies appeared to involve either an implicit or explicit extension of links between the state and private capital. This became the basis for the accumulation strategy of the 1960s.

What is important for understanding Thatcherism is that the first Conservative attempt to grapple seriously with the problem of decline took for granted not only that the solutions could be found within the parameters of the 1940s settlement, but also that they would involve ways of releasing the potential for collaboration between the major producer interests. New tripartite institutions like the National Economic Development Council, and the first serious attempt at an incomes policy, the National Incomes Commission, were launched. But the modernisation drive was perhaps characterised above all by the additional public expenditure which the Conservatives were eager to commit to new programmes to improve health, education and transport. This was accompanied by a commitment to expansion and the preparation of contingency plans to avoid the momentum of growth in the economy being interrupted by sterling crises.[10]

The adoption of this accumulation strategy to modernise the economy could not bring quick results and the Government was an easy target for past errors and past neglect. A reunited Labour party won a narrow victory at the general election in 1964. The election was remarkable for the closeness of the policies of the parties. All three main parties subscribed to the need for substantial modernisation of British institutions to enable Britain to restore competitiveness and improve the rate of economic growth.

Labour built on the initiatives which the Conservatives had started. The Wilson Government when it took office enjoyed a wide measure of support for its programme from all major interests. But the Government proved quite unable to pursue a coherent strategy in the face of repeated pressure on the pound, and in the end it abandoned its expansionist ambitions. The disappointment of the high expectations of the Wilson Government which many on the Left had held was marked and was to have profound long-term consequences for the Labour party. But there were important consequences also for the Conservative party. Conservatives observed the weakness of the Government in the face of corporate interests, and many turned against measures of modernisation which increased the quantity and range of government controls, and involved the major producer groups in economic policy making. The relative failure of the various corporatist initiatives of the Wilson Government, such as the prices and incomes policy, the national plan and the industrial policies, discredited the modernisation programme among Conservatives and helped precipitate the birth of a new right in the party.[11]

This response was all the greater since, although the Labour Government failed to deliver its 'New Britain' through a reversal of economic decline, the pace of change in the 1960s was rapid, particularly in cultural terms. Many Conservatives who were critical of increased state intervention were also worried about threats to the family, public order and national identity.

This period saw the first emergence of a New Right in Britain. It embraced the growing misgivings of economic liberals about the direction of government economic policy, as well as the new concerns of moral campaigners like Mary Whitehouse who launched her National Viewers and Listeners Association to monitor the output of the media in 1965. It was plainly post-imperial with its focus on domestic issues, and it challenged the authority of the Conservative leadership to determine the direction of party policy. The politician who united its different strands and who provided a clear challenge to Edward Heath and his supporters in the party leadership was Enoch Powell.

Powell's career has been much studied.[12] Before Thatcher rose to prominence he was the most important figure on the Right which the Conservative party had produced since 1945. He had been a New Conservative, one of the recruits to the powerhouse of the new thinking, the Conservative Research Department, over which Butler presided in the 1940s. He always remained obstinately loyal to Butler, even refusing to serve in Alec Douglas-Home's cabinet in 1963 after Butler had been denied the premiership for the second time.

Even in the 1950s he was noted for his commitment to free

market ideas. He resigned as a Treasury Minister in 1958, along with Peter Thorneycroft and Nigel Birch, because of a Cabinet decision to increase expenditure by £50 million against Treasury advice. Powell ever after argued that that decision was the beginning of the great inflation which reached its climax in the 1970s.[13]

His reputation as an adherent of liberal economics did not inhibit him as Minister of Health between 1960 and 1963 when he participated fully in the modernisation drive and supervised a large expansion of the hospital building programme. But once he had resigned he began to be noticed more and more as an exponent of what was abusively termed *laissez-faire* economics. His hostility to high levels of public expenditure and taxation and to all forms of government intervention in the workings of free markets made him often appear very isolated within his own party, and still more so in British politics. In the early 1960s his arguments for unfettered markets marked him as an oddity. The tide of opinion was flowing very strongly in the other direction.

Powell returned to front bench responsibilities when the party was defeated in 1964. In 1965 he contested the party leadership – the first open election the Conservatives had ever held – and polled 19 votes. The new Leader, Edward Heath, appointed him defence spokesman. Powell, at one time an ardent imperialist, now emerged as the advocate of a drastic reduction in Britain's overseas military commitments, to create a defence more in line with Britain's reduced capacities in the world. These ideas did not endear him to the traditional imperialist Right in the Conservative party which was still arguing strongly for the maintenance of British bases east of Suez.

What transformed Powell's standing with the electorate as well as his relations with the Tory party was his intervention in the debate on immigration and race relations that had been gathering pace through the 1960s. In his speech at Birmingham in 1968 he was careful to say nothing that was not party policy but the language that he used to say it made the speech an intervention that the party leadership could not ignore. Powell became the first major politician to break the bipartisan consensus that had grown up on immigration. By using his speech to publicise the fears expressed by his constituents he took on the role of a tribune of the people attacking the conspiracy of silence of the progressive Establishment.[14] Powell's speech was of decisive importance in launching a new politics of the nation, and in demonstrating the possibilities of a populist assault upon some of the central aspects of postwar social democracy. In April 1968 one per cent of those questioned by Gallup wanted Powell to be the next Leader of the Conservative party; in May, after the speech, it rose to 24 per cent. As many as two-thirds of those questioned by pollsters said they agreed with what Powell had said. He received 105 000 letters of congratulation and there was a demonstration by dockers in London's East End in his support.[15]

Powell touched off a minor explosion in public sentiment. The frustration and anxiety of white working-class communities at the growing number of immigrants was not being represented by either major political party. Powell's concern with the identity of the nation and the need to preserve its essential character and continuity provided him with a popular cause which free market economics would never have done. Powell's espousal of this cause, however, was not primarily a cynical manoeuvre aimed at advancing his own career and claims to leadership. It flowed from a particular conception of politics, one which emphasised the importance of the nation and its preservation above all else. Powell was drawing on a very old Conservative insight. Making appeals to non-rational instincts and emotions could often elicit a much deeper response than a politics of incentives and material benefits. Even before the boom had cracked Powell showed the potential for reconstructing British politics on very different terrain. He rejected the idea that the only way the Conservatives could compete with Labour was to provide faster economic growth. The claim of the Conservatives to be the national party, able to appeal to all classes and particularly to the working class, depended, in Powell's view, on its ability to protect the nation from its enemies.

Expelled from the front bench, Powell became the severest critic of the Conservative leadership, but Heath's election victory in 1970 ensured that he would remain outside it.

Powell's new nationalism found new causes in the 1970s alongside race: opposition to Britain's entry into the Common Market and the defence of the union with Ulster. Isolated from so much of the political Establishment Powell became increasingly strident in his denunciation of it. He attacked the enemies within, not merely those who by their violent actions and protests were undermining public and social order, but also those in the civil service, in the media and in government who were persistently thwarting popular demands. The gulf between the progressive elite and the people, which was a common theme in radical right rhetoric elsewhere, was deployed with great vigour and skill by Powell.

In appealing to national feeling and attempting to mobilise opinion against the opinion-formers of the progressive Establishment Powell did not neglect his other obsession – the market. Once freed from the restraints which membership of the Shadow Cabinet had placed upon him Powell became a savage critic once more of all the assumptions and priorities of the modernisation programmes of the 1960s, which were still deeply embedded in the thinking of the Conservative leadership. He was particularly scornful of incomes policies and of all tendencies towards corporatist arrangements between government, unions and employers. He also called for wholesale denationalisation of all public enterprises and for income tax to be reduced to 4s 3d (21p) in the pound, and drastic reductions in public expenditure by ending state intervention in the economy and privatising welfare.[16] Above all he was a strong supporter of sound money to prevent the drift towards faster inflation, and he was an early advocate of floating exchange rates.

Powellism as it emerged always contained this mix of free market economics and nationalism. Powell was the first politician in Britain to advocate the doctrine of the free economy and the strong state, which was to dominate the New Right debate in the 1970s and 1980s. Yet Powellism was always much more coherent than Thatcherism as a set of ideas, in part because of the kind of politician Powell was, in part because the package never became the policy of either the party or the government and so was never tested by the kind of pressures to which Thatcherism was subject.

Powellism was important for later developments because it demonstrated not only that there was a coherent intellectual alternative to the modernisation programmes of the social democratic state, but also that there was an alternative politics of support available to the Conservatives. The right did not need to be imprisoned forever within a system of hegemony, much of which was not of their making. If the old politics was breaking down, the opportunity could be seized to forge a new course.

Apart from a few clues, such as her speech to the Conservative Political Centre in 1968, there is little evidence of what Margaret Thatcher thought of the potential of this new politics. But she was known to admire Powell. She was the only member of the Shadow Cabinet to wish him well in the 1970 election, and it is difficult to believe that his example and his ideas did not leave a deep impression.[17]

The Heath Government

The Conservative Government elected rather unexpectedly in 1970 lasted less than four years, but it proved a critical episode in the emergence of Thatcherism. In retrospect it appears both as a first attempt to introduce a 'Thatcherite' programme and as the last phase of the interventionist modernisation programme of the 1960s. Although it seemed radical at the time and was regarded as marking a sharp break with the policies that had been established during the 1960s, in retrospect the Government belongs more to the era that was closing than to the era that was about to be born.

What was radical about the Heath Government was not that it had abandoned the objectives of the postwar accumulation strategy, which had underlain the modernisation programmes of the 1960s, but that it was proposing new means to achieve them. The profound disillusion with the effects of Labour's interventionist policies, the increasing pressure from Powell and his allies in the party, and the need to differentiate the party from its opponents, all combined to promote a policy of disengagement of the state from the economy.[18]

The Heath Government began by dismantling many of the interventionist agencies which Labour had used to implement its policies. The Prices and Incomes Board, the Industrial Reorganisation Corporation and the Ministry of Technology were all axed. The Government declared that it would not intervene in industry, 'lame ducks' would be allowed to go bankrupt to make the economy more efficient, and no pay and price controls would be introduced. A more competitive and more enterprising economy was the goal.

The emphasis upon competitiveness and efficiency was linked with the commitment to entry into the EEC as quickly as negotiations would permit. Membership of the EEC was expected to open the British economy to fiercer competition from European industries and made the achievement of higher levels of investment and productivity in British companies essential for survival. It was also the next stage in the gradual adjustment of British policy to the withdrawal from Empire. Heath had been in charge of the negotiations in 1961–3 and, despite their failure, and the subsequent failure of the Labour Government's bid in 1967, he had never wavered in his commitment to Europe.

Apart from Powell and a small number of backbenchers the party had become reconciled to membership of the EEC by 1970. For Heath and many leading Conservatives the bid to join Europe was an essential part of the bid to modernise the British economy and improve the British version of Fordism. It offered a new and challenging environment in which British industrial practices would be shaken up and their deficiencies exposed. It offered an end to the illusions that Britain was still a great power which could do without co-operation with its closest neighbours and could rely on its 'special relationship' with the United States. Heath's pro-Europe stance and his coolness towards aspects of the American relationship made him the least Atlanticist British premier since the war.[19]

Heath's conception of what a modern Britain would be like was drawn from the models of the successful EEC member states. He wanted to reform British Government and British industrial relations and to inject more competition into industry. The policy of disengagement and the plans for a new legislative framework for industrial relations were integral parts of this strategy.

Entry into the European Community was achieved very smoothly. Heath was able to give the kind of reassurances to the French about Britain's future role in Europe which at last removed their veto. But in their domestic policies the Government faced mounting problems, particularly over Northern Ireland and the trade unions. The worsening disorder in Northern Ireland was to have momentous domestic political consequences for the Heath Government. The decisions which the Government took to impose direct rule, abolish Stormont, and to set up a power-sharing executive eventually brought the severing of the link between Ulster Unionism and the Conservative Party. The refusal of Ulster Unionist MPs to take the Conservative Whip in 1974 prevented the Conservatives being the party with the largest number of seats after the February election.

Still more traumatic for the Conservatives, however, and still more decisive for Health's loss of the party leadership in 1975, was the course of industrial relations. The attempt to impose a comprehensive legal framework on the unions badly misfired. The degree of union resistance and the inflexibility of many of the new institutions (in particular the National Industrial Relations Court under Sir John Donaldson) led to a series of major confrontations with the unions and often embarrassing climb-downs for the Government. The refusal of the unions to co-operate with the Act made much of it ineffective, and by 1974 even the Confederation of British Industry (CBI) was acknowledging that the Act had harmed rather than helped the evolution of better industrial relations.

The central problem with the Act was that it was designed to deal with the problem of unofficial strikes and the growing power of shop stewards in some major industries, and it sought to do this by giving greater authority to the national union leaderships. The refusal of the trade unions, however, to trade some loss of their privileges for greater authority over their members destroyed the plan and soured relations between unions and Government.

The industrial relations reforms of the Heath Government were misconceived in another way. They did not address the central problem which the Government faced – holding down the rise in labour costs. The Government was determined at first to do without an incomes policy, preferring instead to set a good example by restraining pay in the public sector and encouraging a more competitive atmosphere in industry. It had some early successes in public sector pay disputes but it then suffered a major defeat in 1971 against the miners.

The policy of disengagement also had some hard knocks, first from the collapse in 1971 of Rolls Royce, which had to be rescued by being nationalised, and secondly from the long campaign by workers on Clydeside to resist the closure of Upper Clyde Shipbuilders. Events like these, combined with the sluggishness of the economy and the rise of unemployment towards one million during 1971, created pressures for policy changes. The changes when they came were interpreted by Heath's critics in the party as a U-turn.

The term is very inexact when describing what took place in 1972.[20] In many areas of policy there was no significant change, in others there was a slight shift of emphasis. But there were also three more substantial changes. The Government changed its macroeconomic stance, deciding that a substantial reflation was necessary in order to achieve the kind of rapid growth rate which the Government hoped would become routine once Britain was a full member of the EEC. The Government also chose to implement the decision to reflate by increasing public spending programmes. The attempt to hold down or even reduce public spending was substantially modified after 1971. The Government also became much more actively in favour of state intervention to restructure industry. Sweeping new powers were given to the Secretary of State under the 1972 Industry Act.

The biggest change of all, however, and the one which excited the loudest shouts of betrayal, was incomes policy. The manifesto in 1970 had been quite specific that the Conservatives would not introduce a compulsory incomes policy and in the first phase they had remained true to that pledge, dismantling the incomes policy apparatus they inherited from Labour. The experience of trying to manage the British economy convinced ministers that some formal controls on pay were indispensable. It was very difficult to envisage such controls without the active consent and participation of the trade unions.

A peculiarity of the British political system is that the trade unions are not just allied to one political party but are a key element in its internal organisation and finance. This has always made Labour Governments much better placed to secure co-operation from the unions and has made the Conservatives more wary of corporatist institutions. The position was especially difficult for the Heath Government, since its handling of the Industrial Relations Act and its abrasive style during its early period in office had greatly depleted the goodwill which the Government could draw on.

Nevertheless, despite the unfavourable climate, the Heath Government came very close in the summer of 1972 to securing a comprehensive agreement with the Trades Union Congress (TUC) and the CBI over the management of the economy and over the control of pay and prices. When the talks finally broke down the Government moved to impose through legislation a statutory incomes policy. This was the most far-reaching statutory incomes policy ever achieved in peace-time.[21] Trade unions and employers initially acquiesced in it. Stage 1 and Stage 2 of the policy were successful. Only when Stage 3 was reached did the policy come unstuck, owing to the mishandling of negotiations with the miners. This precipitated another clash with the National Union of Mine-workers (NUM), with dire consequences for the Government. But no general trade union offensive materialised against the pay policy. Most workers settled under the Stage 3 limits.

The complaints of the Government's critics were voiced most strongly by Enoch Powell. During the short life of the Heath Government he managed to vote against the Conservative whip on no fewer than 113 occasions. He argued that the Government was pursuing policies which were quite contrary to the prospectus on which they had been elected. He deplored the turn to compulsory incomes policy and to greater intervention in industry and he predicted that by so lightly abandoning their principles they were heading for disaster. The decline of the Conservatives was made all the more certain, Powell thought, because they seemed prepared to abandon their customary role as the national party, embracing the EEC and forsaking their friends in Ulster.

The Heath Government would have had no difficulty in shrugging off these charges if it had had more luck or if its policies had been more successful. The Conservative attitude towards incomes policy had always been pragmatic. Powell had clashed in 1964/5 with Maudling and other senior Conservatives over whether Conservatives should favour incomes policy. The balance of opinion in the party had swung against incomes policy in the late 1960s, owing to dissatisfaction with Labour's record. The pragmatic revival of incomes policy by the Heath Government was not a betrayal of a deep Conservative principle.

What hurt Edward Heath's leadership more than the charge of treachery was the charge of incompetence. So much happened between 1970 and 1974 that in retrospect the record of the Government looked incoherent. It also appeared to have failed in several of its major objectives. Popular memory of that time is of a period of great turbulence. The Government had been forced to declare five states of emergency in those three and a half years. At the height of the miners' overtime ban it had been forced to impose a three-day week on industry. It had confronted the trade union movement and ultimately it was judged to have lost. The Government proved unable to defeat the miners industrially, and by calling and then losing an election in February 1974 it proved unable to defeat them politically either.

The Heath Government left behind it an image of failure. The Government had failed in the end to impose its authority. Union power, far from being less, seemed to have received a significant boost. Legislation on industrial relations proposed by successive Governments had been successfully resisted. The performance of the economy had not improved but deteriorated. The country was coming to seem ungovernable. The decision to impose the three-day week in January 1973 to cope with the shortage of power supplies, and the announcement of major new expenditure curbs shortly before, dramatically signalled the end of the hopes of the Heath Government for a new era of rapid economic growth. The much faster rate of growth which had been achieved in 1973 was cut short by the quadrupling of the oil price and the onset of world recession.

The misfortune of the Heath Government was to have presided over the British economy at a time of major international changes. The breakdown of the Bretton Woods system in 1971 and the acceleration in commodity prices and domestic cost pressures made the monetary and fiscal policies of the postwar policy regime quite inadequate to contain them. A major increase in the rate of inflation was already under way when the Heath Government came into office. A much larger increase was bequeathed to its successor.

The critics of the Heath Government subsequently singled out the reflation of the economy in 1972 as the cause of the high rates of inflation in 1974 and 1975. The record of economic management under the Conservative Government was taken as vindicating the monetarist critique of Keynesianism. To a greater extent than any British Government since the war the Heath Government attempted to spend its way back to full employment during 1972/3. It was able to do so because the constraint afforded by fixed exchange rates had disappeared. But to keep the momentum of the expansion going, the Government found itself obliged to intervene in markets more and more, and to try to control wages and prices directly.

For a time the policy had seemed to carry all before it. But the collapse of the boom in the world economy and the resistance of the miners wrecked the policy and the hopes that were attached to it. Heath called an election and made the main issue 'Who Governs Britain?' To be refused a parliamentary majority on the basis of such a call was a severe rebuff and threw the Conservative party into despair and demoralisation. The political initiative now passed to Labour which formed a minority administration and subsequently won a small parliamentary majority in a second general election in October 1974.

At this second election the Conservative vote fell to 35 per cent, the lowest percentage they had polled this century. The beneficiary was not Labour but the Liberals and the nationalist parties. Nevertheless the Conservative electoral coalition had been severely weakened, and yet one more major modernisation programme had been shipwrecked. The Conservatives seemed more marginal to British politics and the new centres of power than at any time since 1945. In these circumstances, whatever the degree of blame attaching to him, it would have been remarkable if Edward Heath had remained as Leader. The challenge was not long in coming.

The ascendancy of Margaret Thatcher

In 1974 the Conservative party lacked any procedure for challenging an incumbent leader. It was only nine years previously in 1965 that the party had adopted a method of direct election for the party Leader in place of the informal processes of consultation by which Conservative Leaders had previously emerged. Heath was the first Leader to owe his position to direct election by the parliamentary party, but nothing in the rules obliged him to seek re-election.

The peculiar circumstances of 1974, when the Conservative party lost two general elections, created great pressure for Heath either to resign or to renew his mandate. Heath soon made it clear that he had no intention of resigning and his friends in the party then tried to persuade him to submit to an early vote of confidence from the party. Their reasoning was that there was no serious challenger in sight. The Shadow Cabinet was mostly filled with loyal Heath men. Enoch Powell had put himself out of the running, first by refusing to stand as a Conservative in February 1974 and advising his supporters to vote Labour, and secondly by re-entering the House of Commons in October 1974 as an Ulster Unionist.

The only senior Conservative who seemed likely to challenge Heath was Sir Keith Joseph. He emerged during 1974 as the leading critic inside the party of the policy errors of the Heath Government. In a series of speeches he began to develop a free market and monetarist programme, proclaiming that the Conservative party needed to rediscover its principles. He disowned Keynesian economic management, state inter-vention, high public spending and incomes policies. In one speech he announced his conversion to Conservatism. He had always thought of himself as a Conservative, but now he realised he had never understood what being a Conservative meant.[22]

Sections of the Tory press, notably the *Spectator* under the editorship of Patrick Cosgrave, became strong supporters of Joseph and launched a fierce anti-Heath campaign. The anti-Heath forces were considerable because Heath had antagonised many Conservatives during his period as Leader. The defeat of the Conservative Government gave all these elements the chance they needed to begin mobilising against the leadership. Those who had criticised some of the policies of the Government at the time now appeared to be vindicated. Keynesianism and interventionist policies were badly discredited, and to that was added widespread disquiet about the state of the country, the loss of authority and the drift towards ungovernability. In ideological terms the New Right was able to take the initiative. Their distrust of the Tory Establishment and the central party institutions, including Central Office and the Conservative Research Department, was intense. In 1974 Joseph and Thatcher set up an alternative source of policy advice, the Centre for Policy Studies.

Despite the emergence of a strong New Right presence in the party, however, Heath's critics seemed in no position to launch a bid for control of the party. Keith Joseph had an uncertain touch as a politician and torpedoed his own chances of becoming Leader by making a speech in which he gave the impression that curing the problems of poverty and deprivation required restrictions on the right of the lower-income groups to have children. A second difficulty was that any leadership contest would be settled by the votes of the Conservative MPs. This was an electorate likely to be swayed, not by ideological arguments of the kind Keith Joseph offered, but by pragmatic and hard-headed assessments of where their interest and the party interest lay. Joseph's deficiencies as a politician were unlikely to recommend him.

However, although there appeared to be no convincing challenger to Heath in 1974, there was deep unease in the party about his leadership and a strong body of opinion in favour of a change. The problem was that the most promising successors were all loyal to Heath personally and would not agree to stand if they had to fight him. The curious situation

had developed that those who wanted a Leader other than
Heath could only have a chance of getting who they wanted
by voting initially for someone they did not, namely a
candidate from the Right of the party who had no inhibitions
about challenging Heath.[23]

Heath was eventually persuaded to submit himself to a new
election under a new set of rules drawn up by the former
Conservative Leader, Lord Home. This at last provided for
an annual election of the Leader. For such an election to take
place, however, there had to be someone prepared to challenge.
Keith Joseph had seemed certain to fill that role, but, once
he had ruled himself out, the way was cleared for Margaret
Thatcher to step in.

Thatcher had been a relatively junior member of Heath's
Cabinet; her ministerial experience was confined to education.
In 1974 she had become a front bench spokesman on Treasury
matters and had considerably increased her reputation with
MPs by her attacks on the Finance Bill. In Opposition she
had become associated with Keith Joseph's critical assessment
of the record of the Heath Government through her sponsor-
ship of the Centre for Policy Studies, but there was no stream
of ideological speeches from her, nor had she opposed any of
the policies of the Government while she had been in Cabinet.

Her emergence as the standard-bearer of the anti-Heath
forces in the Conservative party was unexpected, but just
credible enough to make her challenge a serious one. Few at
the outset expected her to win, but she did have certain
advantages. Her campaign was very skilfully managed by
Airey Neave, she had few enemies in the party determined to
prevent her election, and she benefited from drawing on the
support of all those who did not want her as Leader but hoped
that a sufficiently large vote for her would persuade Heath to
resign.

Her campaign managers skilfully exploited this last factor,
playing down Thatcher's chances of winning outright, and
fanning the fears of those who knew that, if Heath got a
sizeable majority on the first ballot, it might be impossible to
shift him from the Leadership for a long time. The strategy
worked perfectly. When the vote was announced the confidence
of the Heath camp that they were heading for an easy victory

was shattered. Thatcher had won 130 votes, Heath 119, Hugh Fraser 16.

Heath now departed, and the way was open for all his loyal lieutenants to come forward to join the contest. But now another factor operated in Thatcher's favour. She had set up an irresistible momentum. The *Daily Telegraph* headlined an editorial: 'Consider her Courage'. Thatcher had made the all-important psychological break with the Heath era. Her victory in the first ballot had created a quite new situation. As a result her support did not diminish in the second ballot but increased. She now won 146 votes; Whitelaw received 79, Prior 19, Howe 19, Peyton 11. It was an extraordinary triumph but it was due mainly to the number of Conservative MPs wishing to vote against Heath rather than to the number wishing to vote for Thatcher. Almost by accident the New Right found they had captured the most important position in the Conservative party.[24]

Opposition

Margaret Thatcher had become Leader of a Conservative party which was in disarray and still demoralised after its heavy defeat in 1974. The party badly needed a new strategy and a new self-confidence to allow it to restore its former dominance of British politics. It had to rebuild its electoral appeal and it had to develop a new programme for government. There was widespread gloom in the Conservative party in 1974 and 1975 about the party's future prospects, a gloom which in some parts of the party Thatcher's election did nothing to dispel. Harold Macmillan reflected this mood when he said in 1975: 'The Tory party is not regarded as a national party now. We tried – Churchill, Eden, myself – to make it a sort of jolly for everyone. It was a party for the nation. Now I'm afraid they've lost that'.[25] John Biffen, a leading critic of the policies of the Heath Government reflected:

> Today the Conservative party no longer receives the support of MPs from Northern Ireland, its representation in Scotland is lower than at any time in this century and in England it

has barely a Westminster toe-hold in the large industrial cities. There is a real danger that the Tories will become the middle-class party of the English shires.[26]

What many Conservatives feared also was that their party would be marginalised by the way in which governments responded to the recession. If the trend towards the strengthening of corporatist structures continued, the main beneficiary would be the Labour party with its close ties to the unions. Labour might be perceived as more relevant and more competent as a party of government. If the Conservatives could not win trade union consent how could they govern? And why should voters support them?

The party had climbed back from heavy defeats before, but in 1975 the future did not look hopeful. The decline of the party as a national political force was evident, as John Biffen suggested. The Conservatives had become closely identified with the EEC, which seemed to hand the valuable card of defender of national sovereignty to Labour. The Empire had gone and Britain was no longer a Great Power. Its economy was in a mess and economic performance had been relatively much poorer than that of many of its closest rivals. The Conservatives had become the advocates of modernisation and rapid social change in the interests of improving industrial efficiency. Their traditional role as defender of national institutions and the English Way of Life had become blurred. In the recent past the Conservatives seemed to have cut themselves off from many of their natural supporters, but had lost the wider popular support which they gained in 1970 because they had been unable to sustain their authority as a strong and competent government that was capable of improving the performance of the economy.

Harold Macmillan's advice to the party he had once led was forthright:

Don't be doctrinaire. Reunite the party at the top. Reunite it in the House of Commons. Invigorate the old Tory machine, which has largely been allowed to collapse. The party is in disorder. The Tories have got to get themselves into a position to fulfil their role, whatever that role may be – we can't tell yet.[27]

Few in the Tory Establishment seem to have believed that Margaret Thatcher would be able to reunite the party. Many thought that in electing her the party risked accelerating its decline. Her appeal was regarded as strictly limited. There were numerous jibes about her supposedly suburban and middle-class image. Ian Gilmour warned during the leadership campaign that the party must not retire 'behind a privet hedge' if it wanted to make a broad national appeal.[28] Julian Critchley recalls the occasion when he first met Margaret Thatcher. His companion said afterwards she reminded him of the Chairman of his Women's Advisory Committee 'writ hideously large'.[29]

Curiously, disdain for the new Leader was shared at first by many New Right intellectuals. Thatcher lacked the intellectual qualities of Keith Joseph; her right-wing views always appeared much more a matter of instinct than rational argument. She was seen by some as comparable to a mid-West American politician, strong on first principles, weak on understanding of the complexities of the modern economy. Her lack of political and intellectual sophistication invited ridicule. The Conservative political class had long despised conviction politics and those who practised it. They prided themselves on their intelligence, their flexibility, and their pragmatism. Thatcher's abrasive, direct style swept all that away and threw the devotees of the Tory political arts into panic.

Her leadership in opposition certainly did not follow the pattern prescribed by Harold Macmillan in all respects. Her election unleashed a remarkable outpouring of doctrine in the party, assisted by the highly doctrinaire tone of most of the Leader's own utterances, and there was no reuniting of the party at the top. Thatcher's purge of the Shadow Cabinet she inherited was fairly modest, considering that only three out of 23 are thought to have voted for her in the leadership election. But the victims included some major figures like Peter Walker, who had been a senior Minister in the Heath

Government and had run Heath's campaign, and was younger than Thatcher herself.

The most significant absence, however, in Margaret Thatcher's Shadow Cabinet was Edward Heath. His exclusion advertised the deep division that had opened up in the ranks of the Tory leadership, a division that was to persist even after 1979, although it was to become less significant as Thatcher's dominance increased. Heath moved steadily into a position of bitter personal antagonism towards Thatcher herself and denounced many of the policies she adopted and pursued. In a manner that was unprecedented for a former Tory Leader he carried on the battle in public – at the party conference, in the House of Commons and through the media.

There was never any question of a Heath restoration. But his vocal opposition to the new Leader and the direction she was taking the party did express the views of many of those inside the Shadow Cabinet. Many of the senior Conservatives whom Thatcher did not consider it prudent to remove from her Shadow Cabinet were strong supporters, if not of Heath personally, certainly of the policies he advocated. From the start Thatcher moved cautiously. Her supporters were in a minority in her Shadow Cabinet and in her first Cabinet as well. The Conservative leadership was divided by her style of leadership and the policies with which she was identified to a greater degree than at any time since the 1930s.

The pace at which new policies were developed was, however, very slow.[30] The Conservatives were not committed to a radical Thatcherite programme by the 1979 election. Yet by that date the main outlines of Thatcherism were clearly established. A new political agenda had been marked out, and with it the outline of a new accumulation strategy and a new hegemonic project were becoming visible.

Thatcher attracted enormous attention when she became Leader of the Conservatives, at first because she was the first woman leader of any major British political party, but subsequently because of her very distinctive political style which began to emerge in her responses to the events and crises that destroyed the authority of the Labour Government and undermined the credibility of its policies. Thatcher took full advantage of this. She used every opportunity during her time in opposition to intervene on particular issues.

A firm image of her objectives and her beliefs soon began to crystallise. Her lead encouraged the marshalling of powerful popular and intellectual forces in support of a radical programme. This programme was never adopted as the programme of the Conservative party, but it became the rallying-point for all those groups who wished to overturn the old politics and destroy the old consensus. A thousand flowers began to bloom on the New Right. Enormous hopes and expectations began to be invested in this new leader.[31]

The way in which her image came to be formed can be traced through the major interventions she made between 1975 and 1979. She focused on those areas where the authority of the state had been weakened. The solutions she favoured and the attitudes she struck defined a new role for the Conservative party, but it was a very different role from the one envisaged by Harold Macmillan. Instead of cleaving to the centre and rebuilding an image of soundness, competence and moderation, Thatcher provided something much more exciting and risky – a radical assault on the assumptions of the postwar consensus on domestic policy in the name of Conservative principles.

Yet the intervention which first gave content to Thatcherism and expressed Thatcher's new style was not a radical break with the postwar consensus but a return to one of its most central themes. In a speech in Kensington on 19 January 1976 Thatcher launched a major attack on the policy of *détente* and called for a major new arms build-up by the NATO countries and an ideological crusade against communism.

The speech was one of the opening shots in the new cold war. It brought Thatcher considerable notoriety, especially after she had been labelled the Iron Lady by the Soviet media. The epithet was gratefully accepted and iron became an essential part of the Thatcher image. In her speech Thatcher denounced the Soviet Union, declaring that its leaders were bent on world dominance and that they were 'rapidly acquiring the means to become the most powerful imperial nation the world has seen'. A constant theme was impatience at western weakness: 'They put guns before butter, while we put just about everything before guns'. She warned of the huge gap which she claimed had opened up between the size of the conventional forces on each side. Most striking of all, however, were the constant references in the speech to the need for moral rearmament against the Soviet threat. She quoted Alexander Solzenitsyn approvingly for reminding the West that 'we have been fighting a "Third World War" over the entire period since 1945 – and that we have been steadily losing ground'. She cited the loss of Vietnam and Indo-China and the 'open grab for power' in Portugal, and warned:

> Even now the Soviet Union and its satellites are pouring money, arms and front-line troops into Angola in the hope of dragging it into the Communist bloc . . . the Russians . . . have one great advantage over us – the battles are being fought in our territory not theirs.[32]

Britain must wake up:

> The advance of Communist power threatens our whole way of life. It is not irreversible, providing that we take the necessary measures. But the longer we go on running down our means of survival, the harder it will be to catch up. In other words, the longer Labour remains in government, the more vulnerable this country will be.[33]

The first need therefore was to get rid of socialism and social democratic governments throughout the West. She took comfort from the recent election victories by right wing parties in Australia and New Zealand:

> What has happened in Australasia is part of a wider reawakening to the need to provide a more positive defence of the values and traditions on which Western civilisation, and our modern prosperity, have been based.[34]

The speech was also notable for the firm support which was given to the Atlantic Alliance and the lukewarm endorsement of Europe – Britain's membership had been recently confirmed in the 1975 Referendum: 'We believe in the Conservative party that our foreign policy should continue to be based on a close understanding with our traditional ally, America'. For the EEC she cautioned, 'the interests of individual nations are not identical, and our separate identities must be seen as a strength rather than a weakness. Any steps towards closer European union must be carefully considered.'[35]

This was coupled with the traditional endorsement of Britain's greatness and special mission in the world. Thatcher rejected the idea that Britain was no longer a great power. The decline in Britain's former strength, she declared, was partly inevitable, caused by the rise of the superpowers, and partly avoidable, 'the result of our economic decay, resulting from processes that the Labour Government has assisted'. The speech ended on what was to become a major theme of Thatcherism: 'The Conservative party has a vital task in shaking the British public out of the effects of a prolonged course of sedation.'[36] The shaking was only just beginning.

Thatcher's speeches on foreign policy marked a shift away from the pro-EEC stance of the party under Heath and a reaffirmation of the party's commitment to the Atlantic Alliance. This coolness towards the EEC had already been demonstrated during the EEC Referendum campaign in 1975, when the major Conservative contribution to the pro-Referendum campaign had been left to Edward Heath. There was never any suggestion that the party might reverse the commitment it had made to the EEC, but there was no longer such enthusiasm about Europe and no wish to see the Community develop quickly as a supranational body.

In her onslaught on *détente* Thatcher first demonstrated her ability to define issues in new ways and to change the existing agenda. Her taste for moralising and for seeing problems in simple black and white terms began to delight her followers and enrage her critics. Her interventions on policy were rarely cleared with her colleagues. Reginald Maudling, who had re-entered the Shadow Cabinet as Foreign Affairs spokesman after Thatcher's election, became appalled at the way in which Thatcher chose to make impromptu policy pronouncements. One of these appeared to commit the party, without prior discussion, to a major programme of rearmament. His protests were ignored and he was soon removed from his post.[37]

The attack on *détente* and the reaffirmation that the Anglo-American alliance had greater priority than the EEC were hardly bold positions staked out against the tide of British political opinion. They were attitudes shared entirely by the Labour Governments of Wilson and Callaghan. But Thatcher skilfully exploited the new cold war fears to outbid any position that the Labour Government took up. Labour was condemned for vacillation and weakness in the face of the 'threat to freedom'.

Another area where Thatcher intervened to help shape the agenda of the new politics was economic policy. Once again the radicalism and novelty of the position taken up by the Conservative leadership can be exaggerated. Much of the replacement of a Keynesian by a monetarist policy regime was the work of the Labour Government, responding to the crisis in the world economy between 1974 and 1976. What the Conservatives argued was that Labour's conversion to monetarism was produced by circumstances, not by conviction, and would be reversed at the earliest opportunity. They also claimed that it was too little, too late. The monetary cure had to go much further if sound money was to be restored and if new life was to be breathed into the ailing British economy.

What gave the attacks by the Thatcher leadership such edge was the critical state of the British economy in the 1970s. The failure of successive Governments to reverse the relative decline by trying to modernise the productive base of the economy in line with best practice in Fordist economies elsewhere was evident. The weakness of many British industrial sectors was now painfully exposed by the world recession.

The Labour Government, after dropping its own radical programme after 1975,[38] attempted to cope with the recession by a mixture of pragmatism and opportunism. It used whatever policies and institutions were to hand. It had no coherent accumulation strategy. Its ambitions were aimed at preventing the situation getting any worse. The policies of the Labour Government were quite successful within their limits. After the first two years and a series of major crises involving inflation, public spending and sterling, the situation was stabilised. Inflation fell sharply, the pound began to rise with the prospect of North Sea oil coming on stream, unemployment did not rise beyond 1.5 million, the incomes policy held, and strikes declined to very low levels.

These achievements were, however, scorned by the Thatcherites and the New Right, although for a time during 1978 they were understandably nervous that the economic improvement and the parliamentary pact with the Liberals[39] might help Labour to recover enough electoral popularity to win the election. The basis of their scorn was their conviction that the old political formulas were tired and played out. British decline could not be reversed by Labour's defensive policies: subsidising jobs, propping up or nationalising industries that got into difficulties; protecting and strengthening the position of trade unions; and attempting to control a wide range of wages and prices.

What Thatcher grasped was that the productive base of British capitalism was so enfeebled that it could no longer support the public sector spending programmes and the tripartite structures of economic policy making which gave a veto to producer interests on radical policies. Profitability had to be rebuilt, and to achieve this a new accumulation strategy had to be pursued which would give priority to sound money, free markets, lower taxes and greatly reduced trade union power.

Under Thatcher's leadership the Conservative party first began to signal its interest in a radically different accumulation strategy from the one being pursued by the Labour Government through its enthusiastic embrace of monetarism, even though its policy statements remained cautious and pragmatic. On becoming Leader Thatcher had moved Michael Wolff from his post as head of the Conservative Research Department and had given Keith Joseph the job of co-ordinating policy and research. Both Joseph and Thatcher had become identified with the New Right critique of Keynesian economic management, but while Joseph explored the deeper intellectual arguments in favour of a new policy regime, Thatcher was chiefly interested in finding solutions to inflation. She argued passionately in favour of stable prices as the most important economic objective. Monetarist arguments provided a useful justification for a policy objective she felt should be central to any Conservative programme.[40]

The appeal of monetarism was much more than a set of techniques for controlling the money supply. In Thatcher's hands the arguments against Keynesianism became an opportunity to restate the case for a free society. Stable money was one of its foundations, but limits on public expenditure and the removal of obstacles to free competition were also crucial. The major obstacles to a free economy were identified as the spreading network of corporatist institutions which were encroaching on the functioning of free markets. The main targets were the Labour Government's incomes policy, the influence of the trade unions over Government policy, the proposals of the Bullock report for legislation to enforce industrial democracy by placing with trade unionists on company boards, the new measures of nationalisation in vehicles, shipbuilding and aerospace, and the level of public expenditure, borrowing and taxation.[41]

Thatcher always made it clear that she intended to break with the corporatist style of economic management practised by both Labour and the Heath Government in its last phase. As the party in opposition the Conservatives were obliged to distance themselves from the programme of the Labour Government and revive once more the traditional free market, individualist critique of state power. What was new was that this turn in party policy was not just a matter of electoral expediency but was also now bolstered by a set of doctrines about the way the economy worked and how British decline could best be reversed. The Conservatives now had a leadership which was convinced that a major power struggle was going to be necessary before the economy could be turned round and a new and viable accumulation strategy installed.

Thatcher succeeded in identifying the party with the assumptions and conclusions of monetarist analysis and made it plain that the party would reject corporatism. One of her chief targets was incomes policy. In her Conference speech in 1976 Thatcher supported the return of free collective bargaining in place of the kind of incomes policy achieved through Labour's social contract with the unions. She argued that the only reason there had been a clash between the unions and the Heath Government was because of the imposition of a statutory incomes policy, which the next Conservative Government would not repeat.

Throughout the period of Labour's voluntary policy (1975–8) the Conservative opposition indicated it would scrap all controls. When the policy finally collapsed in the wave of public sector strikes in the winter of 1978/9 Thatcher's stance seemed vindicated. But it had only been maintained against powerful opposition within the party. Many leading Conservatives believed an incomes policy was a vital instrument in the management of the economy, and that the only alternative to it was to permit the creation of much higher levels of unemployment.

Leading figures in the Tory Reform Group urged the creation of a Tory social contract, which would combine understandings on pay with Government commitments on industrial democracy and urban deprivation.[42] There were widespread misgivings about abandoning attempts to secure understanding with the trade unions, and relying on a revival of the disciplines of bankruptcy and unemployment to curb prices. This pressure was resisted, however. Thatcher's repeated denunciations of statutory incomes policy ensured that by 1979 the party was committed to a return to free collective bargaining and therefore to curbing trade union power by other means.

What these other means might be was left vague during the years of opposition. The policy documents *The Right Approach* (1976) and *The Right Approach to the Economy* (1977) promised very little new legislation on unions. The opposition spent a lot of time trying to dispel the idea that any future Conservative Government would be embroiled once again in confrontations with the unions. The leadership gave considerable thought to the question. Two internal reports were prepared, one by Nicholas Ridley and one by Lord Carrington, to advise the Shadow Cabinet on its options in the face of major industrial unrest under a future Conservative Government. Carrington was more pessimistic than Ridley. In his report Ridley argued for a policy of fighting public sector strikes in industries where the Government was confident of winning, and avoiding them where it was not, until it had built up its strength sufficiently to be sure of victory.[43]

Thatcher made her own characteristic contribution in an interview on *Weekend World* in September 1977. Pressed to say how she would respond if a Government led by her were faced by a new miners' strike she said that she would call a referendum. This idea received no favour among her colleagues and was subsequently dropped. The handling of the miners, however, from the payment of subsidy to keep pits open in 1981, followed by the carefully prepared breaking of the strike in 1984/5, showed that Ridley's report was not forgotten.[44]

Thatcher and Joseph seem to have been in no doubt that a major curb on trade union power was indispensable, but in opposition they trod carefully, preparing the ground rather than drawing up the kind of detailed plan with which the Heath Government had entered office in 1970. Important members of the Shadow Cabinet such as James Prior fought a long and successful rearguard action against the rising tide of anti-union feeling in the party. Norman Tebbit, still a backbencher, but by now one of four key advisers to Thatcher,[45] denounced the attitude of some party leaders to the unions as demonstrating the morality of Laval and Pétain, the French leaders who were prepared to collaborate with the Nazis.

Pressure for commitments by the Opposition to tighten the law was particularly strong at the time of the Grunwick dispute in 1977.[46] The party leadership, however, contented itself with denunciations of union power, but made no firm proposals for curbing it. Yet since the party was also committed to do without an incomes policy and to reduce the scope of subsidy and intervention, the need to weaken trade union power became an inescapable necessity. The opportunity to press for new laws finally came with the Winter of Discontent.

Thatcher and Joseph seized on the events of that winter of 1978/9 as a symbol of the bankruptcy of social democracy. It seemed to confirm everything they had been saying about the impossibility of going on in the old way and trying to keep the old consensus together. Trade union power could not be appeased. It had to be destroyed if decline was to be reversed and the authority of the state restored. The myth of the Winter of Discontent, with its images of closed hospitals, rubbish piling up in the streets, and dead bodies rotting unburied in graveyards, was a masterpiece of selective news management in the Conservative interest and even came to surpass that other great myth from which the Conservatives benefited and which has shaped the way the 1970s are perceived, the myth of the 1976 IMF crisis.[47]

It re-awakened all the fears about union militancy which had been stilled by the social contract, and it raised once again doubts as to whether the project of social democracy in Britain still had the capacity to be hegemonic. Its accumulation strategy had proved inadequate to reverse the decline of British capitalism, it had lost the ability to command the support of key sectors of capital and organised labour, its electoral coalition was visibly fragmenting. It could no longer sustain the authority of the state against challenge. It had produced a weak state and a fettered economy.

Thatcherism offered deliverance from all this.[48] Emboldened by the winter carnival, the Conservatives at last made some explicit if still cautious commitments in their 1979 manifesto. There was no great trumpet-call to announce the beginning of the Thatcher Revolution. There were few indications in the manifesto of the storm that was about to break.

4

The Thatcher Government 1979–87

Our country's relative decline is not inevitable. We in the Conservative party think we can reverse it. We want to work with the grain of human nature, helping people to help themselves . . . The Conservative Government's first job will be to rebuild our economy and reunite a divided and disillusioned people.

Conservative Election Manifesto 1979

The Conservatives' victory in 1979 was decisive but not overwhelming. The party's share of the vote recovered from its low point in 1974 to reach 43.9 per cent. The Conservatives won 339 seats, a majority over all other parties of 43. A Conservative victory had seemed probable after the collapse of the authority of the Government during the IMF negotiations at the end of 1976. Labour had trailed the Conservatives by as much as twenty-five points in the opinion polls in some months between the autumn of 1976 and the summer of 1977. The party had suffered some major by-election losses in this period,[1] as well as enormous losses in local government seats.

The by-election defeats had deprived the Labour Government of its overall majority in Parliament, and the Opposition had had some hopes of forcing a general election half way through the Government's term. This was avoided by the conclusion of a parliamentary pact with the Liberals in March 1977. The Government's popularity recovered markedly at the end of 1977 and during 1978, but it chose not to call an election as expected in the autumn after the ending of the Lib–Lab pact. It then suffered the second major blow to its authority with the strikes of public sector workers in early 1979. What brought the Government down, however, was not the Winter of Discontent but its inability to maintain its Parliamentary majority. The crucial event here was the failure of the devolution referenda in Scotland and Wales.[2] This allowed the Opposition to press a vote of no confidence and to force an election at a time of their choosing.

Before May 1979 it was unclear whether the radicalism of Thatcher and her supporters was merely a tactic in the battle for electoral support or the first sign of a major new development in British politics, which would have consequences for the conduct of government. Even for those who accepted that Thatcher's intentions were radical there was still doubt as to how far the Conservatives, if elected, would be able to carry through a New Right programme within the existing state, or how big a restructuring of the state they might authorise in order to overcome obstacles.

Many of the early interpretations of Thatcherism were based on the performance of the Conservatives in opposition. They have often had to be modified in the light of the record of the Thatcher Government, and the different phases of its development. Thatcherism has turned out to be no brief spasm. It has dominated an entire decade. The easiest way to divide up the Thatcher years is by the dates of the general elections; Thatcherism Mark I 1979–83; Thatcherism Mark II 1983–7; Thatcherism Mark III 1987– . This approach is quite useful and it is simple. If the governing party is defeated an election can mark major change in the personnel, the style and the programme of government. Even when the existing Government is re-elected an election means a new manifesto and a new legislative programme, and usually a major Cabinet reshuffle.

What an emphasis on elections may fail to capture, however, are the trends, continuities and patterns which are independent of the election cycle.[3] These are often striking, even between governments formed by different parties, and are particularly strong in the case of governments that are re-elected. They allow different phases in the life of a Government to be identified. They may be created by particular events and issues, by particular policies and doctrines, or by the patterns of party support and conflict.

Of overriding importance in shaping domestic policy in recent years have been events in the world economy. From this perspective there have so far been two crucial phases in the life of the Thatcher Government, determined by the slump in the world economy between 1979 and 1982, and then by the recovery between 1982 and 1987. The slump which brought to an end the partial recovery from the earlier recession in 1974/5 was triggered by the rise in oil prices in 1979. The recovery after 1981 was fuelled and sustained by the budget and trade deficits of the United States. This phase ended with the financial crash which began in October 1987.

Phase I   1979–82: the slump

The monetary cure

The first phase of the Thatcher Government lasted from May 1979, when it was elected, to the March budget of 1982, and was dominated by the consequences of the Government's determination to maintain a strict monetarist policy in order to bring down inflation. The conquest of inflation was the Government's top priority. It had decided to apply a monetary cure for inflation before the onset of the recession, and it persevered with the policy even when the severity of the recession became apparent.

The major rise in oil prices in 1979 reduced world demand and increased industrial costs. At the same time it placed further upward pressure on sterling. The United Kingdom became a significant oil producer at the end of the 1970s. Since 1977 the markets had begun to anticipate this fact and sterling had begun to appreciate markedly in value. OPEC's decision to increase oil prices by 15 per cent was announced on 28 June. Two weeks before, on 12 June, the new Chancellor, Sir Geoffrey Howe, introduced a budget which had two principal objectives – lowering the rate of inflation through a severe monetary and fiscal squeeze and beginning a major restructuring of the burden of taxation. The rate of value-added tax (VAT) was almost doubled, from 8 to 15 per cent, income tax reduced from 33 to 30 per cent, and prescription charges in the National Health Service were increased. At the same time personal tax allowances were raised and the top income tax rate was lowered from 83 per cent to 60 per cent. Dividend control was abolished, a new higher threshold for investment income was announced, and development land tax was cut.

These measures were intended to increase incentives and signal the new direction of government policy. They were accompanied by the announcement of new money supply targets, a pledge to reduce the Public Sector Borrowing Requirement (PSBR) to £8.25 billion, and the immediate raising of minimum lending rate (MLR) from 12 per cent to 14 per cent. Public expenditure was to be cut by £1.5 billion and where annual cash limits on spending programmes were in force they were tightened to reduce planned expenditure by a further £1 billion.

In its first few months in office the Thatcher Government also made some other crucial decisions which signalled its intentions not only to break with many of the policies of the previous Government, but to dispense with several of the key institutions and agencies through which previous Governments had intervened in the economy. It placed its faith in the private sector and the removal of obstacles to the working of free markets.

In July and October 1979 all remaining currency exchange restrictions were removed. This abandonment of exchange controls on capital movements proved permanent. On 19 June the National Enterprise Board (NEB) was ordered to sell assets worth £100 million. On 1 October the British National Oil Corporation (BNOC) was forced to give up many of its interests in oil exploration and its stake in 23 blocks in the North Sea was put up for sale. On 17 July the Government announced that the regional support budget was to be cut by £233 million (one-third of the total budget) within three years.

These early decisions were taking place alongside a growing number of challenges to organised labour. On 1 November, one week after the removal of all exchange restrictions, the closure of the steel works at Corby was announced by the British Steel Corporation. In another nationalised industry, British Leyland, the management began the start of a major crack-down on the shop-floor when they sacked Derek Robinson, the convenor of the shop stewards, on 19 November. The Government made plain that in the public sector it was prepared for closures and redundancies, and would back tough management policies to carry through whatever degree of restructuring was necessary to restore profitability and end public subsidies.

By the end of 1979 the general condition of the economy was beginning to deteriorate rapidly. The Government responded to evidence that money supply growth was accelerating by hoisting MLR from 14 to 17 per cent in November. The year ended with decisions by first Saudi Arabia and then Libya to impose major increases in the price of light crude oil.

The Government had already shown its strong commitment to monetarism by raising interest rates from 12 to 17 per cent within six months of taking office. In the budget in March 1980, however, it went much further by announcing a medium-term financial strategy (MTFS).[4] This aimed to provide greater certainty about future monetary conditions by indicating targets for both money supply and government borrowing. If the targets were not met there would be automatic fiscal or monetary changes in Government policy. The room for discretionary economic management which was held to have been so destabilising in the past would be drastically reduced.

The MTFS, as unveiled in 1980, sought to set targets for money supply growth (using one particular measure of the money supply, sterling M3, as the indicator) over a four-year period. Sterling M3 comprises all notes and coins in circulation plus sterling deposits held by UK residents. It was planned to decline to 6 per cent by 1983/4. Money supply would be tightened by increasing interest rates when necessary in order to achieve this. At the same time the PSBR would be gradually reduced, if necessary by cutting spending or increasing taxes. The government deficit would not be allowed to increase and would not be financed in ways which increased the money supply.

From the outset the control and reduction of public expenditure was an essential part of the monetary cure for inflation. The new assumptions were clearly spelled out in the White Paper on Public Expenditure in November 1979. With its first sentence, 'Public expenditure is at the heart of our current difficulties' the White Paper challenged the bipartisan consensus which had existed since the 1940s on the desirability of high levels of public expenditure. Cuts were no longer necessary simply to meet a short-term fiscal crisis. They had to be permanent and deep in order to lay the foundations for economic revival and long-term economic prosperity.

The White Paper opened a war on all fronts. Specific proposals included the withdrawal of supplementary benefit from strikers' families, the taxing of unemployment benefit, and new increases in prescription charges, excise duties and Petrol Revenue Tax. The White Paper planned a reduction in public expenditure of 4 per cent by 1983/4.

During 1980 the recession deepened rapidly. High interest rates and soaring oil prices combined to push up sterling by 12 per cent. The competitive position of British companies declined by 35 to 45 per cent. Both profits and liquidity were severely squeezed. A mounting wave of bankruptcies, plant closures, and lay-offs was the result. Unemployment rose rapidly month by month. By the end of the year it had reached 2.13 million, an increase of 836 000. Inflation was soaring too, peaking at 21.9 per cent in May 1980.

The severity of the recession brought the first modification in the policy in the autumn of 1980. The MLR was reduced to 14 per cent even though the figures for £M3 were running far above the target range. The Government argued that the figures had been distorted by the removal of the Bank of England's 'corset' on bank lending in July, and that the strength of sterling indicated that monetary conditions must be tight.

The fiscal targets were also proving hard to achieve. Treasury Ministers encountered great problems in forcing the cuts in public expenditure they wanted through Cabinet. Some spending Ministers argued that it was unwise to cut spending when the country was in the grip of such a deep recession.

However expectations that monetarism would be short-lived and that the severity of the recession would oblige the Government to change tack proved mistaken. In the 1981 budget the tight monetary policy was maintained. MLR was again cut and the monetary targets were modified, but what enraged the critics of monetarism within the Cabinet was that direct taxation was sharply increased because tax allowances were not increased in line with inflation. This was done to ensure that the borrowing targets which the Chancellor had fixed the previous year, and which he had been unable to reach through spending cuts, would still be achieved. In the midst of the deepest recession since 1945 the Government made progress towards fiscal balance its priority rather than attempting to counteract the fall in demand.[5]

The application of the tight monetary policy and its consequences dominated the first phase of the Thatcher Government. The depth of the recession had not been anticipated but those Ministers and political advisers who were strongly influenced by monetarist thinking seized on it as an opportunity for forcing through the radical changes in economic policy and economic structure which they wanted to see. An atmosphere of cut-backs, closures and retrenchment pervaded the public and private sectors. By launching a policy blitz and attacking on so many fronts simultaneously the Government encouraged the belief that it was bent on radical change of attitudes, institutions and policies, and that it was determined to see the policies through, whatever the short-term costs.

During its first eighteen months in office there was a spate of decisions announcing closures and cuts in areas of direct Government responsibility. Many of these decisions were aimed at destroying institutions and reversing policies associated with the Labour Government. Fifty-seven quangos were axed, among them the Price Commission. The National Enterprise Board was stripped of most of its functions and after its directors had resigned *en bloc* it was merged into the British Technology Group. The July 1979 Education Act withdrew the instruction to local authorities to organise their schools on comprehensive lines. In November 1980 the Community Land Act was repealed.

Trade unions and the public sector

Despite its eagerness to smash icons and break taboos in order to reshape the policy agenda, the Government's radicalism was most apparent where decisions could be easily implemented and which cost it little. Abolishing boards and public agencies were the best example of this. In several key areas of policy, particularly industrial relations and nationalised industries, the Government initially moved extremely cautiously.

The first trade union bill was put through in 1980. But although it restricted picketing and defined tighter limits for the closed shop, it was a modest measure and was strongly criticised for not going further. James Prior, the Employment Secretary, was one of the leading anti-monetarists in the Cabinet and, although he favoured trade union reform, he was a restraining influence both in Opposition and Government on those who wanted much tougher measures enacted.[6] There was no disposition at first to confront union power directly for fear of presenting the unions with the kind of issue around which they could rally effective protest, as had happened with the Heath Government's Industrial Relations Act.

In opposition the Conservatives had anticipated that major problems with the trade unions would arise in the public sector. The strategy recommended in the Ridley report in 1978[7] was faithfully followed. At first the Government only picked quarrels where it was sure of victory. It backed the management of the British Steel Corporation (BSC) when the first national steel strike for more than fifty years began in January 1980. The strike was defeated after four months. But when, in February 1981, the miners began an overtime ban over pit closures the Government swiftly retreated and found a subsidy to defuse the issue.[8]

Elsewhere in the public sector during this early phase the Government attempted to make nationalised industries more efficient by backing a new breed of managers, often imported from the private sector, to put the industries into competitive shape and staunch the flow of losses. Major confrontations with shop floor power followed. Some of the biggest struggles came in British Leyland, as Michael Edwardes, appointed by the previous Labour Government, reorganised the company by reducing the workforce, closing plants, changing working practices and investing in new models. In 1980 Ian MacGregor was brought in to do the same for BSC.[9]

One radical option that had been canvassed when the Government first took office was for the major lossmakers among the nationalised industries, particularly British Leyland, to be declared bankrupt, and their assets sold off for whatever they might fetch.[10] The Government retreated from this option once the implications for unemployment became clear. Sir Keith Joseph, the leading advocate of free market policies within the Government, was obliged as Secretary of State for Industry to preside over the attempt to make the nationalised industries profitable through state intervention. In the short run this meant a massive increase in subsidies to cover their losses.

This appeared at the time a significant retreat for the Government, since if the Government were successful in making the industries profitable it would demonstrate that public enterprise could work; but if it were not successful it would leave the Government still subsidising the losses. In the meantime it meant that the Government was forced to authorise more public spending on precisely those programmes it most wanted to see cut. Denationalisation of other public sector assets was pursued in part to offset this.

The first move to reduce public holdings was the sale of the assets of the National Enterprise Board, announced in June 1979. The Government stake in the computer company, ICL, as well as in Fairey Holdings and in Ferranti were all sold over the next year. In addition the Government sold five per cent of its stake in British Petroleum (BP) in January 1980. This was followed by the sale of 52 per cent of the Government's holding in British Aerospace (February 1981), the 24 per cent stake in the British Sugar Corporation (July 1981) and 49 per cent of its stake in Cable and Wireless (October 1981). The Government's receipts from these early measures of denationalisation were modest – £377 million in 1979/80 and £405 million in 1980/81 – but their success created a momentum for further sales which was to be carried much further in future years.

The control of public expenditure

The intractability of the problems in the public sector helped throw doubt on whether a key objective of Government economic policy – the need to cut taxation and public spending as a proportion of national income – could be achieved. The control and reduction of public expenditure was seen by the Government as an essential part of the monetary cure for inflation.

But the Government was blown off course almost immediately by the severity of the recession. It increased the subsidies to nationalised industries and it bore the burden of increased spending on social security as the numbers of unemployed soared. In addition the Government was committed to increased spending on a number of programmes. Police and army pay were immediately raised by substantial amounts, as the 1979 manifesto had promised, and the defence budget enlarged. More surprisingly the Government decided to honour the Clegg Commission's verdicts on public sector pay. The Clegg Commission had been set up by the previous Labour Government to investigate the gap that had opened between pay scales in the public and private sectors. Its recommendations kept appearing until the summer of 1980 and meant sizeable additions to public sector budgets.

In the face of this wave of higher spending the Government sought every available means to reduce expenditure. Major spending cuts were announced in November 1979 and in the 1980 budget. Prescription charges were pushed up sharply, the regional aid budget was slashed, overseas student fees were raised, the Parker Morris standards for new council building were abolished, and school meals charges and council house rents were increased. Major reductions in grants to local authorities were announced and university places were cut. A bruising battle at a succession of summits with the other Heads of Government in the European Community resulted in the negotiation of a sizeable rebate on Britain's budget contribution. The overall level of public spending did not fall, but the Government made very plain its hostility to public spending over a wide area and its determination to cut and squeeze wherever it could.

Foreign affairs and defence

The battle over the Community budget was an early sign that the Thatcher Government, like its Labour predecessor, would give greater priority to the relationship of the United Kingdom with the United States than to its relationship with the European Community. There was little enthusiasm, except in the Foreign Office, for the revival of the pro-European policy of the Heath Government.

The worsening of relations between the superpowers after the invasion of Afghanistan in December 1979 led to the American boycott of the Moscow Olympics in 1980 which the British Government strongly supported. Mrs Thatcher's cold war stance enabled her to play a leading role in the new ideological onslaught on the Soviet Union. She became still more important following the election of Ronald Reagan to the United States Presidency in 1980. The close political relationship between Thatcher and Reagan helped underline the continuing importance of the Anglo-American relationship in the political and economic management of the world system. Each was to give the other important assistance in the years ahead.

One tangible sign of the new cold war was the increase in the tempo of the arms race. In July 1980 the Government decided to purchase the Trident missile system to replace Polaris as Britain's nuclear deterrent. The plans to station cruise missiles in Britain had already been laid by the Labour Government and were now confirmed.

The Government enjoyed an early success in foreign policy when, despite initial opposition from the Prime Minister, her Foreign Secretary, Lord Carrington, successfully negotiated a settlement to the civil war in Zimbabwe. This led to the end of the rebellion, democratic elections, and the granting of independence in 1980. The end of the Rhodesian rebellion seemed to mark the end of the Empire as an important factor in British politics. All that remained was negotiating the hand-over of a few far-flung dependencies. The Falklands were soon to confound that notion.

Public order

During this first phase, as the Thatcher Government struggled to make the economy free and to restore the authority of the state, it did not neglect to strengthen the capacity of the state to repress disorder. The Government had to face two major challenges – the Hunger Strikes in Northern Ireland and the inner city riots.

The Government was implacable in its opposition to the republican movement in Northern Ireland, particularly following the assassination of Airey Neave, one of Mrs Thatcher's closest advisers, in March 1979, by the Irish National Liberation Army. In Northern Ireland itself the Irish Republican Army (IRA) remained the greatest security threat. In August 1979 came the bombing at Warrenpoint and the murder of Lord Mountbatten. During 1980 a major challenge developed to the Government's authority through the Hunger Strikes. This protest was organised to win political status for republican prisoners in the H blocks in the Maze prison.

The Hunger Strikes were led by Bobby Sands who, following the death of the sitting MP, was elected MP for Fermanagh and South Tyrone at a by-election in April 1981. The strikes were an early test of Thatcher's political will. She refused to make any concessions to the strikers despite the sympathy which the strikes enabled the IRA to attract both in Ireland and in the United States. After several of the hunger strikers, including Bobby Sands, had died, the strikes were called off.

The inner city challenge came from the riots that erupted in several major cities, including Bristol (St Paul's), London (Brixton), and Liverpool (Toxteth). These riots helped justify a big increase in the range of police equipment and changes in police training. The burning of the cities at the depth of the recession with unemployment climbing towards three million, was seen by many as a direct result of the kind of policies the Thatcher Government was pursuing. Thatcher vigorously denied this, arguing that the problem had nothing to do either with race or unemployment, but was a problem of public order.[11]

Party and electoral support

In 1980/1 the British economy appeared to have gone into a nosedive and one easily identifiable target for blame was the Government's insistence on maintaining a rigid monetary policy. This brought the Government great unpopularity and created considerable dissension within the Cabinet.

During the first parliamentary session, 1979/80, the main beneficiary of the Government's unpopularity was the Labour party, which saw its opinion poll ratings leap. In the Southend by-election in March 1980 Labour came close to snatching the seat. In the autumn of 1980, however, a major internal rift developed in the Labour Party. At the Labour Party Conference two of the three constitutional changes sought by the Left were passed. This was followed by a leadership election in which Michael Foot defeated Denis Healey, and a further Conference at Wembley which decided on the composition of the electoral college to elect the Leader. The largest share, 40 per cent, was given not to the MPs, as the leadership wanted, but to the trade unions. Several prominent Labour MPs, including David Owen and Shirley Williams, then left the party and set up the Social Democratic Party (SDP). Altogether 27 Labour MPs and one Conservative crossed the floor to join the new party in the first six months of 1981.[12]

This major split in the Opposition was eventually to work to the advantage of the Government. During 1981, however, the new challenge from the electoral alliance concluded between the Liberals and the SDP proved formidable. The Alliance soared in the polls, reaching 40 per cent in some months. In October 1981 it won two major by-election victories in Conservative seats – Croydon NW and Crosby. Government popularity fell at the end of 1981 to the lowest level ever recorded by the party in government. Thatcher was also briefly the most unpopular Prime Minister since the war.

The economic blitz, the inner city riots, and the crumbling of Government support caused great unease within the Conservative party. In her first period as Prime Minister Thatcher faced a divided Cabinet and strong opposition to some of her key policies. She compensated for this by concentrating her main supporters in the economic ministries (she took special care with the choice of her Treasury team). She also used the Cabinet Committee system to ensure that she retained control over the policy agenda in crucial fields. Nevertheless the dismay of some Ministers with the direction of policy found expression in an extraordinary spate of leaks about Cabinet discussions, and coded messages of opposition in ministerial speeches.[13]

The Cabinet opposition was dubbed the 'wets' by the media after a phrase of the Prime Minister. The term was used indiscriminately to denote those who either on grounds of principle or grounds of expediency opposed Thatcherite policies. With its public school overtones of spineless opposition the 'wets' came to mean those who lacked the political will and the political courage to take and carry through the hard decisions which the Thatcher revolution required. Thatcher's own personal political style encouraged a cult of toughness, inflexibility and conviction politics. Scepticism was equated with weakness.

The main battle between Thatcher and her Cabinet critics came over public spending. In the autumn spending round in 1980 the wets had some success in resisting the full cuts sought by the Treasury. This meant that the Government could no longer achieve its targets for government borrowing. To remedy this the Treasury team clawed back what had been lost by deciding not to raise tax allowances in line with inflation in the budget. This meant a sizeable increase in direct taxation at a time when the recession was at its most severe.

In line with the normal convention the 1981 budget proposals were not revealed to the Cabinet until the morning of the budget speech. Several ministers contemplated resigning on the spot but none did so. Nevertheless the criticism from inside the Government of the direction of government policy grew. The isolation of Thatcher within her Cabinet and within the party appeared to be increasing, especially after coded speeches by two senior figures, Francis Pym, the Leader of the House, and Lord Thorneycroft, the party Chairman.

Thatcher's response was characteristically defiant. In September she launched a major reshuffle of her Cabinet, bringing in Conservatives committed to her policies, and removing or sidelining several of her most prominent critics. Gilmour, Soames and Carlisle resigned and Prior was removed from Employment and made Northern Ireland Secretary, although he retained his seat on the Cabinet 'E' Committee which discussed economic strategy. Norman Tebbit, at that time one of Thatcher's most trusted allies and advisers, became Employment Secretary, while Cecil Parkinson became Party Chairman and Leon Brittan Chief Secretary to the Treasury.

Thatcher now had a Cabinet more balanced in her favour, although it still contained leading critics like Prior, Walker and Pym. She also had critics in the party. The 1981 Conservative party conference witnessed a fierce denunciation of the Government's economic policy by Edward Heath. At the nadir of the Government's electoral fortunes in late 1981 prospects for the Government's survival looked slim. Most observers thought a Conservative defeat at the next election certain, and the ability of Margaret Thatcher to survive as Prime Minister and Conservative Leader for much longer was questioned. The Thatcher Government seemed to be the latest in a long line of governments which had suffered irreversible damage as a result of bad judgement and ill-fortune. It appeared that the Thatcher experiment would be short-lived.

Phase II   1982–7: the recovery

These years were golden years for the Conservatives. The Government won two general elections by comfortable margins and emerged victorious from a series of major confrontations with its enemies: the Argentinians over the sovereignty of the Falkland Islands; the miners over pit closures; local authorities over rate-capping and the abolition of the Greater London Council (GLC) and the metropolitan counties; and the peace movement over the stationing of cruise missiles in the United Kingdom.

The world economy

Underlying the growing confidence and ascendancy of the Conservatives during these years was the recovery in the world economy. The Thatcherites claimed that the recovery after 1981 was due to the monetary stabilisation achieved between 1979 and 1981. The recovery was however not confined to Britain but was general throughout the capitalist world economy. It was sustained by the supply side policies pursued in the United States which reflated the American economy and increased world demand. This created a boom which brought unemployment down to very low levels and fuelled domestic consumption. This boom was kept going by allowing the budget and trade deficits to rise without check. With the other major economies still pursuing tight monetary policies and refusing to reflate, the world economy became increasingly unbalanced. The position was widely regarded as unsustainable. The financial crash finally came in October 1987, threatening the world economy with a new world recession and a collapse in the value of the dollar.

Foreign affairs and defence

The Conservative Government profited not only from the world economic recovery but also from its victory in the Falklands war in June 1982. A potential disaster for the Government which might have brought its downfall was transformed into a popular triumph. It produced a major improvement in Conservative poll ratings. The display of resolve and the success which it brought lent credibility to other government policies. When the British flag was raised again over Port Stanley Thatcher's reputation as a tough, resolute and trustworthy leader became greater than that of any British Leader since Churchill.

The dispatch of the task force to reconquer the islands after the Argentinian invasion appeared a simple exercise of British power and resolve. But the reality was more complicated, since Britain's freedom to act in the South Atlantic depended on the tacit agreement of its allies and the active assistance of the United States. It demonstrated the continuing importance of the Anglo-American relationship rather than the reassertion of British national sovereignty.

The close relationship between Britain and the United States was symbolised by the close ties between Reagan and Thatcher. Throughout this phase of the Thatcher Government Britain confirmed its traditional postwar role as principal ally of the United States. Britain gave full support to American policy towards the Soviet Union, towards Central America and towards the Middle East. The most striking instance of British support came in April 1986 when the British Government gave permission for American bombers stationed at bases in England to bomb Libya.

In its defence policy the Government gave full support to the deployment of cruise missiles. It fought a major propaganda battle with the revived peace movement over the stationing of these missiles at American bases. The deployment went ahead, despite the demonstrations at Greenham Common and Molesworth. Strains in the relationship came mainly as a result of unilateral American actions which were not cleared in advance with their allies. Prominent examples included the invasion of Grenada, a Commonwealth country, in 1984, and the Reykjavik summit in 1986. At the latter President Reagan appeared prepared to agree to Soviet proposals for a nuclear-free Europe. The British desired to retain nuclear weapons as a deterrent.

The relationship with the European Community improved during this second phase of the Thatcher Government, although the British were still obstructive on many issues. Thatcher continued to veto British participation in the European Monetary System (EMS), and to resist increases in the regional aid budget and other community programmes. On many foreign policy issues Britain more often lined up with the United States than with its European partners. Examples included the boycotting of the United Nations Educational, Scientific and Cultural Organisation (UNESCO), support for the contras in Nicaragua, support for American action against Libya, and resistance to sanctions against South Africa.

The higher priority given to the United States rather than to the European Community was clearly seen in economic policy. Despite the very different emphases of American and

British policy, there was no public criticism from the British Government at the growing American deficits. Similarly there was little encouragement to those attempting to strengthen the European economy. The accumulation strategy the Thatcher Government pursued did not ignore Europe, but at no time did the needs of European capital become its focus.

The Westland affair in 1985/6, although it only concerned a small company, illustrated this. Michael Heseltine, the Defence Secretary, fought inside the Government for a European solution to the problems of Westland helicopters. He wanted the Government to reject the bid from the American firm, Sikorsky, which the company itself wanted, in favour of a bid from a European consortium of helicopter companies. Heseltine broadened the issue into the question of how to ensure the survival of an independent European manufacturing base. Blocked by the Prime Minister, Heseltine resigned from the Cabinet on this issue in 1986, and the decision subsequently went against him.

Economic management

After 1981 it became clear that the worst of the recession was over. Unemployment ceased to rise rapidly, inflation fell sharply, the pound dropped back, and a slow recovery in industrial output began. The devastation of large parts of the economy, particularly the areas of old traditional industry, still loomed large. But the decline had stopped. From 1982 onwards the dominant feature of economic policy and debate was not the recession but the recovery and how far it would go.

Government economic policy in this phase shifted from a concern with monetary targets and the control of inflation to the supply side remedies that were considered necessary to spread prosperity and revive economic activity. Monetarism became steadily less important in Government thinking. Zero inflation remained the Government's objective but it no longer appeared willing to make the sacrifices to achieve it. The medium-term financial strategy still figured prominently in every budget speech, but its targets were now often revised upwards, and the Government began to use more than one indicator of monetary conditions. In this way the main complaint of the wets – that government policy was far too rigid – was overcome. Discretionary economic management was reinstated. By 1987 monetarism was quite unimportant as a guide to what the Government was doing.[14]

With unemployment relatively stable at three million and the rate of inflation falling below five per cent, the Government began to experiment with supply side changes to widen the scope of markets and incentives. The first objective was tax cuts, in the belief that this would provide the incentives that were needed to revive enterprise. Tax cuts and tax reform had long been central to Conservative economic thinking and had featured prominently in the first budget. But the need to cope with accelerating inflation and the deepening recession had deflected ministers away from this part of the strategy. The emphasis had become narrowly monetarist. Many American supply siders were strongly critical of this orientation, arguing that cutting taxes to stimulate enterprise should come before control of the money supply. The Thatcher Government, however, continued to emphasise that tax cuts would only be made when it was safe to do so. This meant when spending had been cut or revenue increased.

The Government's hopes of achieving a major change in the balance between the public and private sectors depended on its success in holding down public spending and finding new sources of public revenue. Certain areas of spending, notably the health and social security budgets were judged too sensitive for major direct cuts. The principal targets in this second phase came to be local authority spending and subsidies for nationalised industries. The Government became involved in major confrontations with local councils seeking to protect their spending and with the National Union of Mineworkers (NUM), seeking to protect jobs and communities.

On the revenue side, the Government already a major beneficiary from North Sea oil revenues, found that the easiest way to increase its income was by selling public companies (denationalisation) and privatising public services. After a slow and hesitant start this programme, which the government referred to misleadingly as its privatisation programme, became a significant factor in the planning of the budget.[15]

Local government

After its earlier failures to control local spending through grant penalties, central government now attempted to achieve control through rate-capping. This involved the Government drawing up a list of councils which it deemed to be over-spending and placing a ceiling on the amount by which they could legally increase their local property taxes (rates). This brought a long struggle with many Labour-controlled councils who tried to avoid the effects of rate-capping by refusing to set a legal rate or by using creative accountancy to raise additional money.[16]

Relations between central and local government, particularly in the big urban centres, deteriorated so badly that the Conservatives began to seek ways to bypass local councils and take responsibilities from them. In their 1983 manifesto they included a pledge to abolish the GLC and the six metropolitan councils. Some of the functions of these councils, such as transport, were to be removed from local authority control altogether. A major battle was waged against the abolition of these councils, which caused grave embarrassment to the Government, but ultimately the abolition was pushed through in 1986.

By the 1987 election the Conservatives were becoming still more hostile towards local government and were proposing a range of new measures to limit the responsibilities and the power of local authorities. These included the replacement of rates by a poll tax to be known as the community charge, the setting of a uniform business rate, educational and housing reforms which would allow schools and council estates to opt out of local authority control, and proposals on inner city redevelopment and higher education designed to reduce local authority involvement.

Trade unions and the public sector

A second major area of confrontation arose over support for industry. The Government was determined to use its control over nationalised industries to force them to become profitable. The big test came with the mines. After giving way in 1981 when faced by the threat of a major stoppage over pit closures the Government had carefully prepared for a major showdown. Little was left to chance. Coal stocks had been built up at the power stations, alternative sources of supply identified, the security forces prepared, detailed contingency plans drawn up by Whitehall, and a new tough chairman, Ian Macgregor, appointed.

The strike began in March 1984 and lasted eleven months. It was enormously costly for the Government, but it ended in complete defeat for the miners, once they had split and been successfully isolated from the rest of the Labour movement. By crushing the miners the Government was able to demonstrate to the whole Labour movement that nothing was to be allowed to stand in the way of restructuring industries to make them profitable again and internationally competitive.[17]

The greater the Government's success in hauling nationalised industries back into profit the more attractive the option of denationalisation. These years from 1982 to 1987 saw a series of major sales of public companies, including British Telecom, British Gas and British Airways. These sales were justified on a number of grounds – as a contribution to Government revenue, as a means of making companies more efficient, and as a way of boosting popular capitalism by increasing the number of shareholders in Britain. These enormous denationalisations came to be used by the Conservatives as the most tangible evidence of the 'Thatcher Revolution'. In the 1987 manifesto the Government promised to denationalise the water and electricity industries during the new Parliament.

Reducing union power and privileges was given a very high priority in this second phase of the Thatcher Government. Two further pieces of legislation were introduced in 1982 and 1984, aimed at restricting union rights and opening their funds to claims for damages. This legislation contributed to the climate, already created by mass unemployment, of trade union demoralisation and retreat. The Government found it increasingly easy to brush aside union resistance. It imposed strict pay curbs in the public sector through cash limits, and it showed itself ready to meet and defeat any strike in the public sector.

The miners' strike was the major test of this resolve. Other important disputes included the print union battles at Warrington in 1983 and Wapping in 1986/7, and the teachers in 1986/7. Throughout this period the TUC was frozen out of participation in central government decision making. The Government made it clear that what it sought was either union-free companies and industries, or single company unions, with no-strike agreements. The new forms of such an industrial relations system were foreshadowed in the experiments promoted by some of the Japanese companies such as Nissan which were now beginning to locate in the United Kingdom.[18]

Unemployment rose above three million in January 1982 and did not fall below it until July 1987. The number of long-term unemployed in the total rose sharply. Controversy centred on the frequent redefinitions of the unemployed which the Government introduced, which had the effect of cutting the headline total by some 600 000 by 1987. The Government's main response to the problem of mass unemployment was the expansion of the Manpower Services Commission (MSC), a quango first established by the Heath Government and developed under Labour. The Thatcher Government in its first phase cut the MSC budget and seemed poised to abolish it altogether. With the rapid rise in unemployment, however, the agency was reprieved and became an extremely powerful and expansionist arm of government. It organised major programmes first for the young unemployed, later for the long-term unemployed, and began to concern itself with all aspects of training and education.[19]

Public order and security

Throughout this second phase the Government continued to arm itself to repress violent protest, breaches of public order and, increasingly, internal dissent. A major initiative on Northern Ireland, the Anglo-Irish Agreement, was signed in 1986. The agreement was a modest document aimed at increasing co-operation between the Irish and British Governments, but it produced fierce opposition from the

Unionists, and attempts by them to make Ulster 'ungovernable'. The Unionists were faced down. The level of IRA activity in Northern Ireland continued to decline during this phase, but they were still capable of major operations. The most spectacular was the bombing at the Conservative Party Conference in Brighton in October 1984, which came close to killing the Prime Minister and several Cabinet Ministers.

There were a number of important controversies about security, amidst fears of growing secret service involvement in domestic surveillance. They included the decision to ban unions at the Government intelligence-gathering centre, GCHQ, in 1983; the revelations of former agents such as Cathy Massiter; the Zircon affair – which involved disclosure of information about the Government's spy satellite; and the attempts by the Government to prevent the memoirs of a former MI6 Officer, Peter Wright, from being published in Australia.

Party politics and electoral support

These years saw a strong recovery in the Government's popularity. In the general election in June 1983 it won a crushing victory in terms of parliamentary seats over a divided opposition. Between May 1982, after the commencement of the Falklands war, and the end of the miners' strike in March 1985, the Government's support in the monthly opinion polls rarely dipped below 40 per cent.

The new strength which the Government enjoyed during this period and the increasing ascendancy of Margaret Thatcher as a national and a world leader owed a great deal to the Argentinians' seizure of the Falkland islands in April 1982 and the Government's response to this unexpected crisis. If the bid to retake the islands had been mishandled and had ended in a costly defeat, or if the Government had agreed to peace terms which conceded part of the Argentinians' claims, the reputation of the Government and of Thatcher herself would have been severely damaged. The successful recapture of the islands created the kind of national euphoria which had long been absent from British politics. It was the first occasion for a very long time that a British Government had succeeded in a major undertaking. The effect upon the credibility of the Government in all its other activities was considerable. The Falklands war more than any other single episode restored the authority of the state and with it the political fortunes of the Conservatives.[20]

Throughout this period, from the beginning of the Falklands war to the victory celebration at the Conservative Party Conference in 1987, the Conservatives were generally in the ascendancy. Only during 1985 after the end of the miners' strike and in the first half of 1986 did Conservative electoral fortunes dip. A succession of events – the Westland affair, the Libyan bombing, the schools dispute, the mishandling of the bill to abolish the GLC, and the attempted sale of part of British Leyland to foreign buyers – put the Government on the defensive and made it look vulnerable. But although it lost some by-elections, its support never crumbled in the way that it did in 1981. Labour gained ground once the miners' strike was finished, but although it led in the opinion polls, it was never able to rise above 40 per cent support. It never established the kind of commanding leads which oppositions in the past had generally achieved prior to victory in a general election.

The two general election results in 1983 and 1987 were remarkably similar. The Conservatives polled almost the same percentage of the vote as in 1979. Labour came second, but 12–15 percentage points behind. The Alliance came third with a substantial vote, 22–26 per cent, but not sufficient to win a large bloc of seats. The economic prosperity (and, even more important, the steady economic improvement) for the majority of those in employment, the divided opposition and the geographical concentration of Conservative support, made the Conservative position an extremely strong one. In both elections the Conservatives entered the election as clear favourites and held their position throughout the campaign. Labour had a new Leader, Neil Kinnock, in 1987 and fought a superior campaign to the Conservatives, but failed to make a major inroad into Conservative support.

In the Alliance David Owen had replaced Roy Jenkins as Leader of the SDP in 1983, but although the Alliance had many electoral successes, it never recaptured the levels of support achieved in its first twelve months. When the election came its vote was squeezed between the Conservatives and a strengthened Labour party. The attempt to merge the Liberals and the SDP immediately after the 1987 election led to a major split within the SDP, and subsequently threatened to split the Liberals also. The disarray of the Centre appeared a direct consequence of the failure of the Alliance strategy between 1982 and 1987.

Throughout this phase the Prime Minister's position was generally unassailable, particularly after the two election victories. The only moment of real danger for her came with the Westland affair, which brought both her veracity and her competence briefly into question.[21] But this moment of danger passed. With the exception of this dramatic episode Cabinet dissent was at a much lower level in this phase of the Thatcher Government than previously. Critics were steadily purged. Francis Pym was removed in 1983, Jim Prior resigned in 1984, Michael Heseltine resigned in 1986, John Biffen was sacked in 1987. The Prime Minister appeared to exhaust and then alienate even some of the colleagues closest to her, such as John Biffen and Norman Tebbit, who left the Cabinet and resigned as Conservative Party chairman in 1987.[22]

Despite its share of scandals – Parkinson, Archer, Proctor, Best[23] – the Conservatives retained their confidence and their unity. The wets disappeared as a visible or coherent force within the party. Thatcherite ideas increasingly dominated the party, and the influence of New Right doctrines and libertarian groups became more pronounced, especially in the Federation of Conservative Students, among some of the younger MPs, and in the Conference itself. Many doubted how far the bulk of the parliamentary party had become doctrinally committed to Thatcherite doctrines. Two decisive election victories, however, and a steadily improving economy were more than enough grounds for loyalty to the incumbent leadership.

The record assessed

In its own estimation the Thatcher Government was a radical

government which sought to reverse British decline. In her foreword to the 1979 Manifesto Margaret Thatcher claimed that the balance had been tilted too far in favour of the State at the expense of individual freedom. The 1979 election, she wrote, was the last chance to reverse that process. It was the most crucial election since the war. She found a feeling of helplessness in the country – 'that we were once a great nation that has somehow fallen behind and that it is too late now to turn things round'.

The Thatcher Government believed that it knew how to turn the country round. It set itself five main tasks:

1. to restore the health of economic and social life;
2. to restore incentives;
3. to uphold Parliament and the rule of law;
4. to support family life;
5. to strengthen Britain's defences.

The first two of these tasks involved the creation of a free economy – a strategy for economic management and accumulation that marked a break with the strategy associated with the Keynesian techniques, and corporatist structures of Fordism. The other three involved the creation of a strong state, to provide the institutions that would support and nourish the free economy. How far have these goals been realised by the Thatcher Government? More specifically, to what extent have the policies of the Thatcher Government realised the objectives of the 1979 Manifesto?

Making the economy free

The economic policy of the Thatcher Government must be assessed under two heads; its conduct of economic management and its strategy for accumulation. The radicalism of the first has been much disputed. The change to a monetarist policy regime had already occurred before the Government took office. Monetarism served important ideological and political needs, but it was less important as a guide to policy. Monetary targeting proved impractical and was abandoned.

Some economists have argued that the reduction in inflation

owed more to the severe fiscal deflation which the Government imposed on the economy.[24] Keynesian techniques continued to be used, only now the objective was to restore financial stability rather than to preserve high levels of employment and growth. This was a major political shift, consolidating the change under the previous Labour Government. But in terms of economic management it was a much smaller shift; economic management remained discretionary and interventionist.

The management of the economy tended to become more discretionary and flexible as time went on. But certain key Thatcherite policy objectives remained. The control of inflation continued to head the list, followed by a reduction in taxation and public spending as a proportion of gross domestic product (GDP). In the early years of the Thatcher Government the trend in both taxation and public spending was up. Aided however by the recovery after 1982 the objectives were reaffirmed and cuts in the rate of income tax were delivered in 1986 and 1987.

What was also delivered, however, were increases in public spending in real terms. Since the economy was growing faster increased public spending was still compatible with the objective of reducing its share in national income. Nevertheless it meant that at best its fall would be very slow. The tax cuts were also very gradual. Income tax had been reduced by 1987 from 33p in the pound to 27p. But after the first reduction to 30p in the 1979 budget which also reduced top rate from 83p to 60p, the next cut had to wait until 1986. Financial stabilisation took priority over more ambitious supply side proposals for boosting growth by encouraging enterprise.

The same picture is apparent if the public spending programmes are looked at in detail. Few programmes were terminated altogether and few radical solutions were applied.[25] Such solutions were canvassed within the Government. The Central Policy Review Staff (CPRS) options to avert a major public expenditure crisis were leaked in 1983. They included privatising the NHS and introducing student loans. They were instantly disavowed by the Government.

The Government's preferred strategy in relation to public

expenditure was to force increases in efficiency by arbitrarily reducing cash limits, and by promoting privatisation and deregulation. This threw most institutions in the public sector into turmoil and created deep demoralisation and a permanent atmosphere of financial crisis and retrenchment. The Government, however, was very slow to take responsibility for reorganising the sectors directly, preferring at first to use central financial pressures.

The deepening conflict which this strategy produced between central and local government and the inability of central government to achieve either control over local spending or the kind of local policies it wanted, produced a marked shift towards centralisation of power, finance and functions away from the Town Halls.

Despite its unwillingness to take radical measures in public spending by closing down major institutions and programmes, the Government's hostility to many forms of public spending was unmistakable, as was its determination to squeeze budgets regardless of the consequences for the organisation and quality of the services that had to be funded from them. The Government had no means of measuring these.

This was clearly unsatisfactory in many areas and gradual recognition of this fact led, not to a restoration of the budgets that had been cut, but to increasing central intervention to reorganise and restructure institutions and programmes. This produced some important changes in the way the public sector was organised, but the overall size of the public sector had not been reduced by 1987. The limited reductions in some areas were more than balanced by increases in others, either through choice, as with defence, or through necessity, as with social security.

The failure to make deep cuts in public spending meant increasing reliance by the Treasury on windfall revenues to control and reduce public borrowing. The two major sources of revenues tapped in this way were the proceeds of Petroleum Revenue Tax on the North Sea producers and the proceeds of denationalisation. This enabled public spending levels to be maintained, and even increased in 1986/7, while at the same time making tax cuts affordable. Without the cushion of asset sales and oil revenues public spending would have had to be cut much more sharply or taxes or borrowing increased.[26]

Denationalisation became a central feature of the Thatcher Government's programme, although it had hardly been mentioned in the 1979 manifesto. It emerged very strongly as a central theme after an initial period in which the Government's policies towards nationalised industries were highly contradictory. The Government did not seem able to decide whether it wanted nationalised industries to be run like private sector companies, subject to the same constraints but allowed the same managerial autonomy, or whether it wished to use them as milch cows for the Treasury or as laboratories for experiments with industrial restructuring. Profitable nationalised industries like gas and electricity were repeatedly forced to raise their prices substantially and to contribute their excess profits to the Exchequer. Those making losses were given tough financial targets and tough new managements.

Ministers gradually became convinced, however, that the political opportunity existed for permanently removing many industries from the nationalised sector. The objective of eliminating losses in the nationalised sector remained but it was rather overtaken by the urge to sell off any assets that could be made attractive to the markets. The success of state restructuring of some of the nationalised industries prepared the ground for denationalisation, because if companies could be made viable commercial entities they became potential targets for denationalisation. This made the most profitable nationalised industries like British Telecom and British Gas, rather than the least profitable like British Rail and the National Coal Board, the most tempting targets.

A major transfer of assets between the public and private sectors took place, mostly during the second phase of the Government, 1982–7. In several cases the need to make the sale as attractive as possible to investors prevented industries being broken up and competition being increased. Few economists thought the sales likely to increase economic efficiency, any more than the original nationalisations in the 1940s had done. But like those nationalisations the denationalisations of the 1980s were a symbol of the changing political climate, and the shift away from collectivist solutions in public policy. The wider share ownership which the sales made possible became a central part of the project of popular capitalism.

The denationalisations were preceded by the dismantling of corporatist institutions like the National Enterprise Board and the Price Commission (even the role of the National Economic Development Council was substantially downgraded). This was part of the Government's drive to reduce the influence of trade unions in the policy-making process and to avoid committing itself to the formulation of an industrial strategy.

In its first two years the Government presided over a major manufacturing recession. Manufacturing employment in Britain fell by 28 per cent between 1979 and 1986, a loss of two million jobs. Manufacturing output fell 14 per cent between 1979 and 1981, and did not regain its 1979 level until 1987. Trade in manufactures swung from a £5 billion surplus in 1978 to a £5.4 billion deficit in 1986. Faced by this decline the Government proposed few specific measures to help industry, other than exhorting firms to reorganise themselves and become more competitive. To aid this process the Government introduced some measures of deregulation; some obstacles to the free working of labour markets were removed; enterprise zones and free ports were established; and foreign inward investment was encouraged.[27]

In general the restructuring of industry was allowed to take its own course. The Government appeared indifferent to the fate of manufacturing industry. Several ministers argued that the only test of whether an economic activity should survive or not was whether it was profitable. The expansion of the service industries was seen as the potential replacement for manufacturing. No strategic priority was given to the need to maintain a strong manufacturing sector.[28] This was reflected in the low importance given to investment in education and infrastructure. The budgets for universities and science were cut, and a huge backlog of spending on infrastructure projects – roads, sewers, communications – was allowed to build up. The Government made it clear that major new infrastructure projects would have to be financed with private money.[29]

In its policy towards the private sector the Government's stated free market position was not entirely borne out by its actions. There remained major protected sectors in the British economy – defence, agriculture and parts of the public sector and their suppliers, such as the nuclear industry. These were not subject to the competitive pressures that devastated so many other parts of the private sector because their markets remained guaranteed by Government spending programmes. Significant areas of investment and employment were thus maintained through Government policies. 52.1 per cent of all government supported research and development expenditure in 1986 went to the defence industries.

There were also brief flurries of more interventionist policies associated with particular Ministers and departments. Some limited support was given for the British information technology industry through Kenneth Baker and Geoffrey Pattie. Michael Heseltine favoured using urban development corporations to deal with inner city problems when he was at Environment and was keen to use Government defence spending to sustain a strong arms industry, if necessary in cooperation with the Europeans. This was the origin of the Westland affair. Successive Ministers of Energy gave full backing to the expansion of the nuclear industry, even though it was difficult to justify on economic grounds.

These remained exceptions however, and no attempt was made to formulate a national industrial strategy. Maintaining the openness of the British economy and forcing companies to be competitive on world markets were the watchwords of Government policy. Under this policy domestic manufacturing contracted, while the financial businesses of the City boomed as did many leading industrial companies whose operations were now international.

Along with manufacturing the position of trade unions suffered an eclipse. The dismantling of corporatism deprived unions of public platforms and public visibility. Mass unemployment brought a substantial drop in union membership (1.8 million or 14 per cent between 1980 and 1983). Union membership as a proportion of those still employed decreased by 5 per cent. The climate of industrial relations was changed in many industries. The legislation passed in 1980, 1982 and 1984 placed important new constraints on trade union activity in relation to strikes, picketing and the closed shop, and exposed unions once more to court action and financial penalties. In several cases the new laws assisted in the defeat of strikes.[30]

The Government would have nothing to do with an incomes policy for the private sector, but successfully imposed pay curbs in the public, and tried to dismantle or weaken collective bargaining arrangements. Public sector strikes over pay or job losses or conditions of service were confronted and defeated. The big set piece strikes, culminating in the miners' strike in 1984/5, were important for demonstrating that a Conservative Government could once more assert its authority over the trade unions. Repeated successes against the trade unions encouraged the Government to give support to the idea of a new industrial relations structure in which unions would either be absent altogether or would be company unions willing to accept no-strike agreements and fully committed to the success of their companies. The developing split among the unions, the establishment of the Union of Democratic Mineworkers in Nottinghamshire, so crucial to the Government's success in the miners' strike, the growth of 'the new realism' associated with unions like the Electrical, Electronic, Telecommunication and Plumbing Union (EETPU) and the Amalgamated Union of Engineering Workers (AUEW), were all seen as aiding the break-up of the traditional Labour movement, and increasing the flexibility of the labour market.[31]

While it welcomed such trends as these, however, the Government still trod cautiously in this field. It rejected proposals to scrap all trade union immunities granted since the 1906 Act. It abolished wage councils and minimum wage legislation and weakened the closed shop, helping to increase the pool of casual part-time workers. Strikes dwindled to very low levels. But trade union organisation remained strong. Examples of union-free industries and no-strike agreements remained rare; and earnings of unionised workers in per-manent employment continued to rise faster than output and inflation. The Thatcher Government presided over a significant shift in the balance of power between labour and capital, but trade union organisation remained formidable. A union-free economy did not look attainable.

The pursuit of this accumulation strategy assumed the

fullest possible integration of the British economy into the world economy. The financial and industrial sectors which benefited most from the increased freedom which the policy gave to them were already operating internationally, and this bias was reinforced.

Making the state strong

Restoring the health of economic and social life in Britain and restoring incentives as the 1979 Manifesto promised meant rolling the state back in many areas. But this could only be successful and a free economy established if the state was simultaneously strengthened in other areas. The Manifesto was very clear about which these areas were – defence; Parliament and the rule of law; and the family.

If the accumulation strategy were to be viable, then there had to be a defence and foreign policy, which would guarantee the continued prosperity and openness of the western capitalist economy. The Thatcher Government sought to ensure this by concentrating on strengthening the Anglo-American relationship. The European connection was given lower priority. This policy was entirely predictable but not without its critics. United States hegemony had been destroyed and there seemed no way of rebuilding it. The political and defence advantages of a strong Atlantic Alliance were allowed to obscure the serious economic imbalance in the world economy which economic management during the Reagan Presidency did so much to create.

The priority given to strengthening the West's defences against the USSR, deploying cruise and Pershing and modernising the British nuclear deterrent by purchasing Trident, overshadowed the relationship with the European Community. But despite the Prime Minister's dislike for the EC the growing integration of the British economy with Europe and the signs of increasing American economic and financial weakness made growing collaboration with Europe in defence as well as economic policy necessary.[32] The British attachment to formal sovereignty, however, still acted as a brake on further co-operation. The most obvious example was the British reluctance to join the European Monetary System.

The need to strengthen Britain's defences was seen almost entirely in relation to the Soviet threat. But the Thatcher Government also had to deal with problems that stemmed from Britain's long imperial past. One of these, the Falklands war, allowed a dramatic demonstration of the strong state in action. But the entire episode belonged to Britain's past rather than its future. Only two years before, the Thatcher Government had attempted to negotiate with the Argentinians the transfer of sovereignty through a lease-back arrangement. The despatch of the task force depended on US and NATO support, and might have been logistically impossible if the plans in the 1981 defence review to reduce the surface fleet had already been implemented.

What the Falklands war demonstrated was that Britain no longer had sufficient strength to maintain defence commitments in Europe and the Eastern Atlantic as well as a capacity to intervene throughout the world.[33] The special circumstances of the conflict were unlikely to be repeated anywhere else. Victory in the war did not encourage the revival of imperial ambitions elsewhere. Agreement to transfer Hong Kong back to China in 1997 was rapidly concluded in December 1984.

The second major area where the state had to be strong was in upholding Parliament and the rule of law. These appeared very traditional, conservative demands. But in the context of the welfare programmes and the corporatist modes of representation which had been established under previous governments they implied a new constitutional doctrine and potentially major upheavals in the way the state was organised.

In formal terms the constitution changed little under the Thatcher Government. In opposition the Conservatives had developed no plans for reforming the constitution to make permanent the changes in the relationship between state and economy which they wished to see. Major constitutional reforms such as proportional representation, devolution of power to the regions, or a bill of rights found no favour.[34] The Government maintained the traditional balance between Parliament and the executive. A new select committee system was introduced, but no major new powers were granted to the committees. Even the limited reform of televising Parliament was resisted.

The Government's constitutional conservatism was quite at odds with the radical constitutional implications of what it was seeking to achieve in many of its policies. The Government believed it had a mandate to undo many of the policies and the institutions which had grown up in the collectivist era. But New Right analysis indicated that it was the way democracy worked that had created the pressure for collectivism and interference in the market order. If the constitution was not changed, how could the Conservatives guarantee that their reforms would not be swept away by a new collectivist Government after some future election? Upholding Parliament meant upholding the system of elective dictatorship which had produced the mass of collectivist legislation in the twentieth century and had provided no safeguards against interventionist government.

The dilemma for the Government was that if it wished its reforms to become permanent it either had to believe that it could hold power indefinitely or it had to reform the constitution so as to make collectivist legislation much harder to introduce in the future. The rather narrow limits of the Government's radicalism and its vision were revealed by its reluctance to examine the ways in which the constitution operated and might be changed. The advantages under the existing constitution of being the incumbent Government inhibited reform.

This pattern was repeated in other areas. The Government did not attempt any major reform of the civil service. The civil service was suspected of being inefficient and likely to obstruct or delay the radical policy changes that the Government wanted to see. Yet the Government did little more than attempt to create a new climate in which civil servants had to work, through some minor administrative changes and appointments of personnel. Many of the Prime Minister's advisers argued that a radical reform of the civil service was desirable. John Hoskyns, head of the Downing Street Policy Unit 1979–82, favoured the creation of an American-style central administration, with many of the top posts being filled by outsiders employed on short contracts and given particular briefs. Each minister would be allowed to appoint some twenty external advisers to civil service posts in each department. To rely on the existing civil service to carry through radical policies, he argued, was to invite frustration and failure.[35]

This advice was never followed. Instead the Thatcher Government relied on a variety of initiatives to make civil service departments more efficient. These included the seconding of Derek Raynor from Marks and Spencer to advise on the management of personnel, money and tasks within the civil service, and the MINIS scheme (Management Information for Ministers) implemented by Michael Heseltine, first in Environment and later in Defence. Substantial savings were identified.

The size of the civil service was cut,[36] and a drive launched to make civil servants more productive. The Prime Minister used her powers of appointment to promote those civil servants who appeared ready to question Whitehall orthodoxies and had the drive and ability to carry through Conservative policies. Several senior appointments were made in this way, sometimes overturning normal seniority.[37] But although such actions shook up the civil service it hardly amounted to a major reform of the way in which the civil service was organised.

The Cabinet also functioned much as before. There were fewer Cabinet meetings and fewer Cabinet committees than under previous administrations. The Cabinet committee system continued to be used as a convenient means of getting the decisions which the Prime Minister wanted before presenting them to full Cabinet for ratification.[38] Like her predecessors Mrs Thatcher soon proved adept at choosing the membership of Cabinet committees to produce the right results. Few decisions appear to have been taken in Cabinet.

None of this was new in British Government, but such was Mrs Thatcher's dominance of her Government by 1983 that there was some speculation that a Prime Minister's department was being created, which might in time lead to a major constitutional downgrading of the Cabinet in relation to the Prime Minister's office. It later became clear that there was no such intention, in part because the power of the Prime Minister in relation to the Cabinet was already so great that no need was seen to formalise the position.

Only minor changes took place. The CPRS, which had served the whole Cabinet, was abolished in 1983 but the Prime Minister's Policy Unit survived. This began to play an increasingly important role in providing alternative policy advice to the Prime Minister, and helped enhance the impression that Downing Street was intent on providing a strategic direction of Government policy.[39] Yet what was distinctive about Margaret Thatcher as Prime Minister was not the new powers she seized for the premiership but her style of conducting it.[40] Most observers believed that the permanent effects on the premiership of her tenure of it would be small. The policy objectives may at times have been radical but the institutional means for carrying them out remained conventional.

Upholding Parliament in Conservative eyes meant making the executive power of the state the supreme authority once again. The influence which producer interests had acquired through corporatist structures was to be diminished. But the Government had no clear idea of how it was to achieve its policy objective of disengaging government from intervention in the economy, when so much of that intervention was managed not by central government but by the quangos and agencies of sub-central government.

Attempting to resolve this problem piecemeal led the Government to become increasingly centralist as time went on. It failed repeatedly to get the co-operation of other bodies, particularly representative bodies, in achieving the objectives it was setting. It then turned to finding ways to impose central control which often involved the creation of new state agencies to supplant the old.

This pattern was seen most clearly in relation to local government. The problems with local authorities arose through the desire of central government to control their spending. The Government succeeded in pushing down the central government's contribution to local authority budgets from 63 to 49 per cent. As the conflict developed so it became clear to central Government that in many areas the old collaborative relationship between central and local government had broken down. Increasingly the Government tried to bypass local authorities. The cumulative steps taken to dispossess local authorities of responsibilities and finance amounted to a major shift in the balance of the constitution between central and local government.

The 1987 manifesto envisaged further major changes. The logic of government policy pointed to eventual abolition of local government altogether, removing education and other major services entirely from local control. The Government disclaimed any such radical ambition, but it seemed reluctant to try to define the appropriate powers and responsibilities for local government in the future.

The same attitude and impatience was manifest in government policy towards many other institutions. In seeking to promote the best possible conditions for profitable private enterprise, as it conceived them, the Government tried to ensure that all institutions over which it had financial leverage should co-operate in helping to achieve them. When financial controls failed the Government resorted to more direct controls.

Upholding Parliament came to mean trying to subordinate all institutions in civil society to the pursuit of the national goals which Parliament had approved. This attempt put the Thatcher Government in collision with many established institutions in civil society, particularly the trade unions. In its legislation the Government was not content with placing restrictions on lawful trade union activity, but forced changes in union rule books on such matters as the holding of ballots before strikes and the election of union officers. This was extremely unusual interference in the affairs of voluntary associations. It did not always prove successful. The attempt to get union members to vote down political funds backfired at the first attempt. Large majorities in every union voted to retain their funds.

The Government also clashed with the media, principally with the television companies. This came to a head in the second phase of the Thatcher Government when open attempts were made to change the editorial policy of the BBC, following the reporting of the American bombing of Libya in 1986. Specific journalists, presenters and programmes were selected for attack. The Peacock Commission was set up to advise the Government on the future of broadcasting, and recommended substantial deregulation and the breaking up of the monopoly of the BBC and ITV.

Clashes also developed with other major institutions in civil society – notably the universities, the schools and the churches. The Government cut education budgets severely in its first few years in office and moved increasingly to impose central control on education – by seeking to determine the content of the curriculum, to weaken the influence of the teaching profession, to allow schools to opt out of local authority control, to end academic tenure, and to place higher education under new funding bodies which could ensure that universities and polytechnics would meet national needs as defined by the Government.

The rule of law was always interpreted rather narrowly by Conservatives to mean internal security. Strengthening the police and restoring public order were major campaign themes in 1979. Substantial increases in police pay, manpower and equipment were made. Several acts were passed to give the police more powers and enforce tougher sentences. The Criminal Justice Act of 1982 introduced a new framework of custodial sentences for offenders under 21. The Police and Criminal Evidence Act, 1984, gave the police new powers in respect of stop and search; entry, search, and seizure; arrest and detention; and the interrogation and identification of suspects. The Public Order Act, 1986, gave the police new powers to control demonstrations and crowds.

The Conservative Government encouraged a trend to tougher sentences, while promoting a better paid, better equipped, and better co-ordinated police force. Co-ordination between police forces, as in the miners' strike of 1984/5, was organised through the National Reporting Centre, which looked like the organisational base for a future national police force. This trend was strengthened by the attempts by some local police authorities to make their police forces more accountable. In this, as in so many areas, however, the Government, while it encouraged Chief Constables to assert their independence, was reluctant to take the final step and formally organise the police as a national force.

The increasing use by the police of firearms and riot equipment was directed at coping with the rise in violent crime and with the picket line violence and inner city riots which erupted in the 1980s. Policing took on a more repressive character as opposition to the Thatcher Government came to be stigmatised as the 'enemies within', likened to Argentinians and terrorists. Repression was particularly severe in some of the inner cities, directed mainly against the black community. The breakdown of relations between the police and black communities was a major factor that led to the riots. By 1987 the police were equipped with massive force sufficient to restore public order whenever it was threatened, and it was clear that there were fewer restraints on its use.

The Thatcher Government also understood upholding the rule of law to mean protecting the secrecy of government, and particularly the operations of the intelligence services. Its period of office was notable for a number of spy scandals, beginning with the belated unmasking of Anthony Blunt in 1980. It became involved in a number of attempts to stop information about the operations of the British secret service and British Government itself reaching the public. The Official Secrets Act was invoked several times in an attempt to suppress embarrassing information and to punish those who were seeking to reveal it. Clive Ponting and Sarah Tisdall were prosecuted, the Government went to enormous lengths to stop the publication of Peter Wright's memoirs, and to prevent details appearing about the Zircon spy satellite project.

The Thatcher Government reinforced the traditional secrecy of British Government while refusing to investigate any of the charges surfacing about the unconstitutional activities of the security services. The obsession with security and secrets was revealed in the GCHQ affair when the Government banned trade unions at its intelligence gathering centre in Cheltenham because of the alleged risk to national security.

The greatest prize for a law and order government – the restoration of capital punishment – eluded Thatcher. The most she could deliver was two free votes in the House of Commons in 1979 and 1983. On each occasion the move to restore hanging was defeated by a large majority. The Cabinet and the parliamentary party remained divided on the issue. Thatcher was able to include in the 1979 Manifesto a pledge that Parliament should have a free vote on whether or not to restore hanging, but further than that she was not able to go.

The Government launched many law and order campaigns aimed at groups like young offenders and football hooligans for special attention, the latter acquiring particular prominence following the Heysel stadium riot in 1985. This led to stringent controls, such as membership schemes and the banning of alcohol at matches being enforced on football clubs. Like previous Governments, however, the Thatcher Government had no ideas of how to turn the rising tide of disorder and crime, and chose for the most part to extract the maximum political advantage by promoting itself as the law and order party.

The third area where the 1979 Manifesto proclaimed a need for a strong state was supporting family life. From the outset the Thatcherite project involved not merely an economic revival but a moral revival. The difficulty was finding ways of promoting it. The most crucial sphere for many Conservatives was the family. But, although the Government set up a Cabinet Committee in 1983 to produce a family policy, the practical results were highly limited. Serious measures to prevent women taking jobs outside the home were ruled out by the increasing importance of women in the labour market. The impact of the recession and many of the cuts in social benefits discriminated most heavily against women, but the Government did not attempt to reinforce this with active policies. It retained the Equal Opportunities Commission and made no direct attempt to challenge the principles on which it worked.

The assumption that the family should be the foundation of social policy and that only nuclear two-parent families were real families influenced much Conservative thinking about social policy. The stripping from the state of functions in social policy, such as care of the elderly, and returning them to the family, was a trend made necessary by budget cuts rather than specific legislation. But it was a trend approved by Conservatives and nothing was done to arrest it. Supporting the family also meant supporting its traditional way of life. This included protecting families from being 'swamped' by alien cultures. This phrase was used by Margaret Thatcher on television in January 1978 in one of her most successful political interventions before she became Prime Minister.[41] Her Government had few ideas on how to convert it into a policy. Immigration controls were tightened further in the British Nationality Act of 1981. But compulsory repatriation was ruled out and the Government made no moves to repeal the Race Relations Acts. It continued to adhere to the bipartisan consensus on equal opportunity and rights for all citizens.

The mounting burdens imposed on black people arose more from the consequences of the recession and the strengthening of internal repression than from deliberate Government policy aimed at the black communities. Nevertheless the association of blacks with the rising crime figures and the inner city riots did ensure a growing polarisation between the state and black communities. The Government commissioned the Scarman report after the Brixton riots but refused to accept any link between unemployment and the alienation of black youth and proposed action on few of the report's recommendations.

Reforming education also became central to the Government's conception of supporting family life. Teaching of the appropriate skills and values was seen as vital in fostering social discipline and cohesion. The reconstruction of education which began to take shape in the Great Education Reform Bill of 1987 was an essential part of the Government's wider plans for encouraging an enterprise culture and popular capitalism. Neither concept was at all well defined in policy terms when the Government was elected in 1979, but they became increasingly important to justify many of the policies the Government adopted and to characterise the long-term objectives of its programme and the kind of society it wanted to see emerge.

The Government argued that the anti-enterprise and permissive culture that had been fostered by social democratic institutions since 1945 had become one of the chief obstacles to reversing decline. The economic and moral regeneration of Britain therefore required putting pressure on every institution to make it supportive of enterprise and capitalism.[42] This was seen as particularly important in the case of the media and education.

Popular capitalism (which had been in fashion once before

in the 1950s)[43] became the term applied to a variety of policies aimed at widening property ownership and consumer choice. The denationalisation measures originally undertaken principally to raise revenue came to be seen as a way of extending share ownership. With the shares of companies like British Telecom and British Gas being offered at levels substantially below their real market value, large numbers of new investors could be tempted to buy shares in order to make quick capital gains. The number of individual shareholders was increased markedly by such means (from three million in 1979 to nine million in 1987), but the overall proportion of shares held by individual shareholders continued to decline. The Government attempted to bolster the growth of shareholding through specific tax concessions. It also raised the thresholds on capital gains tax and capital transfer tax, while reducing the upper tax bands on higher incomes and on investment income.

A key measure to expand property ownership was the extension of the right of council house tenants to buy their houses at substantial discounts. This was one of the most successful and symbolic of all the Government's policies. The Government sought means to extend it into education, pensions and health. The principle, so simple in the case of council houses, proved much harder to put into operation in other areas. In education vouchers were considered but discarded. By 1987 the favoured route for increasing choice in education was to allow parents and governing bodies of a school to decide to take a school out of local authority control.

Conclusion

The translation of the five tasks in the 1979 manifesto into practical policies proved difficult for the Thatcher Government. It stumbled on some of its most successful policies, like denationalisation, by accident. In other areas it felt its way forward cautiously. There were many paradoxes in what the Government was trying to do, and these were often compounded by the Government's own lack of clarity about its objectives, and the means required for achieving them. This was most noticeable in the confusion over the constitutional requirements for a free economy and the strong state.

The meaning of the events and policies of the Thatcher Government has given rise to many varied and conflicting interpretations. A review of these forms the subject of the next two chapters.

5

The pursuit of power

In a progressive country change is constant; and the great question is not whether you should resist change which is inevitable, but whether that change should be carried out in deference to the manners, the customs, the laws, and the traditions of a people, or whether it should be carried out in deference to abstract principles, and arbitrary and general doctrines.

[Benjamin Disraeli (1867)]

We cannot really believe that this is the moment for the party of Baldwin and Churchill, of Macmillan and Butler, of the Industrial Charter and the social advances of the 1950s to retreat behind the privet hedge into a world of narrow class interests and selfish concerns.

[Sir Ian Gilmour (1975)]

Despite the success of Margaret Thatcher in leading her party to three consecutive election victories there are some in the Conservative party who still believe that Thatcherism is an aberration, a deviation from the broad highway of the Conservative tradition, and that sooner or later the Conservatives will return to the politics and values represented by Harold Macmillan and Edward Heath.

Viewed thus what happened in 1975 was that the party was 'hijacked' by its extremist wing. Aided by events and divisions among the other parties it was able to secure itself in power,[1] and banish or win over its enemies within the party. But all the while it has remained illegitimate and those it exiled from

140

influence and office await the day when the Protector will be gone and they will be restored to their rightful place.

New Right Conservatives, however, do not believe there will ever be such a restoration. They see Margaret Thatcher's accession to the leadership as the reassertion of true Conservative principles which had been forgotten during the party's long postwar acquiescence in the regime of social democracy. According to this view it is postwar Conservatism which is the aberration, from which the Thatcher leadership has rescued the party.[2]

Margaret Thatcher's tenure of the Conservative leadership has therefore been accompanied by a fierce debate among some Conservatives over whether 'Thatcherism' is a reassertion of Conservative principles or a major break from them. The party has been riven by ideological and doctrinal disputes to an extent remarkable for a party which has always prided itself on its pragmatic and non-ideological approach to politics. One leading Conservative lamented that the *odium theologicum* had come to infect the Tory party.[3] This debate has been in the first place a debate between two groups involved in a struggle for position and influence within the party. But wider issues are involved in the question 'Is Thatcherism Conservatism?' than which leadership group is to dominate the party. Should the British Conservative tradition be understood as a distinctive tradition of ideology and doctrine, or is it better analysed as statecraft, in which ideas and principles are subordinated to political calculation, the pursuit of office and the management of power? The argument of this chapter is that Thatcherism is much better explained as statecraft than as ideology, and that it is the evaluation of the statecraft of the Thatcher leadership with which the debate in the Conservative party has been principally concerned.

The interpretation of Thatcherism has absorbed a great deal of intellectual energy on the right. The view of Thatcherism as a new ideological doctrine initially commanded most attention. But, although there was some debate as to whether Thatcherism was or was not a Conservative doctrine, the real issue quickly became the relationship of this doctrine to the party's new statecraft. Even if the doctrines of Thatcherism were regarded as alien to the Conservative tradition, the Thatcher

Government could still be judged to be pursuing a Tory statecraft. The finer points of ideological dispute would then become relatively unimportant.

The object of Tory statecraft has always been to ensure that a durable hegemony is achieved and preserved throughout the institutions of state and civil society. Hegemony involves politics, ideology and economics, which is why the agents of hegemony, and the framers of hegemonic projects, are generally political parties. Building support and negotiating power, winning the arguments at all levels of ideological discourse, framing and implementing a viable accumulation strategy, are all involved in a successful hegemonic project. Statecraft is the practice of the politics of hegemony, as Conservatives have long understood. Assessing Thatcherism as statecraft is therefore a central concern for them.

The perils of ideology

The Conservative party has had its share of ideological poison in the past but it has long cultivated an image as a non-ideological party. John Stuart Mill called the Tories 'the stupid party', which was taken by most Tories as a compliment. The squires who thronged the Tory benches were described by Salisbury as 'red hot cannon balls, which they resemble in density if not in weight'.[4] This has not prevented the party being led by a succession of very able and intellectual leaders, who perceived clearly that doctrine and ideology should have a role, but a subordinate one, in the party. The main purpose of the Tory party was to govern, and to remain united for that purpose.

This brought many jibes against the party. The Tories were often portrayed as unprincipled opportunists whose only concern was the gaining of office. This was the Tory party satirised by Trollope:

> At that time we had not thoroughly learnt by experience, as we now have, that no reform, no innovation – experience almost justifies us in saying, no revolution – stinks so foully in the nostrils of an English Tory as to be absolutely

irreconcilable to him. When taken in the refreshing waters of office any such pill can be swallowed.[5]

Many critics of the British Conservatives from Winston Churchill to Friedrich Hayek have also focused on their opportunism and want of principle. In its anxiety to gain office the party's principles have often appeared negotiable, its policies determined by the best means of winning votes. It has seemed at times a party not of principles but of interests. Churchill once called the Tory party:

> a party of great vested interests, banded together in a formidable confederation; corruption at home, aggression to cover it up abroad; the trickery of tariff juggles, the tyranny of a party machine; sentiment by the bucketful, patriotism by the imperial pint; the open hand at the public exchequer, the open door at the public house; dear food for the million, cheap labour for the millionaire.[6]

Despite his admiration for Margaret Thatcher, Hayek has always had reservations about Conservatism as a sound ideological basis for politics. In his postscript to *The Constitution of Liberty*, 'Why I am not a Conservative', he claimed that Conservatives could not be trusted to defend a free society, either because they believed in collectivism, or because, like the British Conservatives, they were opportunists in their political practice and lacked a principled commitment to the maintenance of the conditions for a free society.[7] This made Conservative administrations hardly less likely than Labour ones to embrace collectivist solutions to problems which involved interference and intervention in the workings of markets. Governing according to circumstances meant for Hayek placing public policy at the mercy of the fashions and pressures of the political market-place. All manner of evils, including protectionism, cartels, closed shops and industrial subsidies, could be justified on 'pragmatic' grounds. Conservatives could not be trusted to protect freedom.

Defenders of the British Conservative tradition like Sir Ian Gilmour argue that what Hayek derides as vices in Conservatism are in fact its virtues. Most of his charges against

Conservatism are 'merely pejorative descriptions of attributes in which Conservatives take pride. What to Hayek is opportunism, is to Conservatives paying proper attention to circumstances. What Hayek calls the use of arbitrary power, the Conservative calls the legitimate use of the power of the state to promote the welfare of the people.'[8]

This argument is a long one in the history of Conservatism. Where Conservative parties have become influential in government Conservative statecraft has generally been seen as more important than Conservative doctrine in explaining Conservative actions. Conservatism is understood more in terms of its orientation to government rather than in terms of specific beliefs.

Samuel Huntington in his theory of Conservatism drew a distinction between *doctrinal* and *positional* Conservatism.[9] The former is seen as arising in periods of social and political upheaval, often precipitated by internal revolution or defeat in war. Positional Conservatism by contrast is concerned not with the politics of social breakdown but with the administration of an existing order.

Doctrinal Conservatism has been most in evidence in counter-revolutionary movements which seek either to overthrow a radical regime or to safeguard an existing regime from a revolutionary challenge. Such Conservatism tends to embrace an ethic of will and loyalty, and to seek triumphs rather than reconciliations.[10] It values conviction and commitment, rather than compromise and consensus. It looks for enemies to defeat and thrives on conflict and battle.

Positional Conservatism by contrast shuns ideological certainty and the cult of conviction and struggle. It cultivates instead the art of ruling, in order to maintain a stable social order. Decisions on policy are matters of political calculation, to be arrived at after careful assessment of all aspects of the situation, rather than through a simple-minded application of abstract principles. The need for flexibility is the great virtue.

The opposition between doctrinal and positional Conservatives is perennial. It exists in every period, and to some extent in every Conservative. Whether doctrinal or positional elements are most prominent depends however on the problems Conservatives must confront. The argument between trimmers and realists on one side and diehards and reactionaries on the other goes on in every period, but who gets the upper hand is not determined in advance.

The British Conservative tradition has generally been interpreted as one in which the trimmers have won out over the diehards.[11] The English Tories have always been perceived as positional rather than doctrinal Conservatives. Many Conservatives think that Thatcherism breaks with this tradition. They argue that the emphasis on doctrine, the dislike of consensus, the unconcern about being labelled extreme, and the embrace of radical change and experiment, have made the Conservatives under Margaret Thatcher at times resemble in approach and style more a party of the radical Left than the British Conservatives.

Sir Ian Gilmour in *Inside Right* lists three things the Conservative party is not; it is not averse to change; it is not a pressure group; and it is not an ideological party.[12] The charge against Thatcherism is that it has supported radical and destructive change, that it has represented the interests of only one part of the nation and not the whole nation, and above all that this has come about because it has made the Conservatives an ideological party, dedicated to the pursuit and implementation of a particular doctrine. In doing so it had abandoned the One Nation perspective that had guided its practice and its programme since Disraeli, and contradicted the fundamental principles of Conservative statecraft.

The quest for true Toryism

Debate on the character and future of the Conservative party was ignited by Margaret Thatcher's election as Leader and by the way she then chose to conduct the Leadership. The demoralisation and recrimination that followed the two general election defeats in 1974 increased factional struggle within the party and led to an outpouring of books and articles attempting to define what the party was about, where it had gone wrong and what its future direction should be. A significant feature of the ideological disputes was the readiness of all sides to describe the party in Right and Left terms and to emphasise the fundamental nature of the conflict. Patrick Cosgrave described it as 'a conflict between two wholly different visions of the future, for country as well as party'.[13]

In the past Conservatives had generally trusted their leaders rather than their principles as a guide to politics. Dissenters were often counselled to 'damn their principles' and 'stick to their party'. Such advice embodied an important political truth. Disunity and splits were fatal to a party's prospects of gaining political office.

The Conservative party, like every other political party contesting the terrain of mass democracy, has from time to time been swept by great causes and doctrines. Every party has its men and women of principle. The Conservative party has been unusual in the success it has had in keeping them away from the leadership. In electing Margaret Thatcher, however, the Tories had elected a Leader who became herself the focus of ideological argument. The question she was alleged to put in considering appointments, 'Is he one of us?' came to symbolise her style. From the start she was a very divisive Leader. She invited Conservatives to declare themselves for or against her.

Thatcher was not an intellectual Conservative in the manner of Salisbury or Keith Joseph. But her interest in questioning the legacy of ideas and assumptions which had guided the party throughout the postwar period created a space in which the ideas of the many variants of the New Right could flourish. The apparent legitimacy which such ideas were now given by the party Leader was deeply threatening to other elements in the party.

Extravagant language has been used before about shifts to the right in the Conservative party. After his refusal to serve under Sir Alec Douglas-Home in 1963 Iain Macleod claimed in the *Spectator* that the Conservative party was now being led for the first time since Salisbury from 'right of centre'.[14] Similar charges were made after 1975. One active member of the Tory Left argued in 1978 that the party had been plunged back into the dark days of Salisbury and Balfour.[15] Thatcher's leadership was pictured as regressive, undoing the tradition of One Nation Toryism of Baldwin, Churchill, Macmillan and Heath.

To her supporters in the New Right, however, her leadership offered the first real opportunity for a generation to challenge the ideas and policies of collectivism. Although the New Right did not represent a single coherent perspective all parts of it were united in rejecting the tradition that Heath represented in the party. While the liberal New Right proclaimed the need to commit the Conservative party to a programme of freeing the economy and rolling back the state, the Conservative New Right put the emphasis on the restoration of authority.

New Right institutes, pressure groups and journals sprouted like mushrooms throughout the 1970s and 1980s.[16] The key think-tanks on the liberal and libertarian wing of the New Right were the Institute of Economic Affairs (1957); the Centre for Policy Studies (1974); and the Adam Smith Institute (1981). Long-established campaigning organisations like the business pressure groups, Aims of Industry and the Economic League, were joined by the Freedom Association and the Libertarian Alliance.

On the conservative wing of the New Right, Common Cause, founded in 1952, and the Monday Club, which had been a focus for right-wing dissent since 1961, were now joined in 1977 by the more intellectual Salisbury Group, some of whose meetings Thatcher attended, and by numerous cold war, anti-communist organisations which included the Coalition for Peace and Security, and the Institute for the Study of Conflict. Many of these organisations, like the Freedom Association, had overlapping membership and sponsorship. A network of journalists, lobbyists, academics, business executives and politicians emerged which was committed to spreading New Right ideas and supporting Thatcher against her enemies in the party.

For all sections of the New Right a crucial ideological task was to establish the legitimacy of their ideas within the British Conservative tradition. The Conservatives among them especially wanted to claim that they were the true Tories. The search for 'True Toryism' promised endless writing and rewriting of history. The great Conservatives from the past were scrutinised to determine whether they should hold their place in the Conservative Pantheon or be cast from it.

The Salisbury Club and its journal, the Salisbury Review,

where this kind of writing was particularly noticeable, were named after the former Conservative Leader who was least admired by One Nation Conservatives. A general offensive began against the interpretation of the Conservative tradition that had been dominant in party publications for so much of the postwar period. Gilmour complained that if the inquisition went on much longer the Conservatives would have a gallery of heroes consisting of Lord Eldon and Judge Jeffreys.

The reassessment of the past had a serious purpose, however. The argument of those supporting the new course inaugurated by Margaret Thatcher was that by the mid-1970s the party had lost its way. It no longer offered a distinctive alternative to Labour and was in danger of fighting and losing on ground staked out by its opponents. The call the Thatcherites made was for a major reassessment of the practice of the party since 1945: specifically, its acquiescence in the policies and priorities of the postwar social democratic state.

This kind of argument immediately encountered a major difficulty. The Conservatives had been in office for more than half of the time since 1945. This meant that if the party were to challenge the 'consensus' under which Britain had been governed since 1945 it had to criticise many of the policies and actions not only of the Heath Government between 1970 and 1974, but also those of the Conservative Government between 1951 and 1964. Many of the supporters of the new leadership were prepared to do this. Accusations of appeasement and surrender abounded. Postwar Conservative Governments, it was said, had never put the clock back a single second. Collectivism had crept forward. They had acquiesced in the ratchet of socialism. Periods of Conservative Government had merely administered the *status quo*, while each period of Labour Government had advanced the collectivisation of Britain another notch.[17]

According to this scenario Britain was slipping steadily down the road to serfdom. Conservative Governments had not actively connived in condemning Britain to a totalitarian future, but in failing to reverse the measures which Labour Governments had passed they had failed to arrest the progress of collectivism. They had also been partly responsible for the policies that had led to accelerating inflation, the growth in trade union influence, and the increasing burden of public spending.

What all sections of the New Right demanded was a Conservative party that now sought to regain the ideological initiative and change the policy agenda by challenging the postwar consensus between the parties on domestic policies. They argued that the kind of collectivism practised under postwar social democracy was exhausted and discredited, and that the electoral risk to the Conservatives of deserting the hallowed 'middle ground' of politics was minimal. The middle ground no longer represented a genuine popular consensus, but was a construct of the politicians and the progressive intellectual establishment, and as such was ripe for overthrow.

From the New Right, therefore, came numerous ideas as to how the Conservative party could regain the political initiative, firstly by developing a strategy for reversing decline based on a free economy and a strong state, secondly by winning the ideological struggle against social democracy and One Nation Conservatism, and thirdly by building a strong electoral coalition. The New Right argued that the Conservatives could appeal to all those who were disillusioned with the recent performance of governments, eager for the reassertion of political authority, and open to new populist commonsense arguments about the economy and politics.

The challenge to the Thatcherites came from those Conservatives who identified themselves with the postwar tradition of progressive Conservatism and saw no reason to abandon it. They were not a movement like the New Right, although they created a few organisations like the Tory Reform Group. Their former institutional strength had lain in their control of the Conservative party itself, particularly Conservative Central Office and the Conservative Research Department. This was now lost to them.

The tactic of these Conservatives against emergent Thatcherism was to deny its legitimacy on the grounds that, if the party were to continue as a party of government, it must not become an ideological party, but remain predominantly a party of realists, trimmers and pragmatists; a party that believed in governing in the light of circumstances rather than in accordance with any abstract principle or dogma. Since the aim of the party was to govern, adherence to an ideology, any ideology, was a serious handicap to carry, and risked ceding the priceless asset of being perceived as the party of efficient and pragmatic government to the party's opponents.

A second argument was that the ideology of Thatcherism was the wrong ideology for the Conservative party. The Thatcherite view of what Conservatism was about challenged the carefully constructed interpretation of the Conservative tradition which had become more or less undisputed in the party after 1945, and which had been associated with the leadership style and philosophy of Churchill, Macmillan and Heath.[18]

This interpretation emphasised the identity of the Conservatives as the party of One Nation, the party of the 'Middle Way'. The middle way was between state socialism on one side and *laissez-faire* capitalism on the other. The role of the Conservative party was to curb the tendency of their opponents to push their policies to extremes. Conservatism, according to this view, meant governing a society rather than managing an economy, so what was essential was to pay proper attention to the interests and customs of the society to ensure that all legitimate interests achieved representation and that the continuity of the society was preserved.

This gave government an important role in the management of the economy. Peter Walker's views are representative of his wing of the party:

> In a modern society the government must elaborate national goals, let industry know its target for the rate of growth, and make clear how productive capacity may be increased to make the objective feasible. Governments also have a duty to prevent the unpleasant by-products of growth such as damage to the environment, as well as very wide responsibilities in the fields of housing, education, and the social services.[19]

Walker argued that the problem facing Conservatives was not to argue for the superiority of private enterprise in theoretical terms but to relate those arguments to the hopes and fears of ordinary people. How could private enterprise be made morally legitimate? Harold Macmillan's great insight, according to Walker, was to understand that 'unless capitalism could show sufficient social responsibility it could never win mass support'.[20]

Ian Gilmour in similar vein claimed that 'there is no ideal extent of government intervention. The position of government in industry, as Mr Macmillan once put it, is not a principle, it is an expedient'.[21] The reason was that, in Conservative statecraft, politics is always more important than economics. The choice of policy measures should not be a matter of economic theory or political principle, Gilmour argues, but should be guided by what is compatible with the continued existence of a free society with institutions which command respect and allegiance, which is free from excessive and avoidable social tensions and too much injustice.

Conservatives who were important in this tradition were those who had taken an interest in social reform and had sought remedies for some of the evils of nineteenth-century capitalism. The list includes Peel, Shaftesbury and Disraeli. The reputation of Disraeli as a practical reformer may have waned, but his rhetoric of One Nation and his perception of the role a Conservative party might occupy in an era of mass suffrage allowed him to be presented as the founder of a tradition which was carried on by Randolph Churchill with his call for Tory democracy, by Baldwin and Chamberlain, and finally by Churchill and his heirs, notably Macmillan, Butler and Heath.

The core of this tradition, when it was defined in the 1950s, was held to be the acceptance of state intervention where necessary to remedy evils and abuses and to create the basis for consent. It seeks to incorporate new interests into the governing process by making concessions to them in order to maintain the authority of government and the stability of the state. Policies are judged on whether or not they promote loyalty to the state. As Gilmour puts it:

The preservation of freedom is a complex business. But if people are not to be seduced by other attractions, they must at least feel loyalty to the state. Their loyalty will not be deep unless they gain from the state protection and other

benefits. Homilies to cherish competition and warnings
against interference with market forces will not engender
loyalty. People will not tolerantly sit back and wait for
impersonal forces to overcome disaster. They expect and
demand action, and if they do not get it they are likely to
look elsewhere or take action themselves. If the state is not
interested in them, why should they be interested in the
state?[22]

Gilmour and other One Nation Conservatives in the 1970s
warned against the new statecraft of the Thatcher leadership
because of the damage they expected it to do to prospects of
the party being re-elected. Trevor Russel expressed a common
view (and hope) in the Tory Reform Group when he wrote in
1978:

> Mrs Thatcher's grip on the party may prove short-lived
> . . . Some on the Tory Left, who dismiss her as an aberration,
> or a mistake, already regard the period of her leadership,
> which they expect to be brief, as an unfortunate although
> possibly necessary interlude.[23]

The longer the aberration has lasted the harder it has been
to dismiss Thatcherism as an ideology alien to Conservatism.
It has looked more and more like a new phase in the party's
long development, a new Tory statecraft, that after 1981 was
crowned by success. As the victories have piled up and the
Conservatives have regained their old knack of winning
and holding office (which now rivals the success of the
Conservatives after 1951), the more the grounds for argument
about Thatcherism in the party have shifted. As Sir John
Harington once explained:

> Treason doth never prosper: what's the reason?
> For if it prosper, none dare call it treason.

Three election victories makes Thatcher no longer vulnerable to charges that she has betrayed Conservatism and
threatened its survival by deserting the middle ground of
politics. She has built her new electoral coalition and the

opposition has fallen apart. She has also won the battle inside the party. Many of her earlier critics have fallen silent or been marginalised, while others have learnt to become trimmers in the new Thatcherite ascendancy.

The success of Thatcherism as statecraft has baffled and dismayed many One Nation Conservatives. They had tried to brand it as a species of ideological or doctrinal Conservatism which was alien to the British Conservative tradition, because it subordinated questions of statecraft, of how to win and hold power and preserve hegemony, to questions of ideology, of the correctness of policies measured against abstract principles. But Thatcherism proved to have its own ways of combining the two.

As a result Thatcherism never did subordinate statecraft to ideology as its critics complained. It simply had a different view of statecraft. It rejected the idea that a successful statecraft had to practise opportunism and be ready to surrender principles. This kind of statecraft has often been associated with the British Conservatives, and with the One Nation tradition. Of all ruling groups they have been most ready to pursue strategies of concession and flexibility in the face of new demands and new interests.

A Conservative statecraft, however, need not be defensive, a strategy of delay – as Salisbury wrote, 'delay is life' – or be geared to continual retreat. Henry Kissinger in his analysis of Metternich's politics has pointed up the difference between two styles of Conservative statecraft. Metternich objected to the views of the Peelite, Sir James Graham, who had argued that the statesman's wisdom consisted of recognising the proper moment for making concessions:

> My conception of statesmanship differs completely. The true merit of a statesman . . . consists in governing so as to avoid a situation in which concessions become necessary.[24]

Metternich has had his followers among the British Conservatives, but it is Sir James Graham's approach which has more often been ascendant. Thatcherism represents an endorsement of the Metternich view. Once the authority of the state is restored, no concessions and no compromises with the enemies of Conservatism and freedom are necessary.

This does not convince One Nation Conservatives. Whatever the short-term success of Thatcherism as statecraft, many still think it will end badly. It is taking needless and unacceptable risks. The centralisation of power, the war on so many established institutions, the polarisation of society between North and South, rich and poor and employed and unemployed, and the exacerbation of social tensions have brought the legitimacy of the state to a dangerous degree. Only the economic recovery has enabled Thatcherism to triumph.

The real problem for Conservatives of the Metternich persuasion is that the very strength of their rule and the success which attends it can blind them when the moment for concessions and compromise arrives. Sir Ian Gilmour uses the example of the situation created by the Taff Vale Case in 1901. If the Conservative Government led by Balfour had at once legislated to change the law, it might have forestalled the much more radical reform that was enacted by the Liberal Government after its sweeping election victory in 1906, and might therefore, Gilmour argues, have checked the later growth of trade union influence. Conservatives can pay dearly for such mistakes.

Libertarianism and collectivism

Thatcherism is now accepted as a powerful and successful new statecraft, but there are still many questions to be asked about its relationship to British Conservatism, and the different ways in which this has been conceived and analysed. The nature of the Conservative ideological tradition, the idea of the constitutional state and limited politics, the promotion of a governing class, the practice of high politics and the upholding of authority, are all perspectives which have been used to analyse Thatcherism and evaluate its statecraft.

As a purely ideological phenomenon there is little difficulty in seeing Thatcherism as an authentic expression of one of the two major strands in the Conservative tradition. These two strands have been identified by many political historians but most recently and most persuasively by W. H. Greenleaf. He identifies libertarianism and collectivism as the two axes around which ideological debate has revolved in the Conservative party in common with all other parties.[25] Greenleaf conceives these ideological strands as being much broader than the party system itself, and he has no difficulty in showing how in the British political tradition the balance between them has shifted, so that libertarianism has been dominant in one period and collectivism in another. The charge is often made by critics of Thatcherism that it represents a return to Victorian values and the principles of *laissez-faire* and Gladstonian finance. Statements by John Nott and Milton Friedman that Margaret Thatcher is really a nineteenth-century Liberal have been eagerly seized upon to demonstrate that she is not a true Conservative.

The picture is, however, much more complex than this. It is true that Margaret Thatcher and her supporters can be seen to be reasserting ideas that were dominant in the nineteenth century. But the libertarian tradition at that time spanned all parties, and has continued to have adherents right through the period of the relative dominance of collectivism in the twentieth century. What was at the core of the libertarian tradition was a strong anti-statism. The Manchester School doctrine that, if left alone, any economic or social evil would cure itself, was accompanied by strong beliefs in the advantages of free trade and sound finance, and the importance of individual responsibility. In the 1880s and 1890s the Conservative party was strongly identified with the belief that in matters that concerned the economy and property the role of the state should be limited as much as possible. The role of government was to maintain law and order rather than to interfere with the morals and activities of the people. The party was strongly against intervention.

The growth of collectivist legislation and the power of the Labour movement were fiercely resisted by many Conservatives. A large number were active in organisations like the Liberty and Property Defence League, the Constitutional Association, and later the Anti-Socialist Union.[26] The Liberty and Property Defence League was a major pressure group against collectivist legislation. It organised campaigns to preserve the open shop, to limit picketing, and to prevent the growth of profit sharing. It also helped to break strikes.

What agitated Conservatives was that the extension of the suffrage in stages was leading to an inexorable growth in pressure for class legislation – legislation aimed at redistribution or even confiscation of income and wealth from the propertied groups to the propertyless. As one exasperated Conservative put it, the coming of democracy meant that the traditional checks and balances of the constitution were in danger of being replaced by continual cheques and no balances.

Anxieties about the economic consequences of democracy and the growth of state intervention in the economy did not have to wait for the 1970s to find expression within the Conservative party. Such sentiments were party orthodoxy before 1914. They continued to be strong throughout the period when collectivist ideas had their greatest ascendancy. The defection after 1918 of many Liberals to the Conservatives as the party best placed to resist the advance of Labour further increased the dominance of libertarian ideas about the organisation of the economy and society.

Even after 1945, when the triumph of collectivism seemed assured with the electoral victory of the party most closely associated with it, the libertarian strand of thought in the party was not entirely eclipsed. Waldron Smithers, Nigel Birch and Enoch Powell were prominent exponents of libertarian ideas within the party. The emergence from the 1950s onwards of a new movement of doctrinal anti-statism spearheaded by the Institute for Economic Affairs therefore connects with a long-standing tradition in the Conservative party.

Any examination of the Conservative tradition will therefore find that it offers no one answer to the question 'Is Thatcherism Conservatism?' There are no clear guidelines as to what beliefs a Conservative should hold about the role of government. The Conservative tradition legitimates both liberal and collectivist ideas. Margaret Thatcher and her supporters cannot be excommunicated from Conservatism through the identification of a core strand of doctrinal belief. There is no single core.

This argument has been used to suggest that Thatcherism is indeed a return to true Conservatism. Some historians sympathetic to Thatcher's politics have argued that if there is an aberration in Conservative party history it is the period between 1945 and 1975. Lord Blake, for example, believes that the Conservative tradition is based on four key traditions from which the party deviated between 1957 and 1963 and 1972 and 1974. These traditions are opposition to centralism, defence of the national interest, opposition to equality, and the avoidance of internal splits. The party returned to distinctive Conservative principles in 1970–2 and after 1975. These distinctive principles are reductions in the role of the state measured by spending and the range of decision making, the weakening of trade union power, and a renewed emphasis on individual self-reliance.[27]

The problem with this argument is that in the eyes of many Conservatives the Thatcher Government has deviated from the first and last of the four traditions. In many areas, far from diffusing power, it has centralised it, while internally the party still remains deeply divided. Many One Nation Conservatives doubt that a stable hegemony can be rebuilt in Britain if the problems of polarisation, social division, and poverty and unemployment are not tackled; many remain sceptical that the economic decline has been permanently reversed.

Hugh Thomas, for a time director of the Centre for Policy Studies, echoes some of Blake's ideas. Thomas claims that Thatcherism represents a new libertarian impulse in British politics, and signals the reversal of the trend towards paternalistic collectivism identified by Dicey. Thatcherism's mission, he claims, is to force the middle class to become independent and self-reliant again and to abandon collectivism. Employment has to be drastically reduced in the public sector for this to become possible. Techniques of economic management like monetarism are not important in themselves but are only tactics in a wider war to end government responsibility for problems such as unemployment and recreate the conditions in which a revival of the private sector becomes possible.[28]

In the hands of Blake and Thomas, Thatcherism becomes the quintessence of the Conservative tradition, and collectivism a bad dream which the British people have had to endure and from which Margaret Thatcher now bids them wake. But it is too easy to veer from one extreme to the other. As Greenleaf points out, no party has been more responsible than the Conservatives for introducing and shaping the kind of collectivism that has been introduced in Britain. The debate between liberals and progressives has been a central part of the Conservative tradition throughout this century. Neither side can legitimately claim to be the sole representative of Conservatism. At different times one approach rather than another has been in the ascendancy. The Conservative party would be greatly impoverished for the future if one tendency were entirely to drive out the other. That would be a sign that the party really had become an ideological party.

Limited politics and the constitutional state

One of the most influential characterisations of the British Conservative tradition has come from Michael Oakeshott.[29] He argues that there is a distinct Conservative disposition in politics, which does not need to be buttressed by speculative beliefs of the kind favoured by many European Conservatives. Conservatives engage in political activity in order to resist the 'over-activity' of modern European civilisation and defend traditional institutions and ways of life and the social and political identities established through them from misguided destruction.

The great evil for Oakeshott in modern politics is rationalism, and its avoidance the greatest task for the Conservative. Rationalism is the attempt to plan societies according to some abstract idea rather than forming judgements on the basis of experience and circumstances. What matters for the Conservative is not the content of political programmes but their form. Oakeshott commented acidly on Hayek's famous polemic *The Road to Serfdom*: 'a plan to resist all planning is better than its opposite, but it belongs to the same style of politics'.[30]

For Oakeshott it is rationalism rather than individualism which is the great disease of the modern world and it produces a distinct conception of the modern state – the state as an enterprise. Governing becomes the attempt to organise all resources in a single direction, eliminating conflict. Against this he counterposes the conception of the modern state as a civil association. Here government accepts the current condition of circumstances and does not attempt to interfere with individuals' desire to make their own choices and set their own goals. Such government rests on the current beliefs and practices of its subjects; it acts as an impartial umpire, and its manner of ruling is the making and enforcing of rules of conduct.

For Oakeshott the meaning of British Conservatism has been its desire to maintain the state as a civil association, resisting plans to transform it into an enterprise. In a civil association the function of government is always limited and specific. When rules have to be modified the changes should always reflect, and never impose, a change in the activities and beliefs of those subject to them. Those Conservatives, like Gilmour, who see Thatcherism as a rationalist enterprise importing an alien ideology into the party cite Oakeshott in their support. The desire to impose a blueprint on Britain, whether it is a liberal blueprint or a socialist blueprint is what the Conservative opposes. The ideal of a free economy, and the attempts made to realise it through privatisation, engineering an enterprise culture, centralising in Whitehall powers in education, housing and transport, and the manner in which monetarism has been implemented, do suggest a government which is possessed of a single overriding purpose, and seeks to remove all obstacles to its achievement. If Oakeshott was worried that the rationalist bug had bitten the Conservatives when he read Quintin Hogg's *The Conservative Case* (1947), how much more should the plans of the New Right think-tanks of the 1970s and 1980s alarm him?

Many aspects of Thatcherism are rationalist in Oakeshott's sense. At times Thatcher and her supporters have presented what she is trying to achieve as a grand enterprise – to restore the conditions for a market economy and reduce the role of public decision making in the private sector, and to extend market criteria to as much as possible of the public sector. The Thatcher Government has not hesitated to confront and refashion institutions and to impose solutions against resistance. The practice of the Thatcher Governments has been very distant from Oakeshott's stress on the importance of building a consensus in which every legitimate interest has its rightful place.

But there is an Oakeshottian defence that could be mounted for the statecraft which the Thatcherites have pursued, and it does throw rather a different light on the opposition between libertarianism and collectivism in the British Conservative tradition. It has been the collectivist wing of the party which, until the advent of Margaret Thatcher, has had most success in characterising the libertarian wing of the party as the Diehards and reactionaries, and has been successful in projecting its own views as the expression of the conservative disposition in politics – uniting the concern for governing a society with the belief in the desirability and feasibility of extending state control into new areas.

One reading of Oakeshott, however, would suggest that most collectivist legislation represents a concession to rationalist politics and a move away from conceiving the state as a civil association in which the role of government is to hold the ring and remove obstacles to individuals expressing themselves freely. The Thatcher programme to restore a civil association may be a rationalist enterprise, but it is being undertaken to remove the effects of a long period of collectivist legislation and the resistance of institutions entrenched under collectivism.

Rationalist politics tends naturally towards a strong interventionist state in which the sphere of political decision making is constantly expanding. If it were possible to recreate a civil association and a limited state then the opportunities for rationalist politics would be greatly reduced. If the Thatcherite programme does genuinely seek a limited state, it might be forgiven its rationalist tendency by an Oakeshottian, for its outcome would be the restoration of a situation in which Conservative statecraft could once more be practised, and Conservatives would be freed from pretending to be collectivists or planners.

Such a defence of Thatcherite statecraft would suggest that the heart of the British Conservative tradition is not One Nation Conservatism, an acceptance of the state intervening in the economy to provide welfare and promote prosperity in order to maintain the legitimacy of the state, but libertarian anti-statism. The counter-argument of One Nation Conservatives is that their endorsement of collectivist measures has been based, not on rationalist blueprints for remodelling the whole society, but on the need for measures to remedy specific grievances and shortcomings in current arrangements. Most Conservatives claim the authority of Oakeshott if they can. Nevertheless the basis of Oakeshott's understanding of the modern state does stigmatise enterprise politics as un-Conservative, as well as all policies that lead away from or infringe a civil association. The accumulation of collectivist institutions, attitudes and policies could therefore be regarded as the legacy of rationalist politics, which a genuine Conservative would wish to strip away.

An assessment of Thatcherism using the criteria of Oakeshott's characterisation of Conservative statecraft reinforces the point that ideology and statecraft cannot be neatly separated in an analysis of British Conservatism. Thatcherism cannot therefore be treated simply as a new form of doctrinal Conservatism in opposition to the dominant pragmatic Conservative tradition. Matters are more complex. In reasserting the party's libertarian tradition Thatcher has, at the same time, reasserted a traditional Conservative orientation to government.

Grave doubts remain, however, as to how far the actual statecraft of the Thatcher Government is realising that aim. Here there is a significant conflict between elements of the liberal and the conservative New Right. For the economic liberals the Thatcher Government has not gone nearly far enough in using the powers of the state to create the conditions for a free economy. For many Conservatives on the New Right, however, the chief aim of the Thatcher Government should not be the creation of the conditions for a free economy but the creation of the conditions for strong but limited government. Pursuit of the first objective can lead to never-ending interventions in social institutions. Pursuit of the second encourages Conservatives to concentrate upon upholding the authority of the state within a constitution which limits rather than extends the powers of government.[31]

Roger Scruton has argued that in England conservatism

has sought expression through the activity of a single party, 'a party dedicated to maintaining the structure and institutions of a society threatened by mercantile enthusiasm and social unrest'.[32] More recently this tradition has been threatened because the party has seemed prepared to join 'the competitive market of reform' endorsing such un-Conservative things as the code of economic internationalism and the free market economy, which it once strenuously opposed:

> It has begun to see itself as the defender of individual freedom against the encroachments of the state, concerned to return to the people their natural right of choice, and to inject into every corporate body the healing principle of democracy.[33]

This makes the Thatcher Government as unlikely to restore limited politics and the constitutional state as the much reviled government of Edward Heath. They belong to the same style of politics, just as economists now note the similarities of Keynesianism and monetarism as styles of economic management. Noel O'Sullivan has written on the crisis of identity for Conservatives that has developed since the party abandoned its concern for maintaining limited government. He judges that Thatcherism has not resolved the crisis, but intensified it by substituting for the Middle Way of the progressive Conservatives the free economy of the New Right.[34]

A governing class

A third perspective on Conservative statecraft stresses the importance of the existence of a stable governing class. Such a class is often formed when property ownership and ruling are fused. Land-owning aristocracies are the classic form of such a class, but recruitment from other groups is not excluded.

Members of such a governing class are expected to treat ruling as a highly skilled activity involving obligations as well as privileges. Plato's philosopher-kings are never far away in these conceptions, which helped shape the ethos of the nineteenth-century public schools in which the apprentice rulers of the British state were (temporarily) deprived of property and family, the better to inculcate into them an ethic of public service, and a shared sense of the *patria* they were being called on to defend.

The British governing class has had many admirers, although more recently an increasing number of critics. For its admirers, such as Joseph Schumpeter, the considerable stability and continuity which Britain had enjoyed in comparison to other European states owed much to the capacity of Britain's rulers. The skill of the British ruling class in knowing the right time to make concessions, the best means to maintain and extend its support and divide its opponents made it seem indestructible, in a way that ruling classes elsewhere seldom managed:

> The unrivalled integrity of the English politician and the presence of a ruling class that is uniquely able and civilised make many things easy that would be impossible elsewhere. In particular this ruling group unites in the most workable proportions adherence to formal tradition with extreme adaptability to new principles, situations and persons. It wants to rule but it is quite ready to rule on behalf of changing interests. It manages industrial England as well as it managed agrarian England, protectionist England as well as free trade England. And it possesses an altogether unrivalled talent for appropriating not only the programmes of oppositions but also their brains.[35]

Gaetano Mosca, the analyst of political elites, struck a similar note:

> In the course of the nineteenth century England adopted peacefully and without violent shocks almost all the basic civil and political reforms that France paid so heavily to achieve through the great Revolution. Undeniably, the great advantage of England lay in the greater energy, the greater practical wisdom, the better political training, that her ruling class possessed down to the very end of the past century.[36]

British Conservatism was perceived in this way because it was so successful, and because it appeared free from the doctrinal Conservatism of so many European parties. This in part was the result of the liberal strand within the party's ideological tradition. Doctrinal Conservatism had never become firmly implanted in Britain. The anti-Enlightenment tradition emphasised authority rather than individual liberty, attacked Protestantism and Democracy and regarded individualism as a subversive force, the disease of the modern world. Some of these themes are to be found in some of the writings of the Salisbury Group and the Monday Club, but they have never been influential.[37]

Assessing the skill of a governing class is notoriously difficult. Survival is clearly one criterion. In the case of Britain, however, the most striking aspect of the governing class is how the Conservative party not only established itself as the dominant section of that political class, and united the interests of all sections of property behind it, but went on to dominate the mass democracy as well. Since 1885 the Conservatives have emerged victorious from 16 out of 29 elections and were in government, either alone or in coalition, for 68 of the 102 years between 1885 and 1987.

This degree of dominance by one party is remarkable, especially given the fears that Conservatives themselves expressed at the beginning of the period about the effects of extending the suffrage. The small population still working on the land, and the predominantly urban and industrial character of Britain, made any foothold for a predominantly rural land-owning party associated with the interests and values of pre-industrial England seem precarious.

The Conservatives had no grand design for democratic politics. They felt their way forward cautiously. They became aware, however, that in an electorate which, already after 1885 and still more so after 1918 and 1928, was dominated by the votes of manual workers, they must find ways of winning a substantial section of working-class support. In electoral terms at least, to be a popular party the Conservatives had to be a working-class party.

Without the kind of solid non-industrial base which Conservative parties could rely on the Conservative leadership was unusually conscious of the electoral problem it faced. The other major constraint on its behaviour was its identification with the institutions of the country – the Monarchy, the peerage, the Law, the Army, the Navy, the Universities and the Church. Conservative leaders interpreted their role as defending the interests and privileges of the propertied and the professional classes, upholding the institutions of the country in ways that could command majority support.

In a unitary state like the United Kingdom all contenders for national power are forced to present themselves as national parties. This was particularly true for the Conservatives, since its class base was not nearly big enough to be a substitute for the nation itself. The Conservatives were always anxious, therefore, to find bases for political alignment which did not emphasise class. In this sense they are a One Nation party and must continue to aspire to be a One Nation party, even when in practice they fall short. The content of their national appeal is not fixed, however, but constantly shifting.[38]

The Thatcher Government appears to threaten the traditional Tory conception of a governing class in two ways. Firstly it has been very critical of many of the established institutions of the British State, particularly the civil service. It has not hesitated to have open rows with the leaders of many public institutions, including the Church, the Universities and the BBC. All were once considered sound Conservative institutions whose defence against meddling radicals was one of the main purposes of the Conservative party. Now they are more often viewed as institutions that nurture an anti-enterprise culture and stand in the way of the creation of a free economy. The Thatcher Government has at times deliberately given the impression of being against the Establishment through which Conservative Governments have normally ruled. This may partly reflect the decline of the old governing class itself, and the strengthening of the populist aspect of democratic politics. Peregrine Worsthorne, one of the most persistent advocates of the need for a permanent governing class, wrote in 1978:

There used to be a governing class, whose social position lent them such weight and substance that they could pass through the demeaning processes of democratic politics with their stature and authority intact. Sir Alec Douglas-Home was a splendid relic of those days. But the contemporary politician has no such inherited advantage. Lacking nobility by birth, he must manufacture his own prestige, create his own authority, forge his own claim to rule, in conditions which yearly become more hostile to any such achievement.[39]

A second reason is that, under Thatcher, the Conservatives have finally abandoned the formulas of One Nation politics, which served the party so well for so long – the Union, the Empire and Social Reform. The Empire is no more, even though all its old power to provide the Conservatives with a national cause was displayed in the Falklands conflict. Social Reform, in the collectivist and paternalist sense in which Social Imperialists and Middle Way Conservatives[40] interpreted it, is openly rejected by Thatcherites. Now the Union too is crumbling.

The years of Thatcher's leadership have marked the final moments and exhaustion of the Conservatives' old Unionist formula. The Conservatives are no longer the party of the Union, striving to unite the country on the basis of the attachment of solid bodies of opinion in all regions and cities of the country to the Crown and Parliament. Ulster Unionism is permanently estranged from the British Conservative Party. Since the Heath Government suspended Stormont and imposed power sharing the Ulster Unionist MPs have refused to take the Conservative Whip at Westminster. The signing of the Anglo-Irish agreement by the Thatcher Government in 1986 has further embittered relations. Scotland has drifted rapidly away from Conservatism since the 1950s; the Conservatives have become less representative of Wales, the major industrial cities in England, and the North.

The passing of Unionist politics has made the Conservatives look more than ever the party of the shires and the suburbs, above all the party of Southern England, and of an increasingly remote and alien central state. The Conservatives have so far survived the consequences of the breakdown of their old electoral alliance across all regions because the concentration of population and prosperity means that the Conservatives can win not a single seat in the North of England and Scotland and still have a majority in the House of Commons.

In aspiration Thatcherism remains a One Nation strategy. It seeks to transform the whole country, so that the North becomes like the South, dependency, poverty and unemployment are overcome through a thriving enterprise economy, and all regions vote Conservative. But the actual practice, as Bob Jessop and others have described it, is a two nation politics, which explicitly divides the nation, and seeks to confront and destroy the culture, the communities and the institutions of the minority.[41]

But, as was noted at the end of the previous chapter, the radicalism of the Thatcher Government remains within bounds. It may blame the old governing class for British decline, but its constitutional iconoclasm has not extended to the House of Lords, or Parliament, or the Law. It has been visited on institutions in the second rank. But the central icons in the British state have not been touched.

High politics

There is also another way of looking at Thatcherism which sees a great continuity between the traditional statecraft of the old Conservative Establishment and that of the Thatcher Government. This is the concept of high politics, which has been analysed in great detail and with great insight by Jim Bulpitt.[42]

High politics assumes the existence of a tightly-knit governing class which chooses to reserve certain matters for itself and attempts to exclude the participation of others. The supreme practitioner of high politics was Lord Salisbury. He led the Conservatives in the early period of the enlarged franchise after 1885. He had bitterly opposed Disraeli over the extension of the franchise in 1867, but under his leadership the guide-lines of Tory statecraft in the new conditions of mass democracy were laid down.[43]

Lord Salisbury's period as Leader of the Conservatives has received a great deal of attention in recent years. For a long while Salisbury's reputation has been overshadowed by that of his more flamboyant predecessor. It was Disraeli who was seen as the creator of the modern Conservative tradition – the leadership of Salisbury and Balfour were frequently portrayed as a period of defensive reaction, which culminated in the Liberal landslide of 1906. Recent work on the Salisbury period has considerably changed that assessment. Defensive Salisbury certainly was. He saw the role of the Conservative statesman as trying to make sure that the established institutions would continue to give us 'shelter for our time'. He wanted to defend the existing state and delay the advance of democracy and collectivism for as long as possible. At the same time he fully accepted the need for the Conservatives to participate in the new electoral arena and try to secure a majority in defence of the established order.

The statecraft that emerged, argues Bulpitt, had three elements. Firstly the Conservative party sought to win power at the centre, on its own whenever possible. Secondly the party developed a readiness to seek electoral support from any quarter. Thirdly the Conservatives in office sought to maintain the autonomy of the centre by insulating it from both domestic and external pressures. This meant in practice that the Conservatives tried to restrict the number and the type of issues that were to count as 'high politics'. All other issues were delegated to subordinate bodies where they constituted a sphere of 'low politics'.

One of the Conservatives' main aims, in which they were highly successful, was to resist the emergence of the kind of executive government which was growing up in other parts of Europe. The range of responsibilities of central government remained narrow. Much was left as the responsibility of local Government. These structures were not directly controlled from the Centre; instead the central Government came to rely on various informal mechanisms for ensuring the collaboration of local authorities with the programme of the Centre.

The Centre concentrated on dealing successfully with the issues of high politics – in particular, foreign and imperial affairs. In return for exclusive sway in this sphere the Centre gave autonomy to local authority and other public bodies in their sphere. For the system to work well it was necessary that the citizenry should remain deferential and not seek participation or open government; that local administrators should be prepared to co-operate with the Centre and administer their programmes within parameters laid down by the Centre; and that the principal opposition party which was competing to win power at the centre was prepared to operate the same system.

According to this view of Conservatism what is most important in understanding the practice of the party is not the beliefs and doctrines which leading Conservatives may hold, but the overriding need to preserve the unity of the party and its ability to win power at the Centre, and to maintain the Centre in its traditional form. The formula the Conservatives developed was to maintain the authority of the State by preserving the autonomy of the circles of top decision makers from the pressures of democracy. This was attempted not only for those parts of the state outside the Government, such as the judiciary and the armed forces, but also for the Cabinet and the higher civil servants.

From this perspective the debate on whether Thatcherism is Conservatism looks very different. In terms of this dimension of its statecraft Thatcherism is a return to traditional Tory principles. The Thatcherites argued that the steady growth of corporatist structures and arrangements in British government, and the great increase in the number and range of programmes for which British Government by the 1970s had taken responsibility, meant that the authority of British Government was being seriously compromised. This in turn was weakening Conservatism both because the Conservative party appeared less necessary as an agency of government in such a state and because the party was so strongly identified with the authority of the British State.

However it also involved the Thatcher Government in a paradox. In seeking to restore the autonomy of the Centre the Thatcher Government has been unable to rely on the co-operation of many parts of the State beyond Whitehall, particularly some local authorities and some autonomous public agencies. This has led it increasingly to centralise power in Whitehall and to enlarge the sphere of high politics. The Thatcher Government is likely to bequeath to its successor a state machine with considerably extended powers. This undermines many of the principles, such as local autonomy and the diffusion of power, which Conservatives supported so strongly in the past against the centralist, collectivist doctrines of British socialism. It is a measure of the extent of the decline both of the British economy and of the old governing class that the Conservatives have been willing to pursue policies with such radical implications for the way in which the British State is organised.

Authority

The most basic task of all for Conservatives is to uphold the authority of the state. Despite playing in the party political game Conservatives have generally been anxious to ensure that the authority of the state is not compromised. Roger Scruton has argued that for Conservatives the state is always an end, not a means to some other end, like the achievement of maximum freedom in civil society. Individuals belong to the state, and its authority comes not from the mandate of citizens but from the exercise of established power.[44]

Conservatives have always understood this. The essential task of Thatcherism was therefore to propose ways in which the authority of the state could be restored and the Conservative nation rallied to support it. As J. H. Grainger notes, what Thatcherism set out to do was to mobilise the *patria* against its enemies both within and without: 'In dangerous times the Conservative party is the appropriate party to sustain the country's institutions, to use the authority of the state'.[45]

The Conservatives have always viewed the British state as their state. There may be a Whig history of England, but there is also a Tory history, the history of the nation–state, its expansion within the British Isles and throughout the world. The success of the British state in avoiding both internal overthrow and external defeat for so many centuries has ensured that most of the national myths are Tory myths, and most of the rituals and institutions of the state are Tory rituals and institutions.

As R. W. Johnson and others have argued this makes the

national culture a Tory culture.[46] The assumptions of racial
and national superiority; the deferential attitudes towards
authority; the secrecy surrounding the practice of high politics;
the anti-egalitarian ethos and the status hierarchy, are some
of its characteristic features.

Despite its decline the British governing class remains a
powerful and cohesive social bloc. Only very fleetingly has
Labour looked like challenging its dominance. In this dominant Tory culture, as Johnson points out, the state and its
institutions are synonymous with the nation itself. What is
the meaning then of a Conservative party pursuing an anti-
statist programme? The Thatcherites have argued that the
era of collectivism, far from being an inevitable further stage
in the nation's evolution, is a departure from its essential
traditions. Some judicious rolling back of the state can
therefore be justified to make the state strong again. The crises
of state authority in the 1970s come to be blamed on the
extended state of social democracy which has weakened
rather than strengthened the state by overburdening it with
responsibilities which it cannot discharge. The real anxiety
Conservatives had about British socialism, Worsthorne has
argued, is that it produced ungovernability.[47]

A government that pursued a libertarian programme would
be a profoundly un-Tory thing, but there has been no danger
of Margaret Thatcher's Governments pursuing such a radical
course. The issues which the Conservatives under Thatcher
have taken up – defence, public order, the rule of law, the
power of trade unions, the Falkland islands – are all issues
which have helped to restore the image of British Government
as a strong defender of the state and its institutions. Reasserting
the power and authority of the state have been very popular
things to do, as Johnson points out. Confronting trade union
power, standing firm against the Common Market, going to
war over the Falklands, are all issues readily understood and
communicable in the language of the national culture. It
hardly needs a highly partisan and overwhelmingly Tory
tabloid press to further emphasise it.

There are great advantages to a party which can appear
strong and competent in government. This effect is most easily
communicated in a British context where the responsibilities

of the state are limited, where the governing class is free to define what is to count as high politics, where the authority of the state can be confidently reasserted.

Under Margaret Thatcher the Conservatives have abandoned the hegemonic projects of the past. They have presented a new strategy for accumulation, the free economy and the strong state, and have made this the basis for a new statecraft, a new bid for hegemony, a new political and ideological struggle throughout society. The advocacy of the free market is not in conflict with the state being strong. On the contrary it has been the attempt to restore the free market which has highlighted once more the authority of the state. Many Conservatives now believe that the period of collectivism brought the old Tory state to the point of collapse. Thatcherism has reinvigorated it, and restored the confidence of the party in its basic appeal to the English. This is not Unionism. The Scots, the Welsh and the Irish are increasingly detached; but then, so too are the former colonies of Greater Britain. There can be no return to the dreams of Empire.

Despite its pretensions to making Britain great again, Thatcherism can do little more than aspire to be the latest religion of little England; it is unlikely to be the last. But even while it works to restore the authority of the state and reaffirm the traditional Tory culture, it has had to act in highly un-Conservative ways. This paradox is constantly encountered in Thatcherism and is one reason why Conservatives have been so divided over how to interpret it.

Its critics have noted that there has been a strong rationalist tendency within Thatcherism, and that in practising a Tory statecraft the Thatcher Governments have launched assaults and directed criticism against many of the institutions which Conservatives once took for granted and defended.

One of Mrs Thatcher's hallmarks has been her willingness to acknowledge that a gulf has opened between the people and the institutions of the state. She has always placed herself unequivocally with the people and from that standpoint criticised the institutions of big government and even specific public bodies like the BBC. Remoulding the state to make it once again a true expression of the Tory culture has been an important objective in the Thatcherite project. As J. H.

Grainger notes, Thatcher's success has been due to her ability to combine passion and vulgarity, to develop a popular common sense that finds a response in public opinion: 'Her ultimate appeal is not to classes or interests but to widespread, secular, individualist, conservative, moralising opinion.'[48] As a result, Grainger argues, she has tapped a layer of Toryism running through the whole nation.

As statecraft Thatcherism is certainly no simple return to the practice of Lord Salisbury. Instead of conserving an order and resisting change wherever possible, the Thatcher Governments have attempted to stimulate change and to reshape institutions. The Thatcherites are much closer in this respect to the Chamberlainites who argued for a strong state to remedy the abuses of *laissez-faire* and make the economy more efficient and the society more dynamic. The debate between collectivists and libertarians in the party in the early part of this century has now reappeared. Only this time it is the collectivists who wish to conserve existing institutions and urge caution in making reforms, and it is the libertarians who wish to reshape and remodel society. Margaret Thatcher seeks to restore conditions which would make possible once again the statecraft of limited ends practised by Salisbury. But the means she has used to create those conditions are more reminiscent of the statecraft of Chamberlain.

6
The struggle for hegemony

Those half-formed spectres which once hovered on the edge
of British politics . . . have now been fully politicised and
installed in the vanguard as a viable basis for hegemony,
by the Conservatives. As the span of Labour's fragile base
is eroded, this is the historical 'bloc' poised to inherit the
next phase of the crisis. It is a conjuncture many would
prefer to miss.

[*Policing the Crisis*, 1978, p. 316]

The relationship of Thatcherism to the Conservative tradition
and its character as Tory statecraft is one part of a wider
debate. There has been controversy over the radicalism and
novelty of Thatcherism; whether it is best explained as a new
hegemonic project, an old class strategy, or simply British
government as usual. Does Thatcherism introduce a radical
break in British politics or simply confirm existing trends?
Does it constitute a coherent and credible programme of
modernisation, a viable accumulation strategy for British
capital, an end to the long British decline? Does the election
of the Thatcher Government in 1979 mark a political watershed in British politics, bringing into being a new ideological
map and establishing a new political terrain? How successful
has Thatcherism been as a hegemonic project?

These kinds of question have been much discussed on the
Left of British politics, where debates on Thatcherism have
acquired a wider meaning. They have become debates about
the future of the Labour party, whether it has a future, and
whether socialism still has any political relevance.

174

One of the most important contributions to this debate has been the influential interpretation of Thatcherism developed by Stuart Hall and others and which has become associated with the journal *Marxism Today*. It analyses Thatcherism as a hegemonic project, emphasising its importance and novelty, and its success in recasting the terrain of British politics.

This approach has been strongly criticised from two main standpoints. There are those who agree that Thatcherism is a coherent strategy, but disagree about what it is that gives it coherence, and there are those who believe its coherence is exaggerated, and some even dispute that it has any coherence at all. In the first camp are to be found many of the accounts of Thatcherism as statecraft, reviewed in the last chapter, as well as the interpretations of Thatcherism from the perspectives of class politics and feminism.

From the standpoint of class politics, what gives Thatcherism coherence is the pursuit of class interests. The most basic variant of this approach argues that, though the strategies of the ruling class may shift, the fundamental objectives remain the same. Thatcherism therefore does not represent anything that has not been encountered many times before in the history of capitalism. It is one more episode in the class war between capital and labour. The more sophisticated variants analyse Thatcherism as an accumulation strategy, its relationship to different fractions of capital, and its impact on the existing regime of accumulation.

The feminist perspective sees Thatcherism as a hegemonic project, but argues that New Right ideology on the family is its most important aspect, and that the impact of the policies of the Thatcher Government need analysing in terms of the categories of race and gender as well as class.

In the second camp are, firstly, the sceptics who dispute that Thatcherism is anything more than Conservatism as usual or government as usual. They reject the claims that Thatcherism represents a significant new political practice or a coherent programme of policy. They emphasise the Government's opportunism and pragmatism, and the continuity of its policies with those of previous governments.

Another variant accepts the general analysis of Thatcherism as a hegemonic project but concedes that its radicalism has often been limited, citing by way of explanation the incoherence of the original objectives, the lack of detailed preparation of policies, and the practical obstacles, political pressures and policy dilemmas encountered in government.

The crisis of the regime

The interpretation of Thatcherism which these approaches seek to criticise in different ways has become known as the thesis of authoritarian populism, a phrase first used by Stuart Hall. But its origins lie further back in a series of debates on the British Left about the nature of the British crisis. These debates have centred upon the crisis of the British state, and in particular the problems of sustaining the British *ancien régime*, the impasse of British social democracy, and the relative decline of the British economy.

The seminal writings for these debates were the series of essays published by Perry Anderson, Tom Nairn and other contributors to *New Left Review* in the 1960s and early 1970s.[1] These essays analysed the backwardness of the British state and of British social democracy. They provided a socialist perspective on the British crisis and an important contribution to the extensive discussions taking place in the 1960s on the ways in which the British economy and British society needed modernising.

Anderson and Nairn argued that Britain was ripe for modernisation but that to be successful modernisation would have to involve a thorough restructuring of both state and civil society. Changing a few government policies would not be sufficient. Britain's real problem was that it had a governing elite which was opposed to fundamental modernisation of the domestic economy and society, and it had a Labour movement which had abandoned much of its radicalism for an assured but subordinate place within the British state.

These early analyses in *New Left Review* were influenced by concepts drawn from Gramsci. They were the first major application of the concept of hegemony to the analysis of British politics. The failure of modernisation, according to

Anderson and Nairn, was due firstly to the peculiar character of the English Revolution of the seventeenth century, which broke the back of royal absolutism and accelerated the formation of a capitalist mercantile and agrarian class, and secondly by the failure of the new industrial bourgeoisie in the nineteenth century to wrest hegemony from the representatives of this mercantile and agrarian class. Instead of a clearcut victory for the coalition of industrialists and radical democrats, a fusion took place between the forces of property, which allowed the landed aristocracy to retain predominant influence, and to resist the bourgeois radicalism which was so evident in many other countries. The bourgeois revolution in Britain was therefore incomplete. Britain was modernised but much more slowly than some other countries, and many premodern institutions and practices remained.

In the 1960s the question appeared to be whether the agent of modernisation could come from within the governing elite, or whether the Labour party could assemble a coalition that would permit the modernisation to take place under social democratic auspices. For a brief period in the mid-1960s this appeared possible, but the opportunity disappeared. The failure of the Labour party to constitute itself as a radical force allowed the initiative to pass to the right. The late 1960s saw the first major upsurge of New Right ideas and New Right activities. Enoch Powell was marginalised within the Conservative party but his extraordinary success as a tribune of the people revealed how fragile were the defences of social democracy.[2]

Powell identified the main contours of the political project that became Thatcherism. But his intervention was premature. Labour's modernisation programme was discredited by its failures, but modernisation – the attempt to extend and improve the Fordist regime of accumulation that had been partially installed in Britain – remained the horizon of the Conservative leadership's ambitions. The programme for government developed by Heath was influenced by Powell and by Labour's mistakes, but it remained firmly within the parameters of postwar politics. It was when this programme failed that Powell appeared to be vindicated and many more Conservatives began to question the viability of their continued attachment to the 1940s settlement. A space was created which Thatcherism was to seize.

Heath's programme was analysed by Robin Blackburn in *New Left Review* in 1971.[3] Blackburn noted that the Heath Government was innovative in certain crucial respects. The old political formula inaugurated by the Attlee Government and sustained by the Conservative Governments between 1951 and 1964 had come under increasing strain during the Wilson Government and now appeared exhausted. Blackburn saw Heath making changes in two critical areas: the policy to make Britain part of the European Community and loosen the ties with the United States; and domestic policies aimed at remedying Britain's industrial backwardness through tougher market conditions, lower real wages and weaker trade unions.

When the market cure seemed slow in delivering results and encountered fierce opposition, the Heath Government supplemented it with corporatist and interventionist measures. Before these had a chance to prove themselves the Government was shipwrecked by the oil crisis and its renewed clash with the miners. It was the experience of policy switch and then electoral rejection which, as argued in Chapter 3, provided the launch pad for Thatcherism. Another corporatist and interventionist programme had been discredited. The Conservative Government had compromised its principles by allowing the distinctive programme on which it had been elected to be overridden.

From the Anderson/Nairn perspective the Heath Government, like the Wilson Government before it, was another failed attempt to find a means to modernise state and economy which could command consent from both capital and labour and win electoral endorsement. Their analysis of the deep inertia of the political structures of Britain's *ancien régime* and the paralysis of policy which this induced appeared to be amply vindicated.

Terms like impasse, stalemate and deadlock abounded in analyses of British politics in the mid-1970s. To the apparent inability of the governing elite to modernise itself was added the mounting evidence of the seriousness of Britain's economic position. One influential study, published during the Heath Government in 1972, was Andrew Glyn's and Bob Sutcliffe's

British Capitalism, Workers, and the Profit Squeeze.[4] They argued that, as a result of the industrial militancy of the British working class and the intensification of international competition, profits had been severely squeezed and the rate of profit had declined to levels that were potentially catastrophic for the survival of British capitalism.

To the evidence of low profitability was added evidence of low productivity and low investment. A weak economy placed enormous strains on the government's ability to contain inflation and to fund ever-rising levels of public expenditure. These problems were exacerbated by the world recession that began in 1974. Governments had to cope with its impact against a background of major policy failures, serious industrial conflict and many signs of popular dissatisfaction with government.

This crisis of capitalism in the mid-1970s was also simultaneously a crisis of social democracy. Great opportunities seemed to be beckoning for the Left but even greater ones were seized by the Right. The discrediting of so many of the assumptions on which postwar policy had been based allowed both the New Right and the new socialist Left to argue that a quite new approach to the problems of British decline and modernisation had to be developed. Both rejected social democracy as it had developed in Britain.

The impasse of British politics in the 1970s was symbolised by the weak electoral mandates obtained by Labour in 1974 and the proliferation of new third forces and nationalist movements. Events suggested that a major crisis of hegemony was unfolding. Elements of the Right began to question democracy and endorse violence. The emergence of vigilante organisations, the speculation about military coups, and the plotting of elements of the security services against the Labour Government were signs of the deep disorientation and profound demoralisation which events in the early 1970s had created in sections of the British Establishment.[5]

Authoritarian populism

This exceptional situation in British politics was analysed by

David Purdy in two articles in *Marxism Today* in 1976.[6] The central question Purdy argued was whether the British ruling class could generate a new hegemonic project to overcome its new weakness and to reknit its fractured system of power. Such a new hegemonic project would need at least three elements: a vision of the lines of future economic development; a means to make this vision effective; and a means to make it popular.

Stuart Hall and others came to see Thatcherism as it emerged as just such a project. Following Gramsci, Hall defines hegemony as 'the ceaseless work required to construct a social authority throughout all levels of social activity'.[7] The starting-point for the Thatcherite project was the discrediting of the previous hegemonic project, the project of social democracy, which had achieved partial fulfilment in the settlement of the 1940s. Thatcherism feeds off this failure.

Social democracy as a hegemonic project developed, not in the 1940s with the election of the Attlee Government, but further back in the last great crisis of the state between 1880 and 1930.[8] Hall and Schwarz have argued that during this period there was a succession of crises of the state, and each was only partially resolved. The state that was in crisis was the liberal state of the nineteenth century:

> In the closing decades of the nineteenth century, the liberal state and its attendant modes for regulating civil society could no longer be reproduced by means of liberal policies, practices, and objectives.

One sign of this was the decline of the Liberal party, marked by major internal splits in 1886 and 1916; another was the growth of collectivist legislation and the challenge this presented to the ideologies of individualism – the free individual in civil society as market agent, as the owner of property, as the patriarch in the domestic household – as well as to the idea of the state as a night-watchman with very limited functions. The relevance and coherence of liberal ideas about the appropriate relationship between state and civil society, and the relationship of public and private spheres were also being questioned.

Under the pressures of mass democracy at home and the increasing imperialist rivalries abroad, a major reconstruction of the state occurred. The radical solutions to the problems of the state, whether proposed by socialists, feminists, or Social Imperialists were rejected. But liberal constitutionalism was substantially modified to take account of the pressure coming from both above and below to introduce collectivist legislation. The market remained the most important regulator of social relationships, but it was suspended in some areas and in others the political conditions governing the manner of its employment were changed. The growth of organised labour and organised capital helped legitimate policies of continuous intervention by the state in areas which formerly had been ignored or left entirely to private initiative.

As a result of the upheavals of these years a compromise eventually emerged in the 1920s. Liberalism had been transformed in a passive revolution, a revolution in which the decisive pressure came from above. The new state was launched on a trajectory towards social democracy. It had embraced the notion of universal citizenship and the social rights that went with that; the coming of universal suffrage had established the Labour party as the main representative of the working class and the alternative to the Conservatives; and the rejection of the ambitions of the Social Imperialists to create an integrated British imperial world state had made necessary a new agenda for coping with the problems of empire and a declining world position.

This analysis finds many echoes in other writings, such as Samuel Beer's concept of an 'age of collectivism' and Keith Middlemas's analysis of the rise of corporatism in Britain which he too dates from the 1920s.[9] The ideologies of the new collectivism were supplied by Social Imperialists, by New Liberals and by Fabians. The general intellectual climate became progressively dominated by them.

The advance of collectivism was not smooth or uncontested, but there was a general conviction that collectivism did represent modernisation. In all parties those who considered themselves progressives became collectivists. The legitimacy and effectiveness of state policy came increasingly to be determined by its relationship to group and corporate interests.

Parliament declined in importance and the direct relationship between government departments and the great producer interests increased.

Hall and Schwarz argue that, just as the liberal state entered into a complex crisis and was reconstructed between 1880 and 1930, so the social democratic state entered a similar crisis beginning in the 1960s. The bias towards increasing collectivism and intervention has been halted, the principal political party associated with social democracy, the Labour party, has begun to decline and suffered one major split, and the influence of socialist and collectivist ideas has begun to wane.

There are naturally many contrasts as well as similarities between the two periods. But one parallel is that the social democratic state like the liberal state before it became discredited not only in the eyes of its opponents but in the eyes of many of its supporters. In seeking to cope with the problems of economic decline and the management of an advanced industrial society social democracy tended to degenerate into what Nicos Poulantzas called 'authoritarian statism'.[10] The concept of authoritarian statism has a crucial bearing on the way Thatcherism itself has been explained. Faced with the need to modernise the economy and society, governments experimented with programmes designed to widen the basis of consent for measures of state intervention, such as prices and incomes policies and public investment policies. In some countries such programmes were successful, but in others – Britain is a leading example – the policies failed to gain sufficient co-operation from either labour or capital. This brought a shift away from consent towards coercion. The state took new powers to impose its policies; gradually the democratic aspects of political life began to be eroded and every base of independent countervailing power to the state came under threat.[11]

Poulantzas described this as authoritarian statism because the state was assuming ever more wide-ranging interventionist powers while both parliamentary and corporate mechanisms of representation for conferring legitimacy on the exercise of those powers were increasingly overridden. Greater powers came to be assumed by the permanent agencies of the state in many spheres, but especially in relation to the maintenance of public order, the handling of emergencies and the gathering of intelligence.

There was a clear trend towards authoritarian statism in Britain from the mid-1960s onwards, caused by the breakdown of the attempt to organise corporate consent for modernisation programmes, as well as by rising levels of industrial and political unrest and the renewed conflict in Northern Ireland. But to make it a success governments needed to go much further than they were either prepared or able to contemplate. The result was that, despite incurring increased unpopularity by measures to coerce various groups in civil society to fall in line with state policies, the policies themselves still failed to secure their objectives, and successive governments were defeated at the polls.

The apparent inability of either of the two main parties in the state to organise consent for a programme of modernisation and to govern effectively opened the space for a new right-wing project to develop, the project of Thatcherism. From the start the Thatcherites sought to organise a bloc of interests around the themes of anti-statism, anti-collectivism and anti-socialism. It is this project that Stuart Hall calls authoritarian populism.[12] It is populist because it draws upon popular discontent with many aspects of the social democratic state to win support for a radical right programme. It is authoritarian because in the implementation of its programme it further increases the central power of the state and weakens opposition to it.

As a form of populism Thatcherism feeds off a wide range of discourses that are already established in a number of arenas – discourses on law and order, on the family, on welfare, on education, on race, on economic management and on the trade unions. It is not narrowly concentrated on a single set of issues. But it constantly seeks to explain the ills of society, from permissiveness to industrial militancy, in terms of the malign influence of state collectivism and the activities of bodies like trade unions on which collectivism confers a privileged status.

What makes this a new hegemonic project is the scale of the assault. The attack on social democracy is conceived as a struggle on all fronts and in all institutions. The New Left project of a long march through the institutions becomes the Thatcherite motif. As Stuart Hall puts it, the state is no longer conceived, as Lord Salisbury might have conceived it, as a passive *status quo* to be defended against attack, but as a strategic political field of force to be reconstructed.

One measure of the success of Thatcherism is the extent to which it disrupts the old common sense of social democracy and establishes a new common sense in its place. The market is reconstituted as a major ideological force and crucial distinctions between the productive and unproductive, private and public, wealth creating and wealth consuming, come to be the yardsticks for judging policy.

In seeking to reconstruct the state Thatcherism necessarily appears as a radical political force. It launches a fierce ideological and political assault on old landmarks and the 1940s settlement, specifically on the priority to be accorded full employment, on the collectivist basis of the welfare state, on the principle of redistribution to limit inequality, and on the value of partnership between the corporate interests. In attacking the 1940s settlement it of necessity projects a new one. It seeks to shift the terms of the political debate. The liberal New Right constantly present themselves as the party of progress, and put forward their own Utopia – an economy without unions, markets without rigidities, a minimal public sector and private provision of almost all goods and services.

Such an attempt to redraw the political terrain, to change the scale of political values, and to redefine what is meant by the politically possible, is naturally experienced as deeply threatening by parties and social groups still wedded to the old framework. To the extent that a new project of this kind makes headway, the opposition becomes disorganised and defensive. In Britain the Labour party became deeply divided over how to respond to Thatcherism. Many in the party could not understand how Thatcherite policies could bring the Conservatives electoral success; at the same time there was fundamental disagreement over the achievements of recent Labour administrations and whether the party should defend social democracy as it had come to be understood in Britain, or launch a radical programme to transform it.

The split that occurred in the Labour party in 1981 with

the formation of the SDP came about from the same set of forces that created Thatcherism. The Labour party finally split because the old formula for social democracy no longer commanded wide assent. A divided opposition was a highly favourable circumstance for the pursuit of the radical Thatcherite project, and the Conservatives missed few opportunities to weaken their opponents still further by carefully aimed legislation and propaganda.

Central to Stuart Hall's interpretation of Thatcherism is the idea that the Labour movement is not outside the crisis of hegemony but part of it. The crisis is not a crisis of British capitalism which the Left can watch with folded arms, waiting its turn to take over power. Instead the crisis precipitates the reconstruction of the state and this necessarily involves the Labour movement, both its industrial organisation and its modes of political representation. In the course of this reconstruction the Left is threatened not only with exclusion from the possibility of power, but also with the reversal of the gains which had been won during the rise of the Labour movement and which at one time had seemed inviolable.

The forward march of Labour halted?

The second strand in the *Marxism Today* interpretation of Thatcherism is the analysis of the crisis in the Labour movement, and the problem Labour has encountered in forging a political strategy to defeat the Conservatives. It has been advanced most forcefully by Eric Hobsbawm, starting with an article in 1978 – before the Labour Government had lost office and the Thatcher Government had been installed.[13] Hobsbawm's analysis was prosaic and was criticised for stating familiar facts, but what his analysis focused attention on was the precariousness of the Left's political position. Even the bitterest critics of the Labour party and its policies tended to assume that there was a latent majority for the Left in Britain. The problem was how to mobilise it.

Hobsbawm was less reassuring. He argued that, in the relatively short period in which Labour had been operating as a political party, it had enjoyed a period of steady, and almost uninterrupted advance up to 1951, the year in which it achieved its highest percentage vote, even though it narrowly lost the election. Since 1951, however, support for the party had begun to decline. Only the election in 1966 marked a major exception to the trend. In the elections between 1955 and 1970 the Labour vote ranged between 43 and 48 per cent. In the elections of 1974 and 1979 it ranged between 37 and 39 per cent. In 1983 it fell below 30 per cent, for the first time since 1922, recovering slightly in 1987 to 31 per cent.

Even Hobsbawm cannot have expected that his analysis would be so starkly confirmed. Labour's progress at one time seemed so inexorable and its social base so secure that the Labour movement was sometimes pictured as a machine throbbing its way to socialism.[14] Demography, sociology and psephology all appeared to be on Labour's side. By identifying itself with collectivist legislation and the extension of the role of the state Labour was also identified as the party of progress and the party of the future.

Hobsbawm argues, however, that this optimism was not justified. Long-term changes have occurred which, on balance, have been unfavourable to Labour. Hobsbawm singles out the decline of manual occupations, changes in the organisation of capitalism, and increasing sectional and ethnic and life-style divisions in the working class. The Labour movement as a result has been declining in numbers and importance, and has been handicapped by what Hobsbawm calls the 'pure wage militancy' on display during 1970–4 and the absence of a political strategy to enlarge the appeal of radical and progressive ideas to counter the shrinking of the Labour party's core support in the electorate. He dismissed the increasing strength of the Left in the Labour party as likely to produce only internecine warfare and the pursuit of organisation politics. Meanwhile the vote and membership of the Labour party continued to decline. All factions in the Labour party seemed unaware of the increasing fragility of their support.

This was all written before the Winter of Discontent, before the three major election defeats, and before the split in Labour's ranks over changes in the party's constitution. Reflecting on these events Hobsbawm has argued the need for Labour to reconstitute itself as a people's party, to reforge an alliance between progressive professional and intellectual groups and the working class, and to shed its trade union and class image.[15] From other writers has come the call for Labour to be the party of radical democracy rather than of socialism, in order to begin to tackle Thatcherism on its own ground – to create a new popular mass constituency for radical ideas.[16]

It is argued that Labour has done best electorally in the past – in 1945 and 1966 – when it succeeded in creating a broad coalition of interests around a coherent reform programme. At such times Labour aspired to become the party political agent of hegemony in the state, and for a time succeeded. In the mid-1970s the crisis of hegemony meant that no political party was fulfilling this role. The vacuum was filled by the elaboration of the new Thatcherite project. Labour had no alternative to put against it.

In assessing any movement that aspires to be a hegemonic force Stuart Hall has suggested that there are three questions: can it lead the key sectors; can it win the strategic engagements; can it stay in front when challenged? On such a test the Labour movement was clearly failing in all three in the 1980s.

Class politics

The most widespread alternative on the Left to the interpretation of Thatcherism associated with *Marxism Today* has become known as the thesis of class politics. Sometimes the issue is presented by counterposing the theory of hegemony to the theory of class. Theorists of hegemony are portrayed as being exclusively concerned with questions of ideology. However correct this may be for individual writers, it represents a major impoverishment of the concept of hegemony which, as argued throughout this book, involves ideology, politics and economics. The concept of hegemony makes little sense if it excludes the notion of an accumulation strategy, a fundamental concept of class analysis.

Nevertheless the two terms, hegemony and class, have come to denote very different emphases in political analyses. For proponents of the class politics thesis the *Marxism Today* analysis puts far too much weight on the ideological aspects of Thatcherism. These, it is argued, are secondary. What is of real importance in understanding Thatcherism is the political and economic crisis of British capitalism – the relative economic decline, the impact of the world recession, the weakening of the world power of the British state, and the consequent disorientation of the ruling class and the crisis of legitimacy for state institutions and the political system.

The succession of crises that have engulfed the British state from the mid-1960s have produced, it is argued, a marked polarisation of British politics and the revival of a socialist Left in the Labour party. The forward march of Labour may have been halted for a time in the 1950s, but on this reading of recent history it resumed in earnest in the 1970s.[17]

The evidence cited for this interpretation is varied. There is firstly the industrial militancy of 1968–74 which helped force two Governments to climb down in their attempt to curb shop-floor union power; secondly the growing disillusion with the ideas of the revisionist generation inside the Labour party following the failure of the Wilson Government to carry through the modernisation programme which had owed so much in its formulation to these ideas; thirdly, the rethinking of policy and strategy on the Left in the 1970s which produced the programme that later became known as the alternative economic strategy, and which appeared to offer a clear direction for the party away from the existing orthodoxies of social democracy; fourthly the radicalisation of sections of groups outside the traditional organisations of the working class, such as women, the black communities and students, which created new policy agendas, and a new injection of energy and commitment into the party; and fifthly the growth in influence of the Left inside the Labour party, which enabled it to dominate the NEC during the 1970s, shape the party's policies, and, after 1979, push through major constitutional changes.[18]

The changes in the Conservative party's leadership and policies are seen as the other side of the political polarisation which the failures of social democracy have brought about. But the rise of Thatcherism is regarded by many theorists of class politics as a sign of weakness rather than confidence, a despairing last throw by the ruling class to hold on to power, but quite inadequate as a solution to the problems of British capitalism. It reintroduces the kind of deflationary programme familiar from the past. Unemployment is increased to lower real wages and break working-class resistance to restructuring and reorganisation of production and restore the conditions for profitable accumulation once more.

This kind of interpretation has been put with particular force by Tony Benn. He argued in the 1970s that the choice lay between three broad political economic strategies: the free market policies of Thatcherism, the corporatism of the Labour Right and Tory moderates, and Labour's alternative economic strategy. Only the latter, he believed, was capable of restoring prosperity and extending democracy. Both the free market programme and the corporatist programme would lead to attacks on democracy.[19]

The class politics perspective suggests that, although Thatcherism may be hegemonic in aspiration, it lacks the means to become hegemonic because it cannot overcome the resistance of the working class, and cannot win their consent. A number of analyses also claimed that the class interests which Thatcherism represents are narrow and do not embrace all fractions of capital, so that the base of support for its new regime is fragile.[20]

There is no single 'class politics' interpretation of Thatcherism. A number of different variants have been advanced. One which had brief currency in the 1970s was that Thatcherism represented a radicalisation of elements of the *petite bourgeoisie* who felt themselves squeezed between big capital and the trade unions. This idea appeared to be supported by evidence of mounting middle-class protest against particular aspects of government controls and interventionist policies. The proliferation of ratepayers' groups and organisations like the Small Business Bureau and the Freedom Association, as well as the writings of able polemicists like Patrick Hutber, gave some credence to it.[21] So too did the fact that the Leaders of the New Right in the Conservative party – first Powell and then Thatcher – both came from lower middle-class backgrounds, and the free market ideology they espoused, with its emphasis on self-reliance, independence, small scale enterprise and household economics.

The theory never developed, however, because there was so little evidence to sustain it.[22] Thatcherism was always a passive revolution from above. There was not even the limited mass mobilisation which Powellism briefly created in the late 1960s over immigration. Thatcher gained the leadership of the Conservative party through the votes of her parliamentary colleagues and not in any unorthodox manner. In organisational terms Thatcher has been a conventional Leader of the Conservative party and has done little to transform its internal structures. The point has been well made by Bob Jessop and his colleagues, when they ask:

> Where are the Thatcherite new model unions, the Tebbit Labour Front, the Thatcherite Youth, the women's movement, Thatcherite sports leagues, rambling clubs etc? They do not exist and this highlights a certain vulnerability for the Thatcherite project.[23]

What their absence indicates is that Thatcherism cannot be presented as some kind of Fascist or even Poujadist movement within the Conservative party. There has been no internal purge of those opposed to Thatcher's leadership and little evidence of Thatcherite factions appearing in the constituencies. But the most important evidence is that the programme that Thatcherism has adopted, while containing elements likely to appeal to small businessmen, is supported by and tailored to the needs of the dominant sections of British capital.

A much more influential interpretation of Thatcherism as class politics takes this as its starting-point. Thatcherism is a class response to the strength and militancy of the working class, but it is the response of the dominant fractions of the capitalist class rather than the mobilisation of lower middle-class strata. It is a determined attempt to roll back postwar gains made by the working class in three main areas – welfare programmes, nationalisation and trade union rights.[24]

In the early stages of the Thatcher Government adherents of a class politics perspective often regarded Thatcherism as doomed, a last bid to hold back the working class, to maintain the unity of the Conservative party, and to reverse Britain's economic decline. But the strategy was regarded as flawed because it was economically irrational. This argument rested on two claims. The first was that the interests of banking capital dominated the coalition of interests supporting Thatcher. The second was that monetarism was ideologically archaic and quite unsuited to the complex tasks of managing an advanced capitalist economy. This meant that Thatcherism was a reactionary spasm. Its policies conflicted with the 'objective interests' of the bourgeoisie. The bourgeoisie was defined as large-scale industrial capital, which appeared to bear the brunt of the recession in 1979–81. The optimistic conclusion that was drawn from this was that with capital divided and with the economy plunged into chaos by Thatcherite policies there was a real prospect of winning wide support for a socialist alternative.

This kind of perspective on Thatcherism, although still found among some socialist groups, has generally been abandoned. What it found difficult to explain was why, if the policies were so much against their 'objective interests', corporate capital protested so little. Apart from the brief flurry of CBI opposition in 1981, when the Director General, Sir Terence Beckett, talked of a bare knuckle fight with the Government over the high level of interest rates, capital has seemed remarkably content under the Thatcher yoke. All business organisations gave fulsome backing to the Conservatives in the 1983 and 1987 elections, and the flow of financial contributions to Conservative party funds from business has not diminished significantly.[25]

A second objection to the thesis is that, far from being archaic and a throwback to ideas from a much earlier stage in the development of capitalism, monetarism was a modern doctrine which expressed the logic of the growing financial and commercial integration of the world economy. Its existence as an international orthodoxy belied attempts to portray it as a home-grown British lunacy. It is rather doctrines of political economy based upon national economies, such as most variants of Keynesianism, which became outmoded and 'archaic' in the 1970s. Monetarism prescribed a new and viable programme of policy for national governments within the capitalist world economy.[26]

A third objection, however, was to become the most telling of all. After the initial shake-out of labour and the wave of bankruptcies in 1979–81, the economy stabilised and a slow recovery began. The expectation that the Thatcherite programme would push the British economy into a downward spiral of ever-increasing unemployment and declining production was not borne out. The avoidance of further collapse and the real advance of some sectors of the economy after 1981 made the Thatcherite experiment look very different in 1987 from what it had appeared in 1981. The possibility that it was preparing the way for the emergence of a new post-Fordist regime of accumulation began to be discussed.

Others argued that although Thatcherism might in some respects be considered economically irrational, because of the short-term damage it was doing to the economy and to particular sectors, it was nevertheless politically rational as a strategy for capital.[27] According to this view capital was prepared collectively to accept short-term costs in the form of bankruptcies and losses in order to secure a long-term, lasting improvement in the environment for business in the United Kingdom. The essential requirement for this was a Government prepared to confront and permanently weaken the power of organised labour. The weapons employed included mass unemployment, trade union legislation, the denationalisation of public enterprises and privatisation of public services, and the scrapping of corporatist bargaining structures. The crisis did not therefore come about by accident or because of mismanagement. The crisis was precipitated in order to effect a restructuring of the economy and a change in the balance of power between labour and capital. Mass unemployment in particular was used as a means to break the resistance of labour and introduce a range of changes designed to prevent labour regaining its former strong bargaining position within enterprises.

Many who analysed Thatcherism in this way as a major planned class offensive also claimed that it was doomed to fail because it would not manage to break the resistance of organised labour. Much greater force would be needed. When the economy revived, it was predicted, so would industrial militancy. The economy did revive, but industrial militancy did not.

Apart from its confident predictions about the level of resistance to Thatcherism this interpretation has greater plausibility than some other variants of the class politics thesis. The attack upon the trade unions has been a central feature of the Thatcher Government's programme ever since it was elected, and the Government has fought several major battles with unions. There has been no repetition of the defeats suffered by the Government between 1968 and 1974. In most cases the Government has faced down industrial militancy and contributed to a climate of demoralisation and acquiescence on the shop floor.

The greatest of the industrial battles was with the miners in 1984/5. The events of that strike provide powerful support for this thesis. The short-term economic irrationality of the strike was plain from the start. The cost of the strike to the country and the Government was very high – approximately £2.5 billion. But the Government was prepared to write off this cost for the long-term benefits it expected from a clear-cut miners' defeat. These were not only the effects on the running of the coal industry, but the wider symbolic effects of defeating the group of workers who had successfully resisted the Heath Government. To gain this prize the Government made detailed preparations for a miners' strike, resisted all pressures to compromise, and won a complete victory.[28]

The thesis, however, is more difficult to sustain outside particular examples, because it assumes that the major objective of the Thatcher Government was to crush the organised working class in the interests of reviving industrial capital in Britain. The recession of 1979–81 and the unemployment which resulted are sometimes seen as being deliberately engineered by the Government for this purpose. But there is no evidence that the Government expected the level of unemployment which resulted from its first two years in office. Some transitional unemployment was anticipated from the application of monetarist policies, but the world recession was unforeseen.

What is undeniable is that the Government used the

recession as an opportunity for more radical restructuring. But to argue that the Thatcher Government had a clearly worked out plan for destroying trade union power which it proceeded to implement when it was elected overstates the degree of coherence of the Government's objectives and overlooks the extent of muddle and improvisation in the making and implementing of policies that is apparent from the evidence reviewed in Chapter 4.

Finance and industry

Another objection to many variants of the class politics thesis is that their conception of the British social formation and their understanding of the forces which Thatcherism represents are misleading, because they suggest that the core of British capital is still industrial capital, and that there is something abnormal about banking capital playing such a prominent role. British capital is still analysed as if it were primarily a national interest, and that it was self-evident that every national economy must have a strong national industrial bourgeoisie.

The most valuable class politics interpretation of Thatcherism has come from those who have analysed the significance of the split between industrial and financial sectors in the British economy.[29] What all these writers stress is the rationality of Thatcherism as an accumulation strategy for the dominant sections of British capital. The manner of Britain's integration into the world economy over two centuries has made the bloc of commercial and financial interests dominant over industry in the determination of Britain's foreign economic policy. At times of crisis when major choices have had to be made the issue has generally been resolved in favour of Britain's traditional links with the world economy.

Thatcherism is no exception to this. As John Ross has shown, while there have been some heavy losers under Thatcher, such as heavy engineering and chemicals, a significant bloc of capital has benefited.[30] Oil, food, construction as well as banking and the protected sectors of defence and agriculture all performed strongly right through the recession.

The Thatcher Government has seen a further major move away from manufacturing. Those sectors able to trade and produce internationally have been consolidated as the leading sectors of the economy. From this standpoint it makes no sense to regard Thatcherism as a misguided industrial strategy for reversing Britain's industrial decline. Most of traditional British industry as well as many of the Fordist industries that were the basis of postwar prosperity have been written off. Thatcherism has no industrial strategy except to promote the complete integration of Britain into the world economy. Companies must survive unaided in international competition if they are to have a future in the British economy. Some Ministers in the Thatcher Government doubt that many of the successful companies in the future will be industrial in the traditional sense.

Such a policy has greatly benefited those sectors able to seize the new opportunities as well as the foreign capital which has entered the British economy. The policies of the Thatcher Government have proved most effective in destroying the structures of the (incomplete) Fordist regime of accumulation that was established in Britain.[31] Mass unemployment and trade union laws have helped management in many industries to reorganise industrial relations towards the new model of flexible specialisation, with the work-force divided into core and periphery workers.[32] This appears so far to have been seized upon by multinational companies keen to use Britain as a base for assembly of industrial products for distribution to the European market.[33]

This policy represents the final defeat of the manufacturing interest, since the destruction of the manufacturing base that is involved prevents the possibility of any future revival. Manufacturing will continue to exist in Britain but only subordinate operations will be retained. The design and development of new industrial products will have passed largely elsewhere. Britain's new status as a secondary economic power will be confirmed.

These arguments are powerful. The questions they raise are as follows: why has the manufacturing interest been so weak? Why was the Fordist regime of accumulation never consolidated? Why has Thatcherism received so little opposition from manufacturing companies? The most detailed explanation of the acquiescence of manufacturing industry in the accumulation strategy of the Thatcher Government has come from Colin Leys.[34] He argues that there are four factors involved. Firstly the mode of representation of capital has always been weak both politically and bureaucratically. The main organisation, the CBI, has been a forum for all sections of capital rather than a pressure group for manufacturing. Of its members 30 per cent are not industrial companies at all. The desire to present a consensus has made many of the policy stances taken by the CBI extremely bland and non-controversial.

The second reason was that manufacturing itself is not a single interest but highly divided, in terms of scale, the degree of monopoly and the splits between exporters and domestic producers and national and multinational production. As Leys puts it, the veto on opposition to Thatcherism came

> primarily from distributors and other commercial companies, from the larger, more monopolistic, multinational firms oriented to the domestic market, and from those which had the best chance of restructuring, relocating abroad, or contracting into greater productivity, or which were less affected by the squeeze.[35]

A third reason was the political crisis between 1974 and 1976. A permanent shift in the balance between labour and capital was widely feared throughout industry. This explained, according to Leys, the very strong opposition that was mounted to proposals like the Bullock Report, which would have extended industrial democracy, with strong trade union representation throughout industry. The support which business gave to Margaret Thatcher was forthcoming because she offered a strong stand against the encroachment of labour and trade union influence.

The fourth factor identified by Leys was that British business had never learnt to think in terms of hegemony. British businessmen participate little in politics and have had a low interest in macroeconomic questions. Only two out of 20 business leaders that Leys interviewed in 1983 saw the direction of the state, the definition of national goals and strategies for achieving them as natural concerns for businessmen. Their policy concerns have been more immediate – particular tax rates, tariffs, controls and subsidies. The wider issues of accumulation strategy have been left to the consensus forged in Whitehall.

Gender and race

The writing on authoritarian populism and the writing on class politics have emphasised different things in their understanding of Thatcherism as a hegemonic project. Both have in their turn been criticised for their relative neglect of the issues of gender and race. This failure is most acute in the case of some writing from a class politics perspective. Thatcherism is treated as a return to much more open forms of class struggle. Gender and race issues are part of the struggle that is waged by capital to subordinate labour by dividing it. But the heart of the strategy is a class strategy, and class is the starting-point for understanding it.

The thesis of authoritarian populism gives a much less privileged position to class. Gender and race in theory are regarded as having at least equal importance for analysing the nature of social stratification and for interpreting politics. Such a focus was clearly laid out in *Policing the Crisis*.[36] The question raised by many feminist writers, and by writers on the politics of race, is whether this is carried through in the actual analyses of Thatcherism.[37]

From the feminist perspective the attempt to create a free economy is evaluated not principally as an accumulation strategy but as a much wider political and ideological project to re-establish hegemony. This makes the drift towards a strong state the most significant aspect of Thatcherism. The policies of the Thatcher Governments have greatly damaged the position of women and blacks, but even more importantly consent for these policies has in part been mobilised through a concentrated ideological assault on the new rights which women and blacks secured during the 1960s and 1970s.

This highlights the point already made that, for the theorists of authoritarian politics, what has to be analysed is the crisis of social democracy rather than the crisis of capitalism, because the latter is too often narrowly conceived in terms of the struggles between capital and labour over how to resolve problems of accumulation. A central component of the crisis of social democracy is the erosion of the bases of authority in the state and civil society which results in a widely perceived threat to social order.

From this angle the Thatcherite project is about reclaiming the nation and the family from ideological and political forces unleashed in the 1960s which threaten to subvert both. Thatcherism appears as the authentic voice of white working-class patriarchal values, preaching the importance of a strong nation and a strong family for social cohesion.

One chosen target for attack is the permissive society, which becomes the code in which gender and many race issues are discussed. In the permissive society that developed in the 1960s, it is argued, the public moral code was relaxed to the point where a much wider range of sexual behaviour was tolerated and many taboos were lifted. Activities previously secret become public. Homosexuality was legalised, which enabled gays and lesbians to campaign publicly against discrimination. Abortion was legalised, which allowed many clinics to be opened and brought much wider public awareness of the issues of birth control. Divorce became easier, cohabitation more common, and extended families more fragmented, which focused attention on the loosening of family ties and the growing number of single-parent families and handicapped and elderly people requiring state support.

The greater public freedom accorded sexual behaviour has been blamed by many critics of the permissive society for a general questioning of authority and the undermining of moral community represented by the traditional family. Evidence of indiscipline, whether in the classroom, on the football terraces or in urban ghettos, has been seized on to suggest a general malaise, and a collapse of the firm structure of authority which an ordered society requires. The backlash against permissiveness has been interpreted as a crucial part of the New Right project. Such 'moral majority' politics seeks consent for wider New Right programmes and politicians by speaking to the fears of all those citizens who see their way of life as being under threat.[38]

This makes Thatcherism a deeply divisive hegemonic project, since the unity it is seeking to build cannot be a unity of the whole nation. The nation which is to be restored would render the idea of a plural society in terms of both gender and race illegitimate. The white nation and the patriarchal family as an ideological project marginalises and excludes many of the groups who began to assert their rights to full citizenship in the 1960s and 1970s.

The Conservative New Right has persistently sought to identify social democracy as the breeding-ground for the permissive society, as part of a wider assault on the modernisation projects of Labour revisionists and Tory progressives in the 1960s. As Bea Campbell has argued, the modernisation proposed by the Conservative party under both Macmillan and Heath involved no cultural modernisation.[39] It tended to assume the bedrock of the 'English way of life' – the culture of respectability and patriarchy. Many of the leading Tories were progressive in their views on social policy; the strong grass roots demand for the return of hanging and flogging, much in evidence at party conferences, was successfully resisted throughout the 1950s and 1960s.

However the failure of the modernisation projects opened the way for an increasingly powerful assault on the permissiveness that had accompanied the attempts at modernisation, whether it was the permissiveness towards immigration control in the 1950s or the permissiveness towards sexual behaviour in the 1960s. Both were treated as major threats to the English way of life – the traditional English identity of moderation at home and imperialism abroad, which was already suffering from the precipitate decline in Britain's world status.

The rejection of progressive 'Keynesian' Conservatism was therefore also accompanied by a rejection of progressive social Conservatism, and a marked hardening of the party's attitudes on the questions of immigration, law and order, and the family. From a feminist perspective the Thatcherite project has been very successful in exploiting gender and race issues to win popular support for its wider programme.

Yet important though these populist themes may have been

they did not easily translate into positive government policies. The plural society survived the first eight years of the Thatcher Governments. The Conservatives introduced still stiffer immigration laws and a British Nationality Act, but no moves were made to repatriate immigrants already in the United Kingdom as voices on the Right were urging, nor was any attempt made to repeal existing race relations legislation.

Similarly, despite occasional outbursts from Ministers, little was done positively to reinforce the family. Social engineering on the scale required to refashion social relationships to confirm to the Conservative ideal was too much to contemplate. The proposals of the Cabinet Committee on Family Policy in 1982/3 were leaked in 1983.[40] What was striking about most of the proposals, such as teaching children how to manage pocket money, was that they were little more than the expression of pious hopes. Few serious policy recommendations flowed from them.

Thatcherism as a political project has sought to reassert the importance of a strong nation and the patriarchal family. Both have been significant in the construction of its electoral bloc, and have helped to justify government indifference to the increased burden which the recession and government cuts in welfare services and welfare benefits have inflicted on women and blacks. The 'feminisation of poverty' has become a marked feature of the Thatcher years as it has been in Reagan's America.

The public stance of the Thatcher Government towards women's rights remains ambiguous. It continues to support the principle of equal pay for women in careers. Jobs for women have been less hit by the recession than jobs for men, and the economy during the Thatcher years has become more dependent than ever on women workers. The new pattern of industrial relations with its emphasis on flexible specialisation is particularly suited to the employment of women workers, since they can be more easily recruited and laid off, and because their expectations of pay and conditions of service tend to be lower than those of men. As an accumulation strategy Thatcherism needs more women workers. What it does not want, however, is commitment to the kind of public services and policies which would enable women to combine work and family, and encourage the shifting of child care and housework burdens between the sexes.[41]

Despite its rhetoric the Thatcher Government has tended to lack clear policy ideas as to how the nation might be made more racially and culturally homogeneous and how sexual behaviour can be altered and traditional families recreated. The dilemmas of moral conservatism were exposed by the Aids crisis, which at one level appeared to confirm everything the New Right had ever said about the permissive society, but which still obliged the Government to develop a public health programme whose basis was an acceptance of the facts of sexual behaviour in Britain as they were, not as the moralists of the New Right might like them to be.

Yet, as the Aids crisis reveals, and crises of race relations have revealed in the past, there is an enormous potential for active government policies which make particular minorities scapegoats for major social problems. The Thatcher Government has not moved far in that direction. But Thatcherism has helped create a political climate in which such movement is no longer inconceivable. The weakening of the social democratic idea of universal rights of citizenship is a major step in this direction.

The state and public policy

A different line of criticism of the thesis of authoritarian populism has come from those who have emphasised the dimension of state policy making. It draws upon much detailed work that has been done by analysts of particular Thatcherite policies. It emphasises the continuity of policy and the gap between rhetoric and achievement.

Many political journalists, notably Peter Riddell, have criticised views of Thatcherism which have attributed to it great coherence and novelty.[42] Riddell is responsible for one of the best-known judgements on the Thatcher revolution. 'If there was a Thatcher experiment,' he wrote, 'it was launched by Denis Healey.'[43] In his book on the Thatcher Government up to 1983 he shows how in every policy area the changes are not as great as might be supposed from reading ministers' speeches. The social democratic consensus, he argues, is still intact.

This is a view which many political scientists have endorsed. Richard Rose has analysed the 'moving consensus' that guides policy formation, and has argued that political parties, despite their adversary rhetoric, have little impact on policy outcomes. The constraints on policy makers are so tight that the scope for radical innovations that make big differences to the way the country is governed are small.[44]

This echoes a long-established view of politics and politicians. Christopher Hollis once wrote that 'politics as politicians well know is largely a matter of giving names to what is happening anyway and persuading people to vote for it'.[45] This implies a very sharp disjunction between the politics of support and the politics of power. The means used to construct an electoral majority may have little relevance to the policy agenda in government, although politicians have an obvious interest in pretending otherwise.

As Chapter 4 showed, there is considerable evidence to support this view when the policy record of the Thatcher Government is looked at critically and in detail. The analysis of economic policy under the Thatcher Governments by writers such as Grahame Thompson, Jim Tomlinson, Paul Mosley, and Maurice Mullard also reveal the enormous part played by inertia, rules-of-thumb, crisis management, political pressures and unexpected events in shaping the actual course of policy.[46] Thompson argues, for example, that New Right ideas have only had a limited and uneven impact on policy formation under the Thatcher Governments. They may have served an important function in providing ideological support, but in the actual process of policy formation and implementation they tend to be eclipsed by the instruments of policy that are available and by the constraints which inhibit any actual changes. This makes continuities with the policies of previous administrations still appear stronger than any radical changes that have occurred.

One of the greatest changes in stabilisation policy was the introduction of the Medium Term Financial Strategy. This was certainly an innovation but the real foundations of monetarism had been laid long before. As Thompson notes, the use of the PSBR as a central indicator of the confidence of the private sector financial markets in government policies was an important feature of the Thatcher Governments, but its use as such an indicator dates from 1973/4. Similarly the use of cash limits and monetary targets began in 1975. The MTFS, if it had remained inviolate, would have been a significant innovation, but it was gradually diluted after 1982, particularly under Nigel Lawson, until the range of monetary measures was so wide and the discretion allowed the Chancellor in selecting his monetary and fiscal policy so great that there was little that was distinctively monetarist about the government's policy by 1987.

These doubts about the radicalism and coherence of Thatcherism in practice form the main theme of the critical review of the thesis of authoritarian populism by Bob Jessop and others.[47] They argue that there is a tendency for the thesis to concentrate too much on the ideological aspects of Thatcherism and to fail to analyse it either in the political and institutional context in which it developed, or to assess it as an accumulation strategy. The different levels of analysis of Thatcherism as a hegemonic project have been conflated, and this leads to suggestions not just that Thatcherism is hegemonic in aspiration but that it has already achieved hegemony. They dispute this claim on four main grounds.

Firstly there is little firm evidence that Thatcherism has created a new national–popular consensus. The electoral success of Thatcherism owes as much to shrewd calculation of political interest such as the sale of council houses as it does to any widespread acceptance of New Right ideas. Certain aspects of postwar social democracy, such as nationalisation, may be unpopular, but they were already highly unpopular in the 1950s. What is more serious for the success of the Thatcherite project is the difficulty the Conservatives have encountered in shifting popular attitudes towards collective provision of welfare in areas like health. In the elections of both 1983 and 1987 the Conservatives were, as a result, forced onto the defensive, and obliged to claim that the National Health Service would be safe in their hands. The Conservatives have achieved solid electoral success but with relatively low percentages of the total vote. This allows their success to be explained in terms of the divisions among their opponents, and their own skill in maintaining a bloc of support sufficiently concentrated to assure them of a parliamentary majority. The electoral map of Britain is now so peculiar and the patterns of voting so diverse in different regions that the national Government may not need a national–popular consensus to support it. Power at the centre can be attained by the Conservatives without their being a national party any longer.

A second criticism is that the thesis of authoritarian populism attributes too much dominance to social democracy in the period preceding the rise of Thatcherism. The Thatcherites draw a picture of Britain suffering almost continuously under the collectivist yoke from 1945 until liberation in 1979. The thesis of authoritarian populism also treats Thatcherism predominantly as a response to the failures of the governments which tried to operate within the constraints of social democracy. But social democracy was less developed in Britain than in many other countries. The 1940s settlement was not only about domestic policy; of equal importance was the consensus on foreign policy and foreign economic policy – the Atlantic Alliance, the acceptance of an open international trading order, and the various attempts to rebuild the international business of the City of London and the dominant sectors of British industry, as well as seeking to maintain wherever possible British influence and power through overseas military spending and diplomatic activity.

Britain never was dominated by the Left; indeed it was never properly modernised. The origins of the accommodation between capital and labour that was first worked out in the 1920s led to many important concessions and extensions of public responsibilities but hardly touched either the structure of the state or the manner of Britain's integration into the world economy and the world state system. The 1940s settlement has often been described as producing a social democratic consensus between the parties; the extent of genuine consensus is easily exaggerated, and the extent to which the consensus reflected Conservative priorities easily ignored. Thatcherism's radicalism was limited to attacking aspects of the consensus on the priorities of domestic policy.

It sought to reinforce crucial aspects of the bipartisan consensus on external policy.

A third problem is that, whatever the radical objectives of the Thatcherites, they have encountered serious difficulties in realising them. This is in part due to what Jessop has labelled the 'dual crisis of the state'.[48] The state requires some means to secure consent for its policies, but the two principal modes of achieving this – either through the mobilisation of public opinion through the party system and parliament, or the orchestration of group interests through corporatist bargaining structures – have both, for different reasons, become less and less effective. This has led to the growing autonomy of the state elite in making decisions.

Under the Thatcher Governments this process has been accelerated. The corporatist structures developed by previous Governments have been swept away, but there has been no major restoration of the primacy of party and parliament. Instead other channels, such as the media, have increasingly been relied upon to provide the consent for the policies which are not obtainable from any other source. At the same time the Thatcher Government, in a bid to achieve some of its objectives, has found itself embroiled in major restructuring of the state, in such areas as the relationship between central and local government, but without a very clear set of principles to guide it.

The fourth problem is that the thesis of authoritarian populism is good at analysing some of the key ideological shifts that have changed the relationship of forces between the ruling class, the working class, and the state, but it tends to neglect the relations within the bloc of dominant interests itself and the relationship of those interests to the state. From this standpoint authoritarian populism registers one very important ideological and political shift that has occurred in Britain, but tends to play down or ignore others. Among these others are the constraints imposed by the requirements of economic restructuring on a world level. The great contradiction of Thatcherism is that in the circumstances of modern capitalism it is very difficult for the state to withdraw either economically or politically. Despite the anti-statist rhetoric the Thatcher Governments have proved remarkably interventionist and *dirigiste*. The state has had to be considerably strengthened in order that the Thatcher Governments can press ahead with freeing the economy.

The outcome is, not surprisingly, very confused. There is no comprehensive Thatcherite project which triumphantly seizes hold of the social formation and refashions all the institutions of state and civil society. Instead there is an accumulation strategy which is aimed primarily at liquidating specific sources of weakness of British capital on the world market, eliminating the unfit and freeing the companies able to compete internationally from restrictions and extra burdens at home.

At one level this accumulation strategy is the reassertion of the old commercial and financial logic of British external policy. But it offers little prospect of recovery of all parts of the national economy as previous modernisation plans had done. It is not a programme for extending the Fordist regime of accumulation. It seeks rather to destroy central parts of that regime, particularly the industrial structure and the organisation of industrial relations, and to search pragmatically to establish a new regime of accumulation in Britain based on full integration into the world market, flexible specialisation and the encouragement of new enterprise through deregulation, privatisation, denationalisation and tax cuts.

Jessop has argued that this accumulation strategy was not formulated as a coherent plan before the Thatcher Government took office, but has become more coherent as the Government has experimented with various policies for handling the recession and promoting recovery. One important outcome of these policies has been what Jessop describes as a two nations strategy.[49] The destruction of aspects of the Fordist regime of accumulation and the confrontation with political and social groups seeking to resist or obstruct it have produced a sharp divide between institutions, regions and categories of the population. The metaphor for this old and new Britain has become the North and the South, and has required the formulation of different policies.

The rewarding and encouragement of the prosperous and expanding southern economy has to be accompanied by programmes for managing what threatens to become a new permanent underclass on the margins of prosperity and employment, concentrated in the inner cities, and requiring both increasing income support and surveillance.[50] This tolerance for a two nations outcome to its policies and the evidence of growing regional and social divisions is that has caused most unease among One Nation Conservatives.

Stuart Hall made a sharp rejoinder to these criticisms of the thesis of authoritarian populism.[51] He argued that the thesis had never been intended as a comprehensive explanation of Thatcherism. From the start it had deliberately concentrated on ideological factors without ever suggesting that they were the only important ones. He also claimed, quite fairly, that he had never stated that Thatcherism was in fact hegemonic, only that its project was hegemonic. He agreed that the difficulties encountered by the Thatcher Government in establishing a viable new regime of accumulation meant that, while Thatcherism had become dominant, it had not achieved hegemony. True hegemony requires the economic dominance of a successful regime of accumulation to be combined with the winning of political, moral and intellectual leadership in civil society.

As Stuart Hall readily concedes, an interpretation of Thatcherism in terms of authoritarian populism alone would be inadequate, however valid that perspective may be in pointing to a crucial dimension of the Thatcherite project. What is required is a much broader political analysis which can make sense of this highly confusing and contradictory phenomenon by allowing all the different aspects of it to be given their appropriate weight.

What the debate on the thesis has brought out is not only the different dimensions of Thatcherism that need to be considered in analysing its progress, but also the great differences which exist between the politics of support and the politics of power. Thatcherism was initially a project developed when the Conservatives were in opposition. Quite different problems were encountered after the Conservatives entered government. The experience of the Thatcher Government has substantially changed the way in which Thatcherism has been interpreted.

7
Politics, class and ideology

> The comfortable illusions that accompanied our gradual
> decline have been shattered. The nation has woken up to
> the reality of the need to earn its place in the world.
>
> [Margaret Thatcher, speech to the Institute of Directors
> (1983)]

A new consensus?

From the outset the Thatcher Government intended to be
different. 'Our country's decline is not inevitable', proclaimed
the 1979 manifesto. 'We in the Conservative party think we
can reverse it.' The Thatcherites wanted their government to
be different, not merely from the social democracy of the 1970s
but from postwar Conservatism as well. There was a crusading
mood and a belief that old ways and old values had to be
challenged.

Margaret Thatcher herself scorned consensus. She called
for a return to a politics of principle and urged her party to
occupy the moral high ground and abandon compromise and
retreat. Many Conservatives thought she was leading them
over the cliff. Instead she has led them to three consecutive
election victories. She so dominated British politics in the
1980s that, whatever may happen in the future, this decade
at least is sure to be called after her.

However it will also be called after Ronald Reagan. Thatcherism was only one manifestation of the new politics. New Right
programmes and Conservative administrations triumphed

in many states. Thatcherism has its own local roots and peculiarities, but it was by no means a unique response to the problems of recession and restructuring. The high international profile of Margaret Thatcher and her close political relationship with President Reagan made the decade seem at times like the Thatcher–Reagan years. This rather overstates Britain's importance. These were also the years of Kohl and Nakasone. The crucial axis in world capitalist politics was not the triangle between the United States, Germany and Japan. Despite all the talk of the special relationship with the United States, Britain had become marginal.

Thatcherism needs to be seen in this perspective. It was only one expression of the new conservative politics and occurred within a state no longer in the front rank. The success or failure of Thatcherism depended heavily upon events taking place elsewhere in the world economy. The frequent claims that British sovereignty and autonomy had been restored jarred discordantly with the reality.

Nevertheless the domination of Thatcherism in British domestic politics was real enough. Three election victories gave the Conservatives boundless political confidence. The final demise of the Labour party was confidently predicted after both 1983 and 1987, in the belief that Labour was unlikely ever to recover to win another election. Given the electoral arithmetic and the gap in support between Labour and the Conservatives this view was rather more plausible than it had been after 1959.

The ascendancy of the Conservatives was marked not simply by their success in winning elections, but by their apparent domination of the political argument and the policy agenda. They appeared to have succeeded in reconstructing the political terrain in Britain in such a way that any party seeking to become or remain the main opposition to the Conservatives would be forced to move a long way towards the new policy positions being staked out by the Thatcher Government in order to compete effectively.

The idea of a new consensus had become conventional wisdom in 1987, buttressed by the Conservatives' electoral success and the spread of 'new realism' in the ranks of their opponents. But it remained precarious, heavily dependent upon events outside the control of the British Government, and vulnerable to sudden changes. Even with a new radical manifesto in 1987 many continued to question how far-reaching and fundamental the changes inaugurated by Thatcherism actually were. The gulf between the achievements and the rhetoric of Thatcherism still looked very wide.

The politics of support

Cabinet and party

No one disputes the special character of Margaret Thatcher's premiership. She has been an exceptionally dominant and powerful Prime Minister. This has been enhanced in her case by the character of the Conservative party and the role of its Leader. Conservatives may in the past have been ruthless in disposing of unsuccessful leaders, but so long as a leader is successful, she enjoys great powers of patronage, and influence within the party. Control of the appointments in Central Office, including the Party Chairman, the right to appoint the Shadow Cabinet and to determine what is and is not party policy – all this gives Conservative leaders a dominating role which no other party leaders in Britain enjoy.[1]

From a relatively weak position at first, following her unexpected victory against Heath, Thatcher has gradually consolidated her position in the party, promoted her allies and banished her opponents. Yet it is remarkable how, despite her personal domination of the party, she has been unable or unwilling to assemble a corps of Thatcherite leaders. She has fallen out with political friends, such as Norman Tebbit and John Biffen, and though she has removed many of her critics, like Francis Pym, James Prior and Ian Gilmour, she has come to rely on others like Kenneth Baker and Kenneth Clarke.

What makes Thatcher's period as party Leader look like a personal regime rather than something more lasting is that there is no obvious successor to her, and no certainty that she could hand the leadership on to him even if there were. 'A brilliant tyrant surrounded by mediocrities', was said to be Lord Stockton's judgement. It is unlikely, however, that the

Thatcher years will come to be viewed as an aberration in Conservative party history, and that the party will revert to its true traditions and a traditional Conservative Leader, once Margaret Thatcher departs.

Some Conservatives may continue to believe that their party has been stolen from them and continue to toast the 'King over the water', even though they may differ as to who he is. But, as was pointed out in Chapter 5, Thatcher is in many respects a traditional Conservative, pursuing a recognisable Tory statecraft. Some features of her style are personal to her and will disappear when she does. But other aspects reflect a clear perception of what a modern Conservative politics needs to address. Many of her attitudes and beliefs are mainstream attitudes and beliefs for the modern Conservative party and will survive her.

What may not survive Thatcher's passing are some of the causes of 'radical Thatcherism'. Despite a hefty dose of ideology which Thatcher's election as Leader helped to inject into the party, the Conservative party has remained a party of government. It has not become a party of doctrine. The ideologues among her Ministers have either departed or abandoned their ideology in the face of the pressures of government. What she now has are a number of pragmatists around her, like Lord Young and Nigel Lawson, determined to make the accumulation strategy work.

In the parliamentary party the strong personal loyalty to Thatcher as Leader has not been based upon endorsement of the objectives of radical Thatcherism. Support for the Government's programme has generally been forthcoming, but backbenchers have not hesitated to rebel when particular constituency interests have been threatened. The Conservative MPs alone choose the Leader of the party, and the ideological stance of the contenders is likely to play only a small part in determining the choice. The Conservative party has not become a Thatcherite party. It has remained a Conservative party led by Margaret Thatcher.

This is also apparent when the Conservative party in the country is considered. The Conservatives' enthusiasm for imposing democratic practices on trade unions has not extended to their own party organisation. The annual Conference is still a rally rather than a policy-making body. The officers of the party are still appointed, not elected. The party ethic of loyalty and unity which generally inhibits opposition and dissent is still strong.

These features can make the party, at times, seem very Thatcherite, especially during the adulatory standing ovations given to Margaret Thatcher herself at the annual Conference. She is probably more in touch with the opinions and instincts of the party rank and file than any Conservative Leader has ever been. She shows none of the disdain many previous Leaders have felt for the passions and prejudices of the delegates. She shares them and expresses them. Her stance on crime and punishment (particularly her support for hanging), on defence, on trade union power, on permissiveness and the family, and on immigration, aligns her with the views of Conference delegates. Her populism is first of all a populism of the Tory grass roots. Previous Leaders have been happy to manipulate the sentiments of their supporters but have never been identified with them in the way Thatcher has contrived to be.

But this close relationship between Thatcher and her party does not mean that the Conservative party has become Thatcherite in the sense of embracing a Thatcherite ideology. The party has remained itself, and at last found a Leader to express its dominant emotions and concerns. Ideological ferment there has been but, given the way the Conservative party is organised, the New Right has struggled to gain a secure foothold. It had some success in winning control of the Federation of Conservative Students, but the views of some of its leaders, and the publicity given to the behaviour and views of some of its members, led Norman Tebbit as Party Chairman to close the organisation down in 1986.

Under Thatcher organised ideological groups in the party, chiefly but not exclusively from the right, have flourished. But although these have been important in feeding ideas to the leadership and fighting ideological battles, they have made little impact on the way the party is run. The influence of the New Right on the selection and deselection of MPs has been small. Open critics of the Prime Minister have survived unscathed, and there has been no obvious pattern in the selection of new MPs. New Right groups have not so far been in a position where they could hope to influence constituency selection conferences to choose candidates primarily on ideological grounds.

The Conservative party remains a party of government still; not a party of doctrine and ideology as it threatened briefly to become in the 1970s. Nevertheless doctrine and ideology under Margaret Thatcher have played a more prominent role in the internal life of the party and in the public perception of it.

The electorate

The most tangible sign of the new dominance of the Conservatives has been the three general election victories. The contrast with the party's situation in 1974 is sharp. Yet the extent of the Conservative revival can be overestimated. Their recovery has been dramatic in terms of parliamentary seats, but much less so in terms of votes. In October 1974 the Conservative vote sank to 35 per cent. In 1979, 1983 and 1987 it only climbed seven or eight percentage points above this, considerably below what previous postwar Conservative Governments had achieved; not much above the support when the party lost in 1966, and only four percentage points above the level the Conservatives polled in 1945, the year of the great Labour parliamentary 'landslide'.

The polling evidence does not point to an impregnable Conservative position. The concentration of Conservative support is more striking than its spread. The historic decline of the old Unionist party has continued in the big cities and some of the regions, especially Scotland and Northern Ireland. This process has certainly not been arrested under Thatcher; it has accelerated. Some of the regional differences in voting behaviour have become very marked. The collapse of the Conservative position in Scotland is the most extraordinary example of this. In 1955 the Conservatives had 50 per cent of the Scottish vote and approximately 50 per cent of the seats. In 1987, despite a hundred-seat majority in Westminster, the Conservatives only won 22 per cent of the Scottish vote and 10 seats.

What the Conservatives have learned, however, and particularly during Thatcher's leadership, is that it is no longer necessary or possible to project themselves as the party of the Union in order to win elections. Unionism has declined with the Empire. Conservatism has had to find a new identity. The Conservative Nation now is no longer the nation of Empire and Union. The appeal is directed much more towards England, and towards certain regions of England, the old metropolitan heartland of the Empire.

This is not a new trend. The divide between North and South in the United Kingdom has been steadily becoming more marked throughout the postwar period. But it seemed to have reached a new stage in the elections of 1983 and 1987 when Labour hardly won a seat in the South outside London, and the Conservatives did poorly in many Northern areas, particularly Scotland.[2] This North/South divide is seen to be associated with differential regional prosperity and regional levels of unemployment. Under the impact of the recession and the reorganisation of all parts of capitalist society which it has initiated, many societies have become more segmented. This has led to fears about the rise of a one-third/two-thirds society – the poor, the unskilled and the unemployed forming a minority facing a majority of citizens with jobs, reasonable security and rising real incomes.[3]

The Conservatives' electoral strategy throughout the postwar period has sought to enlarge the base of Conservative support by identifying prosperity and all forms of property ownership with Conservative voting. Thatcher did not invent this strategy, but she pushed it still further, particularly through the sale of council houses and the measures of denationalisation which helped widen share ownership. The creation of a mass of private property interests willing to support market solutions for problems of public policy and antagonistic to state intervention and direction has been a key objective of Conservative statecraft.

Defining the Conservative Nation as a nation of property owners and consumers tended to exclude much more of the actual nation than did some previous versions of Conservatism. The Thatcherites always vigorously denied that they were opposed to the One Nation philosophy of Toryism. Thatcher wanted to see one nation as much as any Tory ever had, but it was to be a nation in which everyone had become a property owner and a consumer. It was no longer to be a nation composed of many different interests and classes, united through a common citizenship and a common loyalty to an ideal of nationhood.

Traces of this older Tory ideal lingered. The Falklands war saw its triumphant return. But the thrust of Thatcherism as an electoral strategy was away from this and towards the consolidation of a bloc of interests rather than the creation of a union of citizens. This necessarily limited Thatcherism's appeal and made it in practice very divisive, since entire sectors, institutions, categories and regions, like the 'North', were stigmatised as problems and in need of reform.

Thatcherism has not abandoned the ideal of One Nation, but if that ideal is to be made reality the existing nation must first be re-formed, and purged of alien elements and practices. Only then can it be truly united. In practice, therefore, Thatcherism constantly splits the nation into two.[4] The world is divided into allies and enemies, those with us and those against us. In Thatcher's New Britain legitimacy is withdrawn from voluntary associations like trade unions and from public institutions like the BBC, the Universities, the state education system, nationalised industries and local government, until they have reformed themselves or been reformed from outside.

This strategy moves away from ideas of the mixed economy and a balance between sectors and interests. It identifies the national interest very firmly with the private sector and downgrades all public sector activities except in privileged spheres such as the police and the military. This takes advantage of the sectoral split that has emerged between public and private sectors, particularly since the 1970s. The Conservatives have sought to align themselves with the private sector both in terms of employment and consumption. This has been most evident in the case of council houses. In health and education the Conservatives have had to be much more cautious, because the private sector has always been so small, but the long-term aim of building up the same kind of lobby for private health and private education that exists for housing is clear enough.[5]

Policy agendas

Winning electoral contests is only part of the struggle to influence policy agendas. Victorious politicians claim mandates for particular policies and programmes, but the link between voting and the endorsement of specific proposals is extremely loose. Electoral attitudes can shift very rapidly and unpredictably, and in practice the setting of policy agendas owes more to the policy debates among the political elite than to the preferences of the electorate.

If this were not so even the limited achievements of the Thatcher Government would not have been possible. The most reliable survey evidence available, the series of *British Social Attitudes Surveys*, shows that remarkably large majorities remain opposed to many of the policy shifts in welfare and social policy most sought by the Thatcher Government. The *1985 Survey*, for example, found the Conservative party was at that time viewed as more extreme than Labour; there was strong support for price controls (66 per cent) and import controls (67 per cent); even wage controls had 42 per cent support (with 53 per cent opposed); on state ownership the argument had shifted from whether there should be more or less nationalisation to the merits of privatisation. But the Survey still found a majority against privatisation among all groups except those identified as Conservative partisans. Even more striking results were found for welfare. Only five per cent of the sample supported reductions in services, even when linked to tax cuts; health and education were easily the most favoured areas for increased public spending. On attitudes to unemployment benefit and the gap between high and low incomes only Conservative partisans thought the former too high and the latter justifiable. On the evidence of the *Surveys* at least, eight years of Thatcher Government have not so far produced a Thatcherite consensus in the electorate.[6] This means that the driving force for changing the policy agenda has had to come from elsewhere. Winning support within the political elite has been essential in translating electoral endorsement into shifts in policy priorities.

Crucial to the success that has been achieved is the degree of support that the Government has received from the media, in particular the newspapers. Since it is the newspapers that provide so much of the material and help fix the parameters for debates and news reporting on television, the active support given to the Thatcher Government by the great majority of the national press has been very important in sustaining the momentum of Thatcherism and projecting its policies as the only right and possible ones.[7]

Under the Thatcher Government the British press has been more one-sided in its partisanship than at any time in the history of British mass democracy. This has made the relative objectivity and pluralism of the television output stand out in comparison, which is why the Thatcher Government became embroiled in arguments with the BBC over the 'bias' of their coverage, and strong efforts were made by the Conservative Chairman, Norman Tebbit, during 1986 and 1987 to influence the editorial and news criteria of the Corporation. This stopped short of dictation, but the message was made clear enough.

The Government looked for full support from the business organisations in its bid to reshape the policy agenda, and in general, after a shaky start, it received it. Apart from the brief outburst in 1980 from the Director-General of the CBI against the policies of high interest rates and an overvalued exchange rate which were doing so much damage to industry, both the CBI and still more the Institute of Directors threw full support behind the changes the Government was attempting to engineer, in the belief that the reforms would put the companies that survived on a stronger footing. Apart from a few rumbles of discontent from some of the regional offices of the CBI, and the contribution from senior industrialists to the 1985 House of Lords report on the state of the economy, manufacturing industry failed to make a significant protest about the contraction which was forced on it.[8]

The uniting of the political representatives of capital behind its programme was of great importance to the construction of the new agenda. It lent enormous weight to the idea that there was no alternative. The credibility of the programmes put forward by the opposition parties and by critics of the Government appeared to founder because no section of British capital was prepared to support an alternative programme. The partisanship of British business increased as the recovery got under way, and by the 1987 election the CBI was openly dismissive of the economic proposals of the Labour party. A sure sign of business approval for the Conservatives was the continuing high level of business contributions to the party. The firms and sectors that were most prominent tended to be those that had gained most from the liberalisation of the economy over which the Thatcher Government had presided.[9]

Support from the trade unions was never very likely for the Thatcher Government, since reform of union law was one of the Government's major priorities, and because the Government was determined to freeze the unions out of the policy-making process. The destruction of the old Labour movement was a key political objective for the Government but this meant a certain ambivalence in government attitudes, since it could not decide whether the objective should be to encourage a union-free economy, or an economy with new model unions, like the electricians' (EETPU) and the break-away Union of Democratic Mineworkers (UDM) in Notting-hamshire, which would provide positive support for the changes the Government was seeking. The continuing high levels of unionisation, despite the falls in total union member-ship due to the recession, suggested that if the Thatcher reforms were to become permanent these new model unions needed to be encouraged, so that eventually a new political settlement might be reached in which they participated.

Securing support from the institutions and organised interests of the private sector was a major goal of the Thatcher Government. This enabled it to pursue more easily its confron-tations with the political representatives of the old Labour movement in the unions and the town halls, and with the representatives of public sector professionals in health and education and housing. In general it made little progress in winning over these groups and sought increasingly to weaken them by cutting their funding, reducing their autonomy, redefining responsibilities, and forcing them to find sponsor-ship and clients directly from the private sector to support their activities.

In its first eight years the Thatcher Government succeeded in shifting the terms of the policy debate, but few of the changes reflected a genuine consensus either within the electorate or the policy-making elite. Major interests and groups remained fundamentally opposed and there were only halting signs of the kind of intellectual revolution the Government wanted to underpin the new policies. By 1987 the Thatcher Government had run up a sizeable legitimacy deficit, only rivalled by the Reagan budget deficit. Both Governments believed that, given time, their policies would bring success, the deficits would vanish, and a true consensus would develop around their programmes.

A key factor here was the attitude of the opposition parties. A major shift in policy becomes permanent when the opposition parties adopt it as their own. That is the common-sense meaning of the term consensus. Here again Conservative attitudes were ambiguous. Ministers sometimes seemed unable to decide whether they wanted the Labour party to reform itself or whether they preferred it to disappear entirely and be replaced by a new party. In either case what was required was the withering away, not just of socialism, but of collectivism. By the latter was understood political and intellectual support for public sector and interventionist solutions to problems of public policy in preference to market ones.

Some success was registered. The split in the Labour party and the emergence of a strong centre alliance in 1981 appeared briefly to be the long-awaited realignment of the British Left. The SDP planned initially to be a Labour Party, Mark II, but increasingly, and particularly under David Owen's leadership, it ceased trying to displace Labour and chose instead to fight the Conservatives as an alternative party for the new South. David Owen went further than any other opposition politician in endorsing major aspects of the Thatcherite policy agenda. He promoted the use of the concept of 'the social market economy'[10] and the need for efficiency and competition in the private sector. Where he stopped short was in endorsing the application of Thatcherite principles in the sphere of social policy.

The Liberal party was much less prepared to abandon the old policy consensus than some in the SDP proved to be. The Liberals in the past had supported incomes policies and industrial strategies, as well as collectivist welfare. In domestic policy it looked more to Beveridge and Keynes than to Cobden and Bright. This ranged it against the drift of the new Thatcherite policy agenda. This tended to be the Conservatives' perception of the Liberals also. The Lib–Lab pact which had sustained the Callaghan Government in 1977–8 accurately pinpointed the position of the Liberals as defenders of key aspects of the old politics.

The Centre parties were thrown into disarray following the 1987 election. The SDP split into bitterly opposed factions over the proposal to merge with the Liberals. The course the merger negotiations took, particularly on policies for the new party, then threatened to split the Liberals. At the heart of the conflicts lay confusion and disagreement about how far a Centre party in British politics should adjust to the Thatcherite interpretation of what the new politics demanded, and how far there was political space for different and much more radical interpretations. Despite David Owen's defeat within the SDP in 1987, the Alliance appeared to be steadily drifting towards his positions, and away from the desire of Liberal activists for a radical, campaigning party.

Within the Labour party the failure of the Left to take control of the party after their conference victories in 1980, followed by the two major election defeats which saw Labour's support fall back to its level in the 1920s, encouraged the spread of a 'new realism' and rethinking of the party's fundamental objectives and purpose. Neil Kinnock's election as Labour Leader after the 1983 election ensured that Labour's rebuilding would be on the basis of the party's labourist traditions. The programme of the fundamentalist Left in the party as well as the ideas of the new urban Left and the new social movements were given much lower priority. The party was to remain a trade union party and seek to re-establish its relevance to the workers in the new South, who had swung in such large numbers to the Conservatives and the Alliance, while retaining its bedrock support in the North.

How far the party would shift its ground to make that appeal possible again was in doubt after 1987. The financial crash in 1987 appeared to vindicate those who argued that the party should offer a genuine alternative programme to Thatcherism, not just an alternative administration. What all sections of the party agreed, however, was that there could be no simple return to the old politics. There was widespread recognition that the new politics was not just a conservative politics, which could be reversed by the election of a Labour Government, but reflected deep and irreversible changes in the organisation of the world economy and British society. Labour was forced to accept that the Thatcher years had permanently changed the agenda of British politics. Changes which looked irreversible included the sale of council houses and the spread of share ownership (notwithstanding the crash); the denationalisation of public sector industries; the abolition of exchange controls and the international integration of financial markets and production; the permanent contraction of manufacturing employment; and the reorganisation of work and industrial relations. Many of these changes were related to the rise of new technological systems and flexible specialisation. What Labour was forced to recognise in the 1980s was that there could be no return to the kind of national economic management and welfare programmes achieved during the postwar boom. A new project of modernisation had to be devised for British capitalism.[11]

Thatcherism perceived the weakness of social democracy in Britain and the national Labour tradition, and it struck several blows at it. Thatcher made no secret of her wish to see socialism destroyed as an effective political force in Britain, and a two-party system organised in which both parties fully accepted the legitimacy of capitalism and markets. A large part of reversing the decline of Britain meant destroying the political and industrial strength of the British Labour movement, eradicating the industries, the communities, the organisations and the institutions associated with it. The attack on unions, on local authorities, on nationalised industries, on public sector employment, on council housing and state education, all fit into this wider attack upon the Labour movement.

The intention, and to some extent the effect, has been to marginalise Labour and the Labour movement, associating it with declining regions, declining communities and declining industries, while successfully identifying the Conservatives with sectors of growth, expansion and prosperity. The sense of a new policy agenda has been created as much by this as by the new policies themselves. The Conservatives have projected themselves as the party of the future, the party of the new politics, the party of modernisation.

The politics of power

The limits of government

Sceptics may find it easy to conclude that, if there is no Thatcherite electorate, no Thatcherite party, no Thatcherite consensus, the term Thatcherism may not explain very much after all. Certainly the transformation of British politics is so far much less than the Thatcherites themselves hoped to see. But there have been several real and significant changes, and the potential for further far-reaching change remains. The capacity of Thatcherism to renew itself and regain its radical momentum has surprised many observers, especially those who expected its radicalism to disappear after six months in office.

The record of the Thatcher Government, like that of all governments, has lacked symmetry, coherence and, often, purpose. What little coherence it has achieved has often been imposed by events and decisions outside its control. It is wrong to see the period from 1979 to 1987 as the unfolding of a New Right masterplan hatched in opposition for overturning social democracy in Britain. The Government reacted pragmatically, its course shaped more by the pressure of events rather than its ideology or strategy.

Nevertheless the Thatcher Government is still unusual for the way in which its Leader and some of its principal figures remained committed to a distinctive ideology, and for the extent to which it did attempt in some areas to formulate and carry through a strategy. Both ideology and strategy were an influence on the way in which the Government behaved. This did differentiate the Government markedly from almost all its predecessors. It was never content simply to administer and react to events, even if for much of the time that was precisely what it had to do.

Throughout this book Thatcherism has been seen as a new

hegemonic project. Such a project involves ideology, economics and politics, a politics of support and a politics of power. The struggle to gather support, to build new coalitions of interests, to win the battle of ideas for a radical change of direction and the dismantling of old structures and old priorities has to be carried through in a programme for government if it is to be durable. A statecraft that was confined to the winning of office would leave few permanent marks.

The Thatcher Government wished to establish a free economy and a strong state, as the new basis for a stable hegemony. Such a project required two things above all: a strategy for accumulation, to reverse decisively the relative decline of the British economy; and a strategy for reorganising the state and civil society, both to make the accumulation strategy work and overcome resistance to it, and to re-establish the authority of the State with the Conservative party as its dominant political force.

The problem with most of the existing interpretations of Thatcherism is that they are too one-sided; they emphasise a single aspect of a highly complex phenomenon. Much of the literature on Thatcherism as Tory statecraft, for example, interprets many of the policy decisions and priorities of the Thatcher Government as guided by calculations of the Conservative party's political interests. This theory provides a plausible explanation of the numerous attempts by the Thatcher Government to weaken the Labour party and the Labour movement. Political parties must first of all win elections and outmanoeuvre their political opponents if they are to survive. The detail of political competition within and between parties, the rise and fall of ministers, and the calculation of party advantage and disadvantage often absorbs the attention and interest of politicians much more than the formulation and implementation of policy.

The statecraft explanation of Thatcherism is a reminder that in Britain no programme for government, however coherent and planned, could ever hope to advance if it were not closely intertwined with party interest. But by itself it is hardly sufficient. It underplays other dimensions of Thatcherism.

Other accounts of the programme of the Thatcher

Government emphasise the constraints of the policy-making process. They analyse how institutions and circumstances tend to determine the way policies are actually formulated and the extent to which they are implemented. This view sees politicians acting out roles and performing actions in which their own ideologies and political preferences play a small part. The politicians exaggerate their own importance. Their role is simply to smooth the path of the changes that are necessary and inevitable. This view punctures the idea that politics is just a matter of will, and that the successful implementation of a radical programme depends solely on having a leadership determined and capable enough to see it through. The importance of individual leaders should not be ignored, however. No radical programme stands any chance at all if the leadership is incompetent or hostile.

While a detailed examination of the policy-making process is essential for understanding how the policies of the Thatcher Government have emerged and changed, there are also wider questions to be asked, for instance about the cumulative impact of the policies on the economy and the society. For even if the policy process is as the sceptics and realists describe, it is still important to ask who is advantaged and who disadvantaged by these policies, and whether or not the various moves to free the economy and strengthen the state are creating the basis for a new and viable regime of accumulation.

Accumulation strategy

Class interpretations of Thatcherism are not short of answers to these questions. Instrumental theories of class suppose that the policies of the Thatcher Government can be shown to benefit the capitalist class and to have been directly inspired by that class. The evidence for that is tenuous and ignores the way in which the modern state is structured. Political organisations like the Conservative party have a great deal of autonomy within their own sphere to determine objectives and policies. There are no mechanisms of representation by which a general capitalist interest could be expressed, other than through the imperfect mediations of the political sphere and the permanent institutions of the state.

This does not make a class perspective on Thatcherism redundant. Thatcherism does not make sense as a capitalist conspiracy, but the question of who has gained and who has lost from the policies, regardless of what may have been intended or planned, remains a crucial one. The principal loser has been the organised Labour movement, but in the process many sections of capital have suffered heavily also. The Thatcher Government's policies ended the prospects of any restructuring based on the traditional manufacturing sectors and regions. Many of these were liquidated in the slump, their work-forces made unemployed and the basis of union strength in those industries destroyed.

The sharp contraction of manufacturing in this second slump has led some to suggest that the policy that is being followed represents the interests of the City. But things are much less simple. It is true that many of the policies, such as the ending of exchange controls, sound finance, the willingness to see sterling and interest rates rise during the first phase, the abandonment of industrial strategy and intervention, the denationalisation of public enterprises, the widening of share ownership and the lowering of taxes on capital and investment, were all favourably received by the City. But important though the City is in the British economy as a source of employment and export earnings, it is not large enough or coherent enough or politically organised enough to determine government policy.[12]

The explanation of the Thatcher Government's policy stance and its effects on manufacturing is not that the Government set out to favour the interests of the City, but that by reasserting the traditional international orientation of British economic policy the Government gave priority to the maintenance of the openness of the British economy over the protection of domestic industry. Given the long relative decline of so much of this industry, such a policy was bound to lead in a sharp recession to the liquidation of many companies.

The accumulation strategy of the Thatcher Government identified the national interest and the general interest of capital with furthering the integration of the British economy into the world economy and, apart from the few protected sectors like defence and agriculture, and to a lesser extent nationalised industries, obliging all other sectors to prove themselves internationally competitive or go to the wall. This policy favoured those industrial sectors which were already dominated by transnational companies – particularly in construction, oil and food – as well as the financial and commercial companies based in the City.

The shake-out that these policies provoked cemented the alliance between British transnationals and the City and made the prospect of a national industrial strategy, which had flickered occasionally in the previous seventy-five years, very remote indeed.[13] The future of the British economy was tied not to a major revival of manufacturing but to the development of (i) *rentier* incomes from the United Kingdom's rapidly growing portfolio of foreign investments;[14] (ii) internationally tradable services, and (iii) the encouragement of inward investment by foreign transnationals establishing plants to assemble products, designed and engineered elsewhere, for sale in European markets.

This was a credible and coherent strategy for British capital and, although sections of British capital complained bitterly about the harsh effects on them, criticism was muted and no effective alternative was canvassed. Despite the efforts of a few Ministers the Government gave little support to developing manufacturing and research capability in new technologies, and reduced spending on science and scientific research.

In the last hundred years British Governments have presided over the decline of the traditional manufacturing base – cotton, coal, iron and steel, shipbuilding and engineering. In the last twenty years they have presided over the decline of many of the mass production industries of the Fordist era, including the manufacturers of consumer durables many of which first became established in Britain in the 1920s and 1930s and expanded in the 1950s and 1960s.

The failure of the attempts to modernise these industries and make them internationally competitive was one of the major sources of the crisis in the 1970s. What the Thatcher Government has done is to abandon the attempt made by earlier Governments to get the old regime of accumulation to work better. This was prompted partly on political grounds – the political costs of earlier modernisation strategies appeared too high and had threatened to marginalise the Conservative party. Another reason, however, was the global economic crisis and the breakdown of American hegemony which made new thinking obligatory. New methods of industrial organisation were going to be required to establish the conditions for a new phase of rapid accumulation.

Recovery or decline?

To adjust to the new conditions that are emerging for accumulation in the world economy and to find a way of reversing decline the Thatcher Government has moved pragmatically. It has tried to redefine what Britain can contribute to the world economy by promoting those activities in which British companies have already shown they can be internationally competitive; it has sought to increase incentives and reduce spending; it has tried to weaken trade unions; and it has attempted to disengage government as much as possible from involvement in the economy and widen the sphere for market criteria and private sector competition in the allocation of resources.

As an accumulation strategy this is fraught with risk, since it depends on ceding ground in most areas of industry to foreign competitors, and trusting to the ability of British companies and new entrepreneurs to seize opportunities in whatever new regime of accumulation emerges that will maintain Britain's status as an advanced industrial society. It does however return to the one constant in British development – the priority given to commerce and finance and therefore to policies that maintained the openness of the British economy even when this was at the expense of domestic production. In a crisis it has generally been this market perspective that has triumphed. Those sectors of the British economy that have grown strong under this policy find their position further reinforced and their political importance enhanced.

Judgements on this accumulation strategy are very divided. What is undeniable, however, is that in the short term the strategy has worked. After a turbulent first two years between 1979 and 1981 when total shipwreck of the Government seemed a possibility, the economy did stabilise and begin to grow again. By the 1987 election the Government was able to boast of record productivity, record output, falling unemployment and low inflation. There was no doubt that the decline had been halted. What was unclear was whether or not it had been reversed.

The doubts were of two kinds. There were firstly empirical doubts about whether the economic success achieved between 1982 and 1987 represented real and lasting improvements in economic performance. Secondly there were theoretical doubts about whether the kind of modernisation envisaged by the Thatcher Government would be sufficient to remedy the deep-seated causes of British decline, and whether the Thatcher Government was prepared to push through the degree of institutional restructuring which its accumulation strategy demanded.

On the first count there has been much discussion of the significance of the improvement in productivity, and whether it was a one-off improvement related to the huge shedding of labour in the recession. What has been much slower to come through has been a major increase in industrial investment in Britain. The productivity gap between British industry and Japanese or German industry in most sectors is so great that only a long period of exceptional investment and growth could close it. What has happened instead is a very big increase in overseas investment by British companies since exchange controls were lifted, and changes in the composition of the British economy. The most striking change has been the way in which trade in manufacturing goods has moved from surplus in 1980 to £5.3 billion deficit by 1986. The overall balance of payments remained in surplus up to 1987, but this was partly owing to the benefits to the balance of payments of North Sea oil production, which was at its height during the 1980s. Oil revenues, which had reached £13 billion per annum by 1985, were also a significant factor in the budget calculations allowing the Chancellor to keep spending higher than it would otherwise have been and to plan for the cuts in direct taxes in 1986 and 1987. This budget strategy was also assisted by the proceeds from denationalisation.

The recovery between 1981 and 1987 was assisted by the

more flexible domestic economic management made possible through the crutch provided for the domestic budget by the oil revenues and asset sales.[15] But an even greater contribution came from the global recovery stimulated by the reflation of the American economy through deficit financing. Even so unemployment only began to fall at the end of 1986, and it was clear that Britain would have to maintain high growth over a long period before substantial inroads were made into unemployment or the gap between itself and other countries was appreciably narrowed.[16]

Britain's 'economic miracle' between 1982 and 1987 was an extremely modest one by the standards of miracles, and for many observers it was a mirage. They doubted that the Government could bring a reversal of decline with an accumulation strategy which involved a reduction rather than an increase in state involvement. This case has been strongly argued by Colin Leys and Perry Anderson.[17] Leys argues that Britain's decline could only be reversed if new comparative advantages could be created. The problem with relying on market forces to do this is that they tend to reinforce existing strengths and weaknesses instead of creating the conditions in which new leading sectors might arise. To create such sectors, Leys argues, a developmental state is needed, a state able to identify sectors capable of long-term growth, and with the power and resources to ensure sustained long-term investment in those sectors, as well as in the support services that the sectors will require to reach their full potential. Such a programme involves a complex interlinking of state planning, the deployment of new technological systems, and extensive institutional and cultural transformation. None of this arises from the free play of market forces, nor, argues Leys, is it envisaged by leading Thatcherites. The Thatcher accumulation strategy destroys the old regime of accumulation but puts nothing in its place.

Perry Anderson agrees substantially with this assessment. The logic of the market, he argues,

left to itself, necessarily tends to be cumulative rather than corrective . . . Deregulation – of labour and capital markets – could only mean still more deindustrialisation, in preestablished conditions. The laws of comparative advantage have continued to work themselves out, by their own momentum. The rectification of disadvantages requires another kind of social logic. For it to occur, a centralising force capable of regulating and counteracting the spontaneous molecular movements of the market must exist.[18]

Anderson identifies four postwar examples of a 'regulative intelligence' in advanced capitalist societies; the state technocracy as in France, the banking system as in West Germany, the interlinking of the planning bureaucracy with the banks, as in Japan, and a politically dominant labour movement, as in Sweden. In each case a supra-market logic was created which laid the foundation for exceptional market performance. Britain failed to establish a similar institutional structure to carry through successful modernisation and safeguard its world market position.

On this kind of reading Thatcherism has not laid the foundations for reversing decline. The Thatcherite accumulation strategy explicitly recognises that the prospects for successful modernisation on the lines previously attempted have vanished. This is not a strategy for reversing decline so much as seeking to come to terms with it, and to reorganise British economy and society to fit a permanently reduced status.

Yet, as Anderson himself notes, the radical internationalisation of the production and finance in capitalism that has accompanied and accelerated the breakdown of Fordism has also undermined the autonomy of every national economy and every national corrector to uneven development within the world economy. 'The British crisis', he writes, 'has no end in sight; and perhaps the time in which one was possible, as a national recovery, has passed'.[19] If this is true, then the accumulation strategy which the Thatcher Government has developed from a mixture of ideological preferences, party calculation, bureaucratic pressures, fiscal requirements and chance events, may prove more successful in reversing decline than many currently expect. The shape of the new regime of accumulation is very unclear, so it may be that a market-oriented programme which allows a period of maximum freedom and experiment may prove better adapted to the new conditions of accumulation than more interventionist programmes, at least in this first phase.

The reorganisation of the state

If a free market programme is to succeed, however, in reversing the long decline, then it will require a much greater degree of state reorganisation than anything yet attempted by the Thatcher Government. The Thatcherite accumulation strategy has aroused many doubts. But its ability to affect the necessary reforms in the state and civil society has aroused even more.

The decline of Britain's postwar manufacturing sector has been accompanied by the weakening of many of the social democratic institutions which were made legitimate by the 1940s settlement. The failure of Britain to develop a viable Fordist regime of accumulation undermined social democracy and exposed its limitations in Britain as a formula for strong and effective government. The 1940s settlement no longer provided a credible or desirable framework for government for a growing number of politicians on both left and right. The crisis of hegemony had begun.

The Thatcher leadership united the Conservative party around the claims that the country had become overtaxed, overgoverned and indisciplined. The traditional distance between the organs of government and the special interests had been eroded. Government had been invaded by pressure groups and too many decisions had been politicised. Government needed to disentangle itself and reassert its authority and independence. This meant reducing the number and the range of government responsibilities. In economic policy it meant asserting that the Government only had responsibility for inflation and the money supply and none for unemployment and growth; it meant abandoning prices and incomes policies and most national tripartite arrangements in which the unions bargained directly with government. It meant promulgating new financial disciplines for public agencies, particularly local authorities, in an attempt to force them to operate within a set of financial constraints determined centrally. It meant launching a major programme of privatisation, giving up many government controls over the way enterprises in various sectors operated. Government functions were to be simplified and government spending reduced. Diagnosing a crisis of hegemony and then remedying it through political action are very different things. The Thatcherites accepted that there was a deep and complex crisis of state authority, but the remedies they recommended pointed in several directions at once. They were not easily reconciled. The Thatcherite project demanded a sweeping transformation of institutions, attitudes and personnel. Yet what was involved in detail in such a radical restructuring and whether it was within the capacity of the Conservative party to deliver was little discussed. Among the intellectuals of the New Right the radical nature of the Thatcherite project was well understood but relatively few of them became Conservative Ministers.

Thatcherism has been such a contradictory phenomenon in government because of the basic practical and theoretical uncertainty about the kind and degree of state restructuring that it sought. Creating a 'free economy' commanded wide support in the Conservative party when it was interpreted to mean lower taxes, lower public expenditure, less nationalisation, weaker trade unions, less government regulation and control, and more inequality. But a free economy was also understood by some to mean a state strong enough to intervene actively in all institutions of civil society to impose, nurture and stimulate the business values, attitudes and practices necessary to relaunch Britain as a successful capitalist economy. This would make the Conservative party for the first time a bourgeois modernising party with no qualms about the radical restructuring of all institutions in state and civil society in the interests of increasing economic efficiency. Such programmes have been proposed before, but foundered because their advocates were never prepared to reshape the British political, intellectual and business Establishment, entrenched in the public schools, the universities, the professions, the civil service and the City.

The Thatcherite project to restore state authority by promoting a free economy would have been feasible if the institutions of civil society had been fundamentally sound, the public sector small, and the economy thriving. Since they were not the Government was drawn into numerous interventions and conflicts to try to transform attitudes and behaviour. Re-establishing the authority of the state required increasing intervention to force the compliance of other agencies and interests with the wishes and plans of the Government. The seriousness of the condition of the British economy and the complexity of the public sector meant that a strategy of disengagement from accumulated responsibilities and commitments had to involve major efforts to reorganise activities and institutions in the public sector and in civil society.

The problem for the Thatcher Government is that its own diagnosis of the crisis of state authority constantly impelled it towards intervention – whether in the internal affairs of trade unions, the spending priorities of local authorities, the curricula of schools and universities, or the patterns of family behaviour. At the same time the Government has been very cautious in creating the kind of state machinery that could make such intervention effective.

Many of the capitalist modernisers among the Thatcherites, such as Sir John Hoskyns, have grown impatient at the slow pace of advance. He has argued forcibly, as a result of his experience in the Downing Street Policy Unit, that decline will not be reversed until major changes in the structure of government have been brought about, particularly the organisation and recruitment of the civil service. In 1986 Hoskyns set out his own radical manifesto for the next Parliament. Imaginative thinking, he declared, was needed now, in advance of declining North Sea oil revenues. The measures included the immediate scrapping of rent and minimum wage controls; abolishing the letter post monopoly and denationalising the coal industry; outlawing strikes in all private and public monopoly services; introducing tax relief on fees for private health and private education; allowing parents an absolute right to choose which state school to send their children to, and allowing successful schools to expand to meet demand; and abolishing the rate support grant by transferring education spending to central government.[20]

In order for such a radical set of measures to have a chance of success, Hoskyns' proposed reforms of British Government would first have had to be carried through and an executive government created that was capable of formulating, implementing and monitoring a co-ordinated programme of policies.

Hoskyns and many like him believe that the Thatcher Government's radicalism has been constantly frustrated by the inadequacy of the civil service and the present organisation of government. The changes that have been made (reviewed in Chapter 4) do not add up to radical overhaul of the state machine. Despite its misgivings about civil servants and its determination to reduce their numbers and contain their pay, the Thatcher Government still relies on the traditional civil service to carry through its programme.

The Thatcher Government has been most successful when it has faced major challenges to its authority and has been able to win a trial of strength against an identifiable opponent. It has triumphed over the IRA Hunger Strikers, the Argentinian military junta, the miners and the rebel local authorities. Here the strong state has had a clear and obvious meaning. But such an approach has been of little use in dealing with long-term problems like the control of public expenditure or the refashioning of education.

The Government's main success in reorganising state and civil society has been in industrial relations. It has achieved a large reduction in trade union influence and visibility, and reversed the trend towards greater corporate representation. It has put more reliance on Parliament as the source of government authority and as the main intermediary between government and civil society.

This change has increased the power of the executive considerably. The party system and the powers of patronage, allied to a strong Prime Minister, allow the Thatcher Government to dominate Parliament in a way it could never have dominated the corporate interests. But the modern Parliament is a fragile base on which to exercise state authority. The interventionist actions of the Thatcher Government have exposed the absence of constitutional safeguards on the exercise of government power in Britain. Commanding only 43 per cent of the popular vote the Thatcher Government has still embarked on deeply unpopular and divisive policies. Parliamentary Government has become more arbitrary and less consensual. The drift towards a more authoritarian style of rule has become marked.

But, despite the initiatives the Government has taken to re-establish its authority, they are still judged by observers like Sir John Hoskyns to fall far short of what is required. To deal with short-term crises and problems the Government has steadily taken more powers, and centralised more functions in its hands. But this has not necessarily increased its effectiveness. One analysis of the Government's handling of the state system beyond Whitehall has concluded that, although the Government has formally more power, its ability to implement the policies it wants across the whole public sector has diminished.[21]

The institutional and cultural transformation required to make the free economy a reality, and a plausible accumulation strategy for the 1990s, has faltered because the Thatcher Government has so far rejected the need, except in a piecemeal and reactive fashion, to create the kind of state machinery that might carry through such a programme. Such a state would have to be a strong state indeed, not tied down by any liberal or democratic scruples or institutional constraints. Only in respect of trade unions and public order has the state under Thatcher moved in this direction, and then only partially.

The result is a restructuring of the state that has gone some way to achieving a free economy but has not so far demonstrated that it can reverse the decline. What it has discovered is a formula for managing the decline and its consequences. The economy is to be an open economy integrated into the world economy, with transformed industrial relations and deregulated markets, and a considerable enlargement of the private sector. But it will also be an economy with sharp disparities between regions, and between the majority of workers in secure employment and a minority composed of the poor, the unemployed and those in low-paid and casual employment. As the labour market has become more segmented, the inequalities of income and wealth more marked, and the decay of the inner cities and public services more evident, so the pressures have grown towards a 'two-nation' politics – on one side policies that increase repression, subsidy and dependence for the minority of the poor and disadvantaged, and on the other policies that maintain the physical security and economic prosperity of the majority.

The strong state that is needed so that this economy may remain free is a state able to conduct effective surveillance and policing of the unemployed and the poor, able to confront and defeat any union challenge, able to contain any upsurge of terrorism or public disorder. But it has not yet proved capable of becoming the kind of strong state needed to break out of the cycle of decline.

The future of Thatcherism

Hegemony is often misrepresented as meaning simply ideological domination, but properly understood it involves the successful interweaving of economic and political as well as ideological domination. Gramsci emphasised this point:

the fact of hegemony presupposes that account be taken of the interests and the tendencies of the groups over which hegemony is to be exercised, and that a certain compromise equilibrium should be formed – in other words, that the leading group should make sacrifices of an economic–corporate kind. But there is also no doubt that such sacrifices and such a compromise cannot touch the essential; for though hegemony is ethical–political, it must also be economic, must necessarily be based on the decisive function exercised by the leading group in the decisive nucleus of economic activity.[22]

The main conclusion of this book is that Thatcherism should be seen as an attempt to clear the way for a new hegemony, not as that new hegemony itself. The Thatcher Government has shown little evidence at any time of being prepared to make sacrifices or seeking compromise. But, now that some of the shifts in policy, attitudes, behaviour and relationships of power which Thatcherism wished to see have been accomplished, it is not hard to see the kind of compromises that a future government, under a different leadership, might concede in order to win the kind of legitimacy that has so far eluded the Thatcher regime.

Looked at in this way two of the central mysteries about Thatcherism – its relationship to Conservatism, and the gulf between its ambitions and its achievements – can be unravelled. The kind of task which Thatcherism has been called on to perform is an unusual one in the history of Conservatism. British Conservatives have generally been used to operating within an established hegemony. Attempting to dismantle and discredit institutions, structures and policies which once carried the full authority of the state is not normally characteristic of Conservatives. The crusading style and the ideological certainties evident among Thatcherites seem alien to traditional Conservatism. But understood as statecraft, aimed at determining the Conservative party interest and restoring the freedom of action and the authority of the party in government, Thatcherism is placed firmly in the most central Conservative tradition of all.

Similarly the gulf between ambition and achievement is explicable, given the scale of the task that was being attempted. The Thatcher Government willed the ends but had no way of organising effective means to see the policies that might achieve them implemented. Since it was committed to overturning many aspects of the 1940s settlement it was obliged to confront and attempt to reconstruct many of the institutions not only of the state and the public sector, but in civil society as well. Many of the institutions that had been important buttresses of the old order were obstacles to the creation of the new. Establishing a fresh basis for a stable hegemony required their reconstruction or, in some cases, their destruction.

It is hardly surprising if after a mere four years in opposition and eight years in government, neither a new political settlement from which a consensus might develop, nor a remodelled society and economy are very close to being achieved. The last period (the 1880s) when hegemony broke down led to several decades of political turbulence and conflict. It is unlikely too that the policy agenda that has been dominant under the Thatcher Government will prove to be more than one phase in the development of a new political settlement. The construction of a new and stable hegemony is rarely the work of a single party.

Nevertheless it is the Thatcherites who are the first group in Britain to grapple with the problem of turning their criticisms of the postwar social democracy into practical programmes and policies. The success they have had so far does not amount to the 'Thatcher revolution' that is sometimes spoken of, but the Thatcher years look certain to be important in demolishing old assumptions, challenging institutions and policies, clearing the ground for future initiatives and changes.

The year 1987 saw the triumph of a third election victory and the stock market crash. The first appeared to indicate the arrival of a new dominant party system. The second was a reminder of the shallow and unstable foundations on which the economic recovery since 1982 had been based. It brought to an end the second phase of the Thatcher Government.

To ask any longer whether Margaret Thatcher is a worthy representative of the British Conservative tradition seems curious when under her leadership the party has won such electoral success. If the main purpose of the Conservative party is to govern, Thatcher has provided it. She has been a more ideological Conservative Leader than her predecessors, but in office, with some exceptions, she has generally shown the required blend of caution and pragmatism that the Conservative party expects from its leaders. Her ideology in any case is hardly an alien importation into the party but a restatement of the libertarian strand of Conservatism, which tended to be eclipsed during the ascendancy of Social Imperialism and Social Democracy, but never entirely disappeared.

In party terms what Thatcherism represents is the conviction that the accommodation of labour and its interests is no longer necessary, and that the forms which this accommodation have assumed are the biggest single obstacle in reversing British decline and positioning British capital to take advantage of the whatever pattern of accumulation becomes established. This means in some respects a reversion to the old Tory politics – reasserting the autonomy of Government from special interests, breaking free from the entanglements of social democracy, abandoning ideas of politics as an enterprise and trusting once again in the powers of British society as a civil association to renew itself.

The Conservative critics of Thatcherism have stressed the neglect of legitimacy and the neglect of production which the vigorous pursuit of these policies entails. A third election victory and a growing economy in 1987 appeared to silence these objections. The political formula of a free economy and a strong state appeared triumphant. The obstacles in the way of free markets had been reduced in a number of fields and, after weathering the shake-out of jobs and companies, the economy appeared to be growing slightly faster than any other major capitalist economy, and the unemployment trend was pointing downwards. At the same time the state had been strengthened both by reducing the range of its responsibilities and activities and by arming itself to meet and overcome any internal or external challenge to its authority. Under Thatcher the balance of state policy shifted away from consent towards coercion.

The Thatcherite vision of the future is that the attack upon collectivism will continue, and that gradually it will be eroded and overcome in more and more areas. The old Labour movement will decline further and cease to be an important force in politics or industry, and the Labour party will decline with it. Political realignment will eventually produce an electoral challenger for the Conservatives but on the ground of the new policy agenda, not the old.

This agreeable political scenario makes a number of assumptions, the most important being that the improvement in the economy since 1982 can be maintained. It is this recovery which has been crucial for the Conservatives' electoral success and for sustaining their claims that the decline is now over and that Britain can look forward to a prosperous economy, declining unemployment, steadily rising living standards and increasing investment. The main difficulty with this scenario is that whether it is fulfilled or not appears to lie outside the power of the British Government to provide. The financial crash in 1987 had been looming for several years, and was caused principally by the political impossibility of sustaining any further the growth in the United States trade and budget deficits which had fuelled the recovery. The capitalist economies that pursued relatively tight monetary policies through this period benefited from the rapid growth of the American market. If this stimulus to growth is removed, and cannot be replaced by co-ordinated reflationary action from Japan and Europe, the world economy faces a major recession, possibly more serious than the two already experienced since 1973.

The economic policy of the Thatcher Government depends for its credibility on the avoidance of recession and the continuation of world economic growth. When the financial crisis hit the Government first blamed the markets for over-reaction, then blamed the United States for running a budget deficit. This was contrasted with the 'sound economy' brought about by 'sound money policies' in Britain. The Government's stance appeared to be what Patrick Dunleavy has labelled 'Thatcherism in one country' – the delusion that so long as Britain applied 'correct' policies the British economy can be insulated from what is happening in the world economy.

The Thatcher Government in its first eight years put great weight on increasing the openness of the British economy, on furthering the internationalisation of the financial markets and on giving full support to many of the United States' policies, such as the arms build-up in the 1980s, that directly contributed to the deficit. The limited economic revival in Britain also owed much to the stimulation of the American economy through Reagan's supply side policies. British criticism of the United States for causing 'unjustified' falls on the British stock market by not curbing its deficit appeared to repudiate the main theme of the Thatcher Government's foreign policy – the strong support given to the United States' attempts to restore its political, military and economic leadership of the West, which had produced the deficit and the boom in the first place.

If the Thatcher project is to continue along its current lines the Government must hope for political deals that will avoid a plunge into world recession. In the bids that will be made over the next few years to maintain a liberal world economic order the British Government has only a marginal role to play, but its stake in the outcome is very high. Britain faces growing trade deficits. Maintaining growth in productivity, investment and new jobs in sectors that might counter these deficits will become much more difficult if the world economy moves back into recession. Manufacturing industry in Britain remains weak. As a result of the contraction of manufacturing under the Thatcher Government the outlook for the British balance of payments looked alarming by 1987. Manufacturing output had recovered in 1987 to the level it had reached in 1979 but this still contrasted sharply with the real growth in manufacturing which other leading capitalist economies experienced through the 1980s. In order to rebuild a strong manufacturing sector on present government policies, a long period of sustained growth in the world economy is necessary, and much higher levels of investment in British industry. The prospects for that at the end of 1987 looked bleak.

The financial crash threatened not only the continuance of the recovery, but also the credibility of many aspects of the Thatcherite project, particularly the privatisation programme and the priority to be given to markets in guiding the government's accumulation strategy. It raised the possibility that the next phase of political development may not be towards ever-increasing extension of market solutions, but towards new forms of collectivism and state intervention. If this occurred the Thatcher years might appear in retrospect not the dawn of a new era, but a transitional period. The phase of the Thatcher Government which commenced in the Autumn of 1987 is likely to determine whether this is the case.

Notes and references

Chapter 1: A crisis of hegemony

1. Analysis of the world system has been greatly influenced in recent years by the work of Immanuel Wallerstein. See *The World System* (New York: Academic Press, 1974).
2. For analysis of the long boom see E. A. Brett, *The World Economy since the War* (London: Macmillan, 1985).
3. See P. Armstrong, A. Glyn and J. Harrison, *Capitalism since World War II* (London: Fontana, 1984).
4. The concept of Fordism has been developed particularly by the French regulation school. See M. Aglietta, *A Theory of Capitalist Regulation* (London: New Left Books, 1979); M. Aglietta, 'World Capitalism in the 1980s', *New Left Review*, 136 (1982) pp. 5–41; Alain Lipietz, 'Towards Global Fordism', *New Left Review*, 133 (1982) pp. 33–47.
5. The course of the 1974/5 crisis is described by Ernest Mandel, *The Second Slump* (London: Verso, 1978).
6. See tha analyses by Ajit Singh and Alec Cairncross in F. Blackaby (ed.) *De-industrialisation* (London: Heinemann, 1979).
7. See Scott Lash and John Urry, *The End of Organised Capitalism* (Cambridge: Polity, 1987).
8. The existence of a new division of labour is controversial. See the discussion by Rhys Jenkins, 'Divisions over the international division of labour', *Capital and Class*, 22 (1984) pp. 28–58.
9. For analyses of the development of the postwar global political and economic order, the international monetary system, and the imbalances and conflicts of the 1980s see E. A. Brett, *International Money and Capitalist Crisis* (London: Heinemann, 1983); R. Parboni, *The Dollar and its Rivals* (London: Verso, 1981); and Kees van der Pijl, *The Making of an Atlantic Ruling Class* (London: Verso, 1984).
10. One of the most influential characterisations of collectivism came from A. V. Dicey, *Lectures on the Relation between Law and Public Opinion in England during the Nineteenth Century* (London: Macmillan, 1905); see also Keith Middlemass, *Politics in Industrial Society* (London: André Deutsch,

242

1979) and W. H. Greenleaf, *The British Political Tradition*, vol. i, *Rise of Collectivism* (London: Methuen, 1983).

11. See A. Przeworski, *Capitalism and Social Democracy* (Cambridge University Press, 1985); R. Miliband, *Capitalist Democracy in Britain* (Oxford University Press, 1982).

12. See Daniel Bell, *The Cultural Contradictions of Capitalism* (London: Heinemann, 1976) and John Urry, *The Anatomy of Capitalist Societies* (London: Macmillan, 1981).

13. This is discussed by David Coates, *The Context of British Politics* (London: Hutchinson, 1984).

14. See David Edgar, 'The Free and the Good', in Ruth Levitas (ed.) *The Ideology of the New Right* (Cambridge: Polity, 1986) pp. 80–106; Stuart Hall *et al.*, *Policing the Crisis* (London: Macmillan, 1978).

15. See Bill Jordan, *The State* (Oxford: Basil Blackwell, 1985).

16. See Nevil Johnson, *In Search of the Constitution* (London: Methuen, 1977).

17. On corporatism see Alan Cawson, *Corporatism and Welfare* (London: Heinemann, 1982).

18. See A. H. Birch, 'Overload, ungovernability, and delegitimation: the theories and the British case', *British Journal of Political Science*, 14:2 (1984) pp. 135–60.

19. See A. Crosland, *The Future of Socialism* (London: Jonathan Cape, 1956).

20. See R. C. O. Matthews, 'Why has Britain had full employment since the war?' *Economic Journal*, 78:3 (1968) pp. 555–69.

21. See Milton Friedman, *Inflation and Unemployment* (London: IEA, 1977); Tim Congdon, *Monetarism* (London: Centre for Policy Studies, 1976).

22. Tony Benn, *Arguments for Democracy* (Harmondsworth: Penguin, 1982).

23. Peter Riddell, *The Thatcher Government* (Oxford: Basil Blackwell, 1985).

24. As Balfour did to the rise of Social Imperialism in the first decade of the century.

25. Martin Jacques, 'Breaking out of the Impasse', *Marxism Today*, 23:10 (October 1979) pp. 6–15.

Chapter 2: The New Right

1. There is a rich and growing literature on the New Right. See especially Ruth Levitas (ed.) *The Ideology of the New Right* (Cambridge: Polity, 1987); Gillian Peele, *Revival and Reaction: the Right in Contemporary America* (Oxford: Clarendon Press, 1984); Norman Barry, *The New Right* (London: Croom Helm, 1987); Desmond King, *The New Right* (London: Macmillan, 1987); and David Green, *The New Right* (London: Wheatsheaf, 1987).

2. For typical writing on this theme see Robert Moss, *The Collapse of Democracy* (London: Temple Smith, 1975).

3. For an initial exploration of this idea see 'The Free Economy and the Strong State', in R. Miliband and J. Saville (eds) *Socialist Register 1979* (London: Merlin, 1979) pp. 1–25.

4. An example of this is the very good study of what is here termed the liberal New Right by Nick Bosanquet. See *After the New Right* (London: HEB, 1983).

5. See the excellent analysis in Peele, *Revival and Reaction*.

6. David Edgar provides a powerful treatment of the new politics of race and gender in 'The Free and the Good', in Levitas (ed.) *The Ideology of the New Right*, pp. 55–79.

7. Sam Brittan is one example. See, among his many writings, *Capitalism and the Permissive Society* (London: Macmillan, 1973).

8. One of the best analyses of the internal tensions in New Right thinking can be found in Patrick Dunleavy and Brendan O'Leary, *Theories of the State* (London: Macmillan, 1987) ch. 3.

9. Moss, *The Collapse of Democracy*, p. 46.

10. See the illuminating discussion by Andrew Belsey, 'The New Right, Social Order, and Civil Liberties', in Levitas (ed.) *The New Right*, pp. 167–97.

11. See Roger Scruton, *The Meaning of Conservatism* (Harmondsworth: Penguin, 1980).

12. See Ferdinand Mount, *The Subversive Family* (London: Jonathan Cape, 1982).

13. I have explored the different components of the liberal New Right further in 'The Political Economy of Freedom', in Levitas (ed.) *The Ideology of the New Right*, pp. 25–54.

14. For a succinct summary see Alec Chrystal, *Controversies in Macroeconomics* (London: Philip Allan, 1979).

15. For one of the best analyses of the international economic order see E. A. Brett, *International Money and Capitalist Crisis* (London: HEB, 1983).

16. See Milton Friedman, *Inflation and Unemployment* (London: IEA, 1977) and Bosanquet, *After the New Right*.

17. See M. Kalecki, 'Political Aspects of Full Employment', *Political Quarterly*, 14 (1943) pp. 322–31.

18. For the main themes of Hayek's writings see Norman Barry, *Hayek's Social and Economic Philosophy* (London: Macmillan, 1979).

19. See W. Rees-Mogg, *The Reigning Illusion* (London: Hamish Hamilton, 1974).

20. See F. A. Hayek, *Denationalisation of Money* (London: IEA, 1978).

21. This has been put forward in a paper by Kevin Dowd, 'The State and the Monetary System' (Fraser Institute, 1988).

22. Hayek, *Denationalisation of Money*.

23. See the discussion by Bosanquet in *After the New Right*. A representative supply side text is B. Bartlett and T. P. Roth (eds) *The Supply Side Solution* (London: Macmillan, 1983).

24. See the criticism by George Gilder, one of the leading American supply siders, in the preface to the English edition of *Wealth and Poverty* (London: Buchan & Enright, 1982).

25. For the inter-war debates on the feasibility of socialism see F. A. Hayek (ed.) *Collectivist Economic Planning* (London: Routledge, 1935).

26. See the Omega Project of the Adam Smith Institute. It is described and analysed by Ruth Levitas in 'Competition and Compliance: the utopias of the New Right' in Levitas (ed.) *The Ideology of the New Right.*
27. For contrasting estimates see Bosanquet, *After the New Right* and Barry, *The New Right.*
28. Robert Nozick is professor of philosophy at Harvard, best known for his *Anarchy, State and Utopia* (Oxford: Basil Blackwell, 1974).
29. Hayek's theory of how knowledge is dispersed in social institutions is one of his most important contributions to social analysis. See 'The Use of Knowledge in Society' in *Individualism and Economic Order* (London: Routledge & Kegan Paul, 1949).
30. Milton Friedman, 'The line we dare not cross', *Encounter* (November 1976).
31. For an analysis of the public choice school see Bosanquet, *After the New Right*, ch. 4, and Buchanan J. *et al.*, *The Economics of Politics* (London: IEA, 1978).
32. Nozick, *Anarchy, State and Utopia.* Nozick's positions are criticised in several of the contributions to J. Paul (ed.) *Reading Nozick* (Oxford: Basil Blackwell, 1982).
33. See Hayek, especially *Law, Legislation, and Liberty, vol. II: The Mirage of Social Justice* (London: Routledge & Kegan Paul, 1976).
34. For the extreme Austrian position see Murray Rothbard, *Power and Market* (Kansas City: Sheed Andrews & McMeel, 1977).
35. The analysis of the new class has been developed particularly by the American neo-conservatives such as Irving Kristol. See I. Kristol, *Two Cheers for Capitalism* (New York: Basic Books, 1978) and Peele, *Revival and Reaction.*
36. Representative examples of conservative New Right writing are Roger Scruton, *The Meaning of Conservatism*; Maurice Cowling (ed.) *Conservative Essays* (London: Cassell, 1978); and Rhodes Boyson, *Centre Forward* (London: Temple Smith, 1978).
37. The impact of the cold war on postwar politics is emphasised by Phil Armstrong, Andrew Glyn and John Harrison, *Capitalism since World War II* (London: Fontana, 1984).
38. Those who moved right in the 1950s included the former Trotskyists such as Irving Kristol, and former Communists such as Alfred Sherman. There was a further wave later among those repudiating social democracy. See, for example, Patrick Cormack, *Right Turn: Eight Men who changed their minds* (London: Leo Cooper, 1978). The eight included Max Beloff, Lord Chalfont, Paul Johnson, Reg Prentice and Hugh Thomas.
39. The origins and course of the new cold war are traced by Fred Halliday, *The Making of the Second Cold War* (London: Verso, 1983).
40. Moss, *The Collapse of Democracy*, is a good guide to subversion. See also the publications of the *Freedom Association*, and Brian Crozier's Institute for the Study of Conflict. The flavour and tone of this literature can be sampled in Brian Crozier, *Socialism: Dream and Reality* (London: Sherwood, 1987).
41. F. A. Hayek, *The Road to Serfdom* (London: Routledge, 1944).

42. Colin Leys in *Politics in Britain* (London: HEB, 1983) ch. 15, analyses right-wing scenarios of political collapse.
43. The ideas and politics of the American New Right has been analysed by Mike Davis in 'The Political Economy of Late-Imperial America', *New Left Review*, 143 (1984) pp. 6–38; and 'Reaganomics' Magical Mystery Tour', *New Left Review*, 149 (1985) pp. 45–66.
44. Irving Kristol, *Two Cheers for Capitalism.*
45. Gilder, *Wealth and Poverty.*
46. See Scruton's criticisms of Nozick in *The Meaning of Conservatism.*
47. A rich source of this writing is the *Salisbury Review*, which is published quarterly.

Chapter 3:   From Butler to Thatcher

1. Ian Gilmour, *Inside Right* (London: Hutchinson, 1977).
2. See Rhodes Boyson, *Centre Forward*; and Andrew Gamble, *The Conservative Nation* (London: Routledge & Kegan Paul, 1974) ch. 5.
3. See J. D. Hoffman, *The Conservative Party in Opposition* (London: MacGibbon & Kee, 1964); Gamble, *The Conservative Nation*, ch. 3.
4. *The Conservative Nation*, ch. 4.
5. The Institute of Economic Affairs was founded in 1957.
6. See also Macmillan's shrewd analysis of the result of the 1959 election in his memoirs, *Pointing the Way* (London: Macmillan, 1972) p. 15.
7. R. T. McKenzie and A. Silver, *Angels in Marble* (London: Heinemann, 1963).
8. See the excellent analysis of why British Fordism was relatively unsuccessful in Henk Overbeek, *Global Capitalism and Britain's Decline* (University of Amsterdam, 1988).
9. For the debate on modernisation see Andrew Gamble, *Britain in Decline* (London: Macmillan, 1985).
10. *Britain in Decline*, ch. 4.
11. *The Conservative Nation*, ch. 5.
12. See T. E. Utley, *Enoch Powell* (London: Kimber, 1968); and D. Schoen, *Enoch Powell and the Powellites* (London: Macmillan, 1977).
13. See Enoch Powell, *Freedom and Reality* (Kingswood: Elliott Rightway Books, 1969) ch. 9.
14. See Schoen, *Enoch Powell and the Powellites*, ch. 2.
15. Schoen provides the most detailed examination.
16. Enoch Powell, *Income Tax at 4/3 in the £* (ed. A. Lejeune) (London: Stacey, 1970).
17. Nicholas Wapshott and George Brock in their study, *Thatcher* (London: Futura, 1983) note the similarities between Thatcher's 1968 CPC lecture, 'What's Wrong with Politics' and the ideas Powell was expressing. She was known to admire Powell's book of speeches *Freedom and Reality*, she attended meetings at which he spoke and she was the

only member of the Shadow Cabinet to wish him well in the 1970 election.

18. For writing on the Heath Government see M. Holmes, *Political Pressure and Economic Policy: British Government 1970–74* (London: Butterworth, 1982); Douglas Hurd, *An End to Promises* (London: Collins, 1979).

19. See Robin Blackburn, 'The Heath Government: a new course for British capitalism', *New Left Review*, 70 (1971) pp. 3–26.

20. The idea of a U-turn was critically examined by Michael Moran, 'The Price for Conservatism', Political Studies Association, 1978. See also Andrew Gamble and Stuart Walkland, *The British Party System and Economic Policy 1945–83* (Oxford: Clarendon Press, 1984).

21. See Hurd, *An end to Promises*, and Holmes, *Political Pressure and Economic Policy*.

22. Two published collections of Sir Keith Joseph's speeches are *Reversing the Trend* (London: Barry Rose, 1975) and *Stranded on the Middle Ground* (London: Centre for Policy Studies, 1976).

23. Accounts of the 1975 leadership election are contained in Wapshott and Brock, *Thatcher*; Robert Behrens, *The Conservative Party from Heath to Thatcher* (London: Saxon House, 1980); and Patrick Cosgrave, *Margaret Thatcher* (London: Hutchinson, 1978).

24. The office of leader is very difficult to capture, but since 1965 it has been subject to election. This is not the case for other offices in the party.

25. Lord Stockton, *The Times*, 9 October 1975.

26. Quoted by Behrens, *The Conservative Party from Heath to Thatcher*, p. 3.

27. Lord Stockton, *The Times*, 9 October 1975.

28. Ian Gilmour, speech at Amersham, 1974.

29. Julian Critchley, *Westminster Blues* (London: Futura, 1985) p. 32.

30. J. Ramsden, *The Making of Conservative Party Policy* (London: Longman, 1980) ch. 10; Behrens, *The Conservative Party from Heath to Thatcher*; and Z. Layton-Henry (ed.) *Conservative Party Politics* (London: Macmillan, 1980).

31. Cosgrave, *Margaret Thatcher*.

32. Margaret Thatcher, 'Britain Awake', *Let Our Children Grow Tall* (London: CPS, 1977) p. 43.

33. Ibid., p. 44.

34. Ibid., p. 46.

35. Ibid., p. 46.

36. Ibid., p. 47.

37. For Thatcher's style as opposition leader see Martin Burch, 'Approaches to leadership in Opposition', in Z. Layton-Henry (ed.) *Conservative Party Politics*, pp. 159–87.

38. See David Coates, *Labour in Power* (London: Longmans, 1980).

39. The Lib/Lab pact was negotiated in March 1977 and preserved the minority Labour Government from defeat in Parliament for a further two years.

40. See W. Keegan, *Mrs. Thatcher's Economic Experiment* (London: Allen Lane, 1984) Part I.

41. See Coates, *Labour in Power*, and M. Holmes, *The Labour Government 1974–79* (London: Macmillan, 1985).
42. Trevor Russel, *The Tory Party* (Harmondsworth: Penguin, 1978) p. 78.
43. 'Appomattox or Civil War', *Economist*, 27 May 1978.
44. See Bill Schwarz, 'Let them eat coal: the Conservative party and the strike', in H. Beynon (ed.) *Digging Deeper* (London: Verso, 1985).
45. The others were Airey Neave, George Gardiner and John Biffen.
46. See J. Rogaly, *Grunwick* (Harmondsworth: Penguin, 1978).
47. See Steve Ludlam, 'The myth of 1976', mimeo, Department of Politics, University of Sheffield, 1987.
48. Keith Joseph, 'Solving the Union problem is the key to economic recovery' (London: CPS, 1979).

Chapter 4:   The Thatcher Government 1979–87

1. Walsall and Workington were won by the Conservatives in November 1976, Stechford in March 1977, and Ashfield in April 1977.
2. On the devolution bills see Coates, *Labour in Power*.
3. See Richard Rose, *Do Parties Make a Difference?* (London: Macmillan, 1984).
4. See William Keegan, *Mrs. Thatcher's Economic Experiment*; Colin Thain, 'The Medium Term Financial Strategy', paper presented to the Political Studies Association Conference, April 1985; and Grahame Thompson, *The Conservatives' Economic Policy* (London: Croom Helm, 1986) ch. 2.
5. For contrasting assessments of the 1981 budget see Keegan, *Mrs. Thatcher's Economic Experiment*, and Alan Walters, *Britain's Economic Renaissance* (Oxford: Clarendon Press, 1986). Patrick Cosgrave judged it to be the 'true strategic beginning of the introduction of Thatcherism into government'.
6. Prior's caution over trade union reform and the conflict this created is described by Patrick Cosgrave in *Thatcher: The First Term* (London: Bodley Head, 1985).
7. See Chapter 3, note 43.
8. Her attitude was like Baldwin's in 1925. Cosgrave reports her as saying of the Government's climbdown 'It gives us time to get ready'; *Thatcher: The First Term*, p. 131.
9. A transfer fee of £1.8 million for MacGregor's services was negotiated with his employers, Lazard Freres.
10. See John Burton, *The Job Support Machine* (London: CPS, 1979) and Jock Bruce-Gardyne, *Mrs. Thatcher's First Administration* (London: Macmillan, 1984).
11. Michael Heseltine, Secretary of State for the Environment, took a very different line.
12. See Ian Bradley, *Breaking the Mould* (Oxford: Martin Robertson, 1981); D. Kogan and M. Kogan, *The Battle for the Labour Party* (London:

Fontana, 1982); and Patrick Seyd, *The Rise and Fall of the Labour Left* (London: Macmillan, 1987).

13. The internal splits in the cabinet are detailed by Patrick Cosgrave, *Thatcher: The First Term*; Peter Riddell, *The Thatcher Government* (Oxford: Basil Blackwell, 1985); Martin Holmes, *The First Thatcher Government 1979–1983* (London: Wheatsheaf, 1985); and Dennis Kavanagh, *Thatcherism and Britain Politics* (Oxford: Clarendon Press, 1987).

14. This is argued strongly by Grahame Thompson, *The Conservatives' Economic Policy*; William Keegan, *Mrs. Thatcher's Economic Experiment*; Nick Gardner, *Decade of Discontent* (Oxford: Basil Blackwell, 1987); and David Smith, *The Rise and Fall of Monetarism* (Harmondsworth: Penguin, 1986).

15. For a full account see Cento Veljanovski, *Selling the State* (London: Weidenfeld & Nicolson, 1987).

16. See Mike Goldsmith, 'The Conservatives and Local Government, 1979 and after', in D. Bell (ed.) *The Conservative Government 1979–84* (London: Croom Helm, 1985); and Patrick Dunleavy and Rod Rhodes, 'Government beyond Whitehall' in Henry Drucker *et al.* (eds) *Developments in British Politics 2* (London: Macmillan, 1986) ch. 5.

17. See Huw Beynon, *Digging Deeper*; and Martin Adeney and John Lloyd, *The Miners' Strike: loss without limit* (London: Routledge & Kegan Paul, 1986).

18. See Michael Moran, 'Industrial Relations' in Drucker, *Developments in British Politics 2*, ch. 12, and Tony Lane, 'The Tories and the Trade Unions' in Stuart Hall and Martin Jacques (eds) *The Politics of Thatcherism* (London: Lawrence & Wishart, 1983) pp. 169–87.

19. The Labour Research Department estimated that in June 1986 the official government figure of 3 229 400 would have been 3 865 000 on the same basis as the 1979 count. In addition MSC programmes increased the numbers on special training and community schemes from 250 000 in 1979 to 737 000 in 1986; of these an estimated 561 000 would otherwise be registered as unemployed. See Labour Research, *A State of Collapse: The UK economy under the Tories* (London, 1987) pp. 24–5.

20. See Anthony Barnett, 'Iron Britannia', *New Left Review*, 134 (1982) pp. 5–96; and Hall and Jacques, *The Politics of Thatcherism*, Part III (chapters by Eric Hobsbawm, Robert Gray and Tom Nairn).

21. See Peter Jenkins, *Mrs. Thatcher's Revolution* (London: Jonathan Cape, 1987) ch. 9.

22. See Peter Hennessy, *Cabinet* (Oxford: Basil Blackwell, 1986) ch. 3.

23. Cecil Parkinson resigned from the Cabinet in 1983 following publicity of his affair with Sara Keays; Jeffrey Archer resigned as Deputy Chairman of the Conservative Party in 1986, following press allegations about his association with a prostitute (he subsequently won substantial damages in a libel action); Harvey Proctor resigned as an MP in 1987 after pleading guilty to involvement with homosexual prostitutes; and Keith Best resigned as an MP in 1987 after being found guilty of making multiple applications for British Telecom shares.

250   *The Free Economy and the Strong State*

24. See Thompson, *The Conservatives' Economic Policy*, and Smith, *The Rise and Fall of Monetarism*.
25. See Maurice Mullard's analysis of the Thatcher Government's record on public spending, *The Politics of Public Expenditure* (London: Croom Helm, 1987) ch. 6.
26. Between 1979 and 1987 asset sales raised £12 billion for the Treasury. By 1985 the Chancellor was planning for receipts of £4.7 billion per annum for the next three years. See Veljanovski, *Selling the State*, ch. 1. Oil revenues expanded swiftly during the 1980s to reach £10–£12 billion a year, which was larger than the Public Sector Borrowing Requirement.
27. See Thompson, *The Conservatives' Economic Policy*, and Wyn Grant, *The Political Economy of Industrial Policy* (London: Butterworths, 1982).
28. See evidence from Ministers to the House of Lords Select Committee in *Report from the Select Committee on Overseas Trade* (House of Lords, 1985).
29. Eurotunnel and the Dartford Bridge across the Thames to relieve congestion on the M25 orbital motorway were two examples.
30. See Hans Kastendiek *et al.* (eds) *Economic Crisis, Trade Unions and the State* (London: Croom Helm, 1986).
31. John Lloyd and Charles Leadbeater, *In Search of Work* (Harmondsworth: Penguin, 1987).
32. See Bob Rowthorn, 'Britain and Western Europe', *Marxism Today*, 26:5 (May 1982) pp. 25–31.
33. See Barnett, 'Iron Britannia'.
34. See Nevil Johnson, 'Constitutional Reform: Some Dilemmas for a Conservative Philosophy', in Z. Layton-Henry (ed.) *Conservative Party Politics*, pp. 126–55; and Gillian Peele, 'The state and civil liberties', in Drucker (ed.) *Developments in British Politics 2*, ch. 6.
35. Sir John Hoskyns, 'Whitehall and Westminster: An outsider's view', *Parliamentary Affairs*, 36 (1983); and 'Conservatism is not enough', *Political Quarterly*, 55 (1984).
36. Civil Service numbers were cut from 732 000 in 1979 to 624 000 by 1984 and were planned to decline further to 593 000 in 1988. See G. K. Fry, 'Inside Whitehall' in *Developments in British Politics 2*, ch. 4.
37. A number of such appointments were made. See Kavanagh, *Thatcherism and British Politics*, ch. 9, for an assessment.
38. See Kavanagh, *Thatcherism and British Politics*, and P. Hennessy, *Cabinet*.
39. The Policy Unit is discussed by Fry, Hennessy and Kavanagh. See also, for an insider's view, David Willetts, 'The role of the Prime Minister's Policy Unit', *Public Administration*, 65:4 (1987). Willetts reveals that the first two questions asked by the Policy Unit about every departmental paper are (i) is there a less interventionist solution which has not been properly considered or has been wrongly rejected and (ii) is there a less expensive option?
40. For Thatcher's style as Prime Minister see Anthony King, 'Margaret Thatcher: the style of a Prime Minister', in A. King (ed.) *The British Prime Minister* (London: Macmillan, 1985).
41. After the speech the Conservative party's poll rating leapt nine points.

For a discussion of race and the Conservative party see Z. Layton-Henry, *The Politics of Race in Britain* (London: George Allen & Unwin, 1984).

42. Two influential treatments of this theme are Martin Wiener, *English Culture and the Decline of the Industrial Spirit* (Cambridge University Press, 1981) and Corelli Barnett, *The Audit of War* (London: Macmillan, 1986); see also David Coates and John Hillard (eds) *The Economic Decline of Modern Britain* (London: Wheatsheaf, 1985).

43. See, for example, David Eccles, *Popular Capitalism* (London: Conservative Political Centre, 1954).

Chapter 5:   The pursuit of power

1. William Keegan, *Mrs. Thatcher's Economic Experiment*.

2. Rhodes Boyson, *Centre Forward*, and Patrick Cosgrave, *Margaret Thatcher: A Tory and her Party*.

3. T. E. Utley, 'The Significance of Mrs. Thatcher', in Maurice Cowling (ed.) *Conservative Essays* (London: Cassell, 1978) p. 44.

4. For a study of Salisbury's political thought see M. Pinto-Duschinsky, *The Political Thought of Lord of Lord Salisbury* (London: Constable, 1967).

5. Anthony Trollope, *The Bertrams*, quoted by W. L. Burn, 'The Conservative tradition and its reformulation', in M. Ginsburg (ed.) *Law and Opinion in the Twentieth Century* (London: Stevens, 1959) p. 43.

6. Quoted in Bernard Semmel, *Imperialism and Social Reform* (London: George Allen & Unwin, 1960) p. 100.

7. F. A. Hayek, 'Why I am not a Conservative', postscript to *The Constitution of Liberty* (London: Routledge & Kegan Paul, 1960).

8. Ian Gilmour, *Inside Right* (London: Hutchinson, 1977) p. 115.

9. S. Huntington, 'Conservatism as an Ideology', *American Political Science Review*, 51:2 (1957) pp. 454–73. See also R. Eccleshall, 'Conservatism' in R. Eccleshall et al. (eds) *Political Ideologies* (London: Hutchinson, 1984).

10. See, for example, Henry Kissinger, 'The Conservative Dilemma: Reflections on the political thought of Metternich', *American Political Science Review*, 48:4 (1954) pp. 1017–30.

11. H. Glickman, 'The Toryness of English Conservatism', *Journal of British Studies*, 1:1 (1961) pp. 111–43.

12. Gilmour, *Inside Right*, Part III, ch. 2; see also Robert Blake, *The Conservative Party from Peel to Thatcher* (London: Fontana, 1985).

13. Cosgrave, *Margaret Thatcher*, p. 36.

14. Iain Macleod, *Spectator*, 17 January 1964. See also the attacks on the Tory Party's rightward drift by Humphrey Berkeley, *Crossing the Floor* (London: George Allen & Unwin, 1972).

15. Trevor Russel, *The Tory Party* (Harmondsworth: Penguin, 1978).

16. Details on these organisations are given in 'Right Thinking People',

Labour Research, 73:2 (1984) pp. 37–42; and updated in *Labour Research*, 76:10 (1987) pp. 7–11.

17. Keith Joseph, 'The Quest for Common Ground', in *Stranded on the Middle Ground* (London: CPS, 1976).

18. See Gilmour, *Inside Right*, and *Britain Can Work* (Oxford: Martin Robertson, 1983); Andrew Gamble, *The Conservative Nation*, especially chs 2 and 3. For a typical statement of One Nation Conservatism see Sir Geoffrey Butler, *The Tory Tradition* (London: CPC, 1957).

19. Peter Walker, *The Ascent of Britain* (London: Sidgwick & Jackson, 1977) p. 29.

20. Ibid., p. 18.

21. Gilmour, *Inside Right*, p. 236.

22. Ibid., p. 118.

23. Russel, *The Tory Party*, p. 167.

24. Quoted by Kissinger, 'The Conservative Dilemma', p. 1020.

25. This distinction between libertarianism and collectivism is drawn by W. H. Greenleaf in his study *The British Political Tradition*, vol I, *The rise of Collectivism*, and vol II, *The Ideological Heritage* (London: Methuen, 1983). Greenleaf prefers 'libertarianism' to 'liberalism' because of the associations the latter has acquired. His concept of libertarianism corresponds to the conception of the liberal New Right developed in Chapter 2.

26. See N. Soldon, 'Laissez-faire as dogma: the Liberty and Property Defence League 1882–1914' in K. Brown (ed.) *Essays in Anti-Labour History* (London: Macmillan, 1974).

27. Robert Blake, *Conservatism in an Age of Revolution* (London: Churchill Press, 1976) and *The Conservative Party from Peel to Thatcher*, chapter 11 and postscript.

28. Hugh Thomas, *History, Capitalism, and Freedom* (London: CPS, 1979).

29. Michael Oakeshott, *Rationalism in Politics* (London: Methuen, 1962) and *On Human Conduct* (Oxford: Clarendon Press, 1975).

30. Oakeshott, *Rationalism in Politics*, p. 21.

31. Noel O'Sullivan *Conservatism* (London: J. M. Dent, 1976). A major expression of this approach can be found in Maurice Cowling (ed.) *Conservative Essays*.

32. Roger Scruton, *The Meaning of Conservatism* (Harmondsworth: Penguin, 1980) p. 15.

33. Ibid., pp. 15–16.

34. Noel O'Sullivan, 'Conservatism, the New Right, and the Limited State' in J. Hayward and P. Norton (eds) *The Political Science of British Politics* (Brighton: Wheatsheaf, 1986), pp. 21–36.

35. J. A. Schumpeter, *Capitalism, Socialism, and Democracy* (London: George Allen & Unwin, 1949) p. 229.

36. Gaetano Mosca, *The Ruling Class* (New York: McGraw-Hill, 1939) p. 119.

37. See *Monday World*, the former journal of the Monday Club, and the quarterly *Salisbury Review*.

38. See the discussion in chapter 5 of *The Conservative Nation*.

39. Peregrine Worsthorne, *Sunday Telegraph*, 15 October 1978. The need for a governing class is also one of the major themes of Worsthorne's book, *The Socialist Myth* (London: Cassell, 1971).
40. It is important to note that the tradition of Social Imperialism and the tradition of the Middle Way are frequently the same.
41. Bob Jessop *et al.*, 'Authoritarian Populism, Two Nations, and Thatcherism', *New Left Review*, 147 (1984) pp. 32–60.
42. Jim Bulpitt, 'The Discipline of the New Democracy: Mrs. Thatcher's Domestic Statecraft', *Political Studies*, 34:1 (1985) pp. 19–39; and *Territory and Power in the UK* (Manchester University Press, 1983).
43. See P. Marsh, *The Discipline of Popular Government: Lord Salisbury's Domestic Statecraft* (Brighton: Harvester Press, 1978).
44. Scruton, *The Meaning of Conservatism*.
45. J. H. Grainger, 'Mrs. Thatcher's Last Stand', *Quadrant*, 3 (December 1980) p. 6.
46. R. W. Johnson, 'Pomp and Circumstance', *The Politics of Recession* (London: Macmillan, 1985) pp. 224–55.
47. Peregrine Worsthorne, 'Too Much Freedom' in M. Cowling (ed.) *Conservative Essays*, pp. 141–54.
48. Grainger, 'Mrs. Thatcher's Last Stand', p. 5.

Chapter 6: The struggle for hegemony

1. Perry Anderson, 'Origins of the present crisis', *New Left Review*, 23 (1964) pp. 26–53; Tom Nairn, 'The Twilight of the British State', in *The Breakup of Britain* (London: New Left Books, 1981) and 'The Future of Britain's Crisis', *New Left Review*, 113/4 (1979) pp. 43–70.
2. Tom Nairn, 'Enoch Powell: the New Right', *New Left Review*, 61 (1970) pp. 3–27.
3. Robin Blackburn, 'The Heath Government: A new course for British Capitalism', *New Left Review*, 70 (1971) pp. 3–26.
4. Andrew Glyn and Bob Sutcliffe, *British Capitalism, Workers and the Profit Squeeze* (Harmondsworth: Penguin, 1972).
5. See Colin Leys, *Politics in Britain* (London: HEB, 1983); and Stuart Hall *et al.*, *Policing the Crisis* (London: Macmillan, 1978).
6. David Purdy, 'British Capitalism since the War', *Marxism Today*, 20:9 (1976) pp. 270–7 and 20:10 (1976) pp. 310–18.
7. Stuart Hall, 'Popular democratic versus authoritarian populism', in A. Hunt (ed.) *Marxism and Democracy* (London: Lawrence & Wishart, 1980).
8. Stuart Hall and Bill Schwarz, 'State and Society 1880–1930' in M. Langan and B. Schwarz, *Crises in the British State 1880–1930* (London: Hutchinson, 1985) pp. 7–32.
9. See S. Beer, *Modern British Politics* (London: Faber & Faber, 1965) and *Britain Against Itself* (New York: W. W. Norton, 1982); Keith Middlemas, *Politics in Industrial Society* (London: André Deutsch, 1979).

See also Bill Schwarz's assessment of Middlemass's work, 'Conservatives and Corporatism', *New Left Review*, 166 (1987) pp. 107–28.

10. Nicos Poulantzas, *State, Power, Socialism* (London: NLB, 1978); and Bob Jessop, *Nicos Poulantzas* (London: Macmillan, 1985).
11. Dominic Strinati, 'State intervention, the Economy, and the Crisis', in A. Stewart (ed.) *Contemporary Britain* (London: Routledge & Kegan Paul, 1983); and Stuart Hall *et al.*, *Policing the Crisis.*
12. Stuart Hall *et al.*, *Policing the Crisis*; 'The Great Moving Right Show', *Marxism Today* (1979) pp. 107–28 – revised version printed in S. Hall and M. Jacques (eds) *The Politics of Thatcherism* (London: Lawrence & Wishart, 1983); 'Popular democratic versus authoritarian populism', in Hunt (ed.) *Marxism and Democracy.*
13. M. Jacques & F. Mulhern (eds) *The Forward March of Labour Halted?* (London: Verso, 1981). Eric Hobsbawm's article was first published in *Marxism Today* (September 1978).
14. Raymond Williams in *The Forward March of Labour Halted?*, pp. 142–52.
15. See especially Eric Hobsbawm 'Labours' Lost Millions', *Marxism Today* (October 1983).
16. See Gavin Kitching, *Rethinking Socialism* (London: Methuen, 1983); Ernesto Laclau and Chantal Mouffe, *Hegemony and Socialist Strategy* (London: Verso, 1985). Strong criticism of these positions has come from Ellen Meiksins Wood, *The Retreat from Class* (London: Verso, 1986) and Ralph Miliband, 'The New Revisionism in Britain', *New Left Review*, 150 (1985) pp. 5–26. See also Ben Fine *et al.*, *Class Politics: An Answer to its Critics* (London: Central Books, 1985).
17. See the critics of Hobsbawm in Jacques and Mulhern (eds) *The Forward March of Labour Halted?*; and Wood, *The Retreat from Class.*
18. See Patrick Seyd, *The Rise and Fall of the Labour Left* (London: Macmillan, 1987).
19. Tony Benn, 'Who Dares Wins', *Marxism Today* 29:1 (January 1985) pp. 12–14. See also the reply by Stuart Hall.
20. This is discussed further below.
21. Patrick Hutber, *The Decline and Fall of the Middle Class and how it can fight back* (Harmondsworth: Penguin, 1977).
22. Roger King and N. Nugent, *Respectable Rebels* (London: Hodder & Stoughton, 1979).
23. Bob Jessop, Kevin Bonnett, Simon Bromley and Tom Ling, 'Authoritarian Populism, Two Nations, and Thatcherism', *New Left Review*, 147 (1984) pp. 32–60.
24. Andrew Glyn and John Harrison, *The British Economic Disaster* (London: Pluto, 1980).
25. The details of company donations to political parties and other organisations are listed every year in *Labour Research.*
26. See E. A. Brett, *The World Economy since the War* (London: Macmillan, 1985).
27. See John Ross, *Thatcher and Friends* (London: Pluto, 1983); also 'Does Thatcherism have a Future?', *International*, 7:2 (March 1982) pp. 4–10.
28. See H. Beynon (ed.) *Digging Deeper* (London: Verso, 1985).

29. See Geoffrey Ingham, *Capitalism Divided?* (London: Macmillan, 1984); and F. Longstreth, 'The City, Industry, and the State', in C. Crouch (ed.) *State and Economy in Contemporary Capitalism* (Oxford: Martin Robertson, 1979).
30. Ross's inclusion of construction as a sector that benefited from the policies of the Thatcher Government has been questioned by Overbeek in his book, *Global Capitalism and Britain's Decline*, University of Amsterdam.
31. Colin Leys, 'Thatcherism and British Manufacturing: A Question of hegemony', *New Left Review*, 151 (1985) pp. 5–25; Henk Overbeek, *Global Capitalism and Britain's Decline*; Bob Jessop, 'The mid-life crisis of Thatcherism and the Birth-pangs of post-Fordism', *New Socialist*, 36 (March 1986).
32. See the analysis in Charles Leadbeater and John Lloyd, *In Search of Work* (Harmondsworth: Penguin, 1987).
33. Ben Fine and Laurence Harris, *The Peculiarities of the British Economy* (London: Lawrence & Wishart, 1985).
34. Colin Leys, 'Thatcherism and British Manufacturing'.
35. Ibid., p. 16.
36. Stuart Hall *et al.*, *Policing the Crisis*.
37. See Tessa ten Tusscher, 'Is Thatcherism anti-feminism?' and John Solomos, 'Racism, Political Action and the State in Britain: Trends in political analysis', papers presented to the Political Studies Association Conference, April 1985.
38. See Miriam David, 'Moral and Maternal: the Family in the Right', Gill Seidel, 'Culture, Nation, and "Race" in the British and French New Right', and David Edgar, 'The Free or the Good', in Ruth Levitas (ed.) *The Ideology of the New Right* (Cambridge: Polity, 1986). See also Lynne Segal, 'The Heat in the Kitchen', in Hall and Jacques (eds) *The Politics of Thatcherism*.
39. Bea Campbell, *Iron Ladies* (London: Virago, 1987).
40. Miriam David, 'Moral and Maternal: the Family in the Right'.
41. Jean Gardiner, 'Women, Recession, and the Tories', in Hall and Jacques, *The Politics of Thatcherism*.
42. Peter Riddell, *The Thatcher Government* (Oxford: Basil Blackwell, 1985) p. 59.
43. Riddell's scepticism is shared by several other leading journalists including Ian Aitken, Hugo Young and Peter Jenkins. There are others, however, notably Brian Walden, Ronald Butt and Paul Johnson, who argue that the Thatcher Government has introduced radical and irreversible changes.
44. Richard Rose, *Do Parties Make a Difference?* (London: Macmillan, 1984). See also Dennis Kavanagh, *Thatcherism and British Politics*.
45. Christopher Hollis, 'The Merits and Defects of Marx', in G. Woodcock (ed.) *A Hundred Years of Revolution* (London: Porcupine Press, 1948) p. 87.
46. See Grahame Thompson, *The Conservatives' Economic Policy* (London: Croom Helm, 1986); Maurice Mullard, *The Politics of Public Expenditure*

(London: Croom Helm, 1987); Paul Mosley, *The Making of Economic Policy* (London: Wheatsheaf, 1984); and Jim Tomlinson, *Monetarism: Is there an alternative?* (Oxford: Basil Blackwell, 1986).
47. Bob Jessop *et al.*, 'Authoritarian Populism, Two Nations, and Thatcherism'; *New Left Review*, 147; 'Thatcherism and the Politics of hegemony: a reply to Stuart Hall', *New Left Review*, 153 (1985) pp. 87–101; 'Popular Capitalism, Flexible Accumulation, and Left Strategy', *New Left Review*, 165 (1987) pp. 104–22. See also Fiona Atkins, 'Thatcherism, populist authoritarianism, and the search for a new left political strategy', *Capital and Class*, 28 (1986) pp. 25–48.
48. Bob Jessop, 'The Transformation of the State in Post-War Britain', in R. Scase (ed.) *The State in Western Europe* (London: Croom Helm, 1980).
49. See Bob Jessop, *The Capitalist State* (Oxford: Martin Robertson, 1982) pp. 244–5.
50. See Bill Jordan, *The State* (Oxford: Basil Blackwell, 1985).
51. Stuart Hall, 'Authoritarian Populism: a reply to Jessop *et al.*', *New Left Review*, 151 (1985) pp. 115–24.

Chapter 7:   Politics, class, and ideology

1. See Anthony King, 'Margaret Thatcher: the Style of a Prime Minister', in *The British Prime Minister* (London: Macmillan, 1985); Philip Norton and Arthur Aughey, *Conservatives and Conservatism* (London: Temple Smith, 1987); Dennis Kavanagh, *Thatcherism and British Politics* (Oxford: Clarendon Press, 1987); and Martin Burch, 'Mrs. Thatcher's Approach to Leadership in Government', *Parliamentary Affairs*, 36:4 (1983).
2. See Doreen Massey, 'The Contours of Victory', *Marxism Today* 27:7 (July 1983) pp. 16–19; and 'Heartlands of Defeat', *Marxism Today*, 31:7 (July 1987) pp. 18–23. For psephological analysis of the Conservative vote see Dunleavy and Husbands, *British Democracy at the Crossroads* (London: George Allen & Unwin, 1985); R. Rose and I. McAllister, *Voters Begin to Choose* (London: Sage, 1986); A. Heath *et al.*, *How Britain Votes* (Oxford: Pergamon Press, 1985).
3. The term comes from Peter Glotz. See Andrew Gamble, 'The Great Divide', *Marxism Today*, 31:3 (March 1987) pp. 12–19.
4. See Jessop *et al.*, 'Authoritarian Populism, Two Nations, and Thatcherism'.
5. See Patrick Dunleavy and Chris Husbands, *British Democracy at the Crossroads*.
6. R. Jowell *et al.* (eds) *British Social Attitudes: the 1985 Report* (London: Gower, 1985). The most recent, the 1987 report, appears to confirm that the broad trends away from Thatcherite values identified in the earlier surveys are continuing. John Curtice argues, however, that this trend is less important for voting decisions than the level of 'economic optimism' which most voters now feel. See 'Interim Report: Party

Politics', in *British Social Attitudes: the 1987 Report* (London: Gower, 1987).

7. Knighthoods were given to loyal Thatcherite tabloid editors like Larry Lamb and David English. For an analysis of the press see J. Curran and J. Seaton, *Power Without Responsibility* (London: Methuen, 1985).

8. See Colin Leys, 'Thatcherism and Manufacturing', and the 1985 report of the Select Committee of the House of Lords set up to examine the results of the run-down of manufacturing on the British balance of payments. For a summary of its conclusions see Lord Aldington, 'Britain's Manufacturing Industry', *Royal Bank of Scotland Review*, 151 (1986) pp. 3–13. See also the different views collected in David Coates and John Hillard (eds) *The Economic Revival of Modern Britain: The Debate between Left and Right* (London: Edward Elgar, 1987).

9. See Ross, *Thatcher and Friends*, and *Labour Research*.

10. The concept of the social market economy was at first adopted by the Centre for Policy Studies. See *Why Britain needs a social market economy* (London: CPS, 1975). It has since been appropriated by David Owen and the SDP.

11. See Scott Lash and John Urry, *The End of Organised Capitalism* (Cambridge: Polity, 1987); and Henk Overbeek, *Global Capitalism and Britain's Decline*.

12. See Stephen Blank, 'The Politics of Foreign Economic Policy', *International Organisation*, 31:4 (1977) pp. 673–722. See also Joel Krieger, *Reagan, Thatcher, and the politics of Decline* (Cambridge: Polity, 1986).

13. Hugo Radice, 'The National Economy: a Keynesian myth?' *Capital and Class*, 22 (1984) pp. 111–40.

14. Foreign investments, both direct and portfolio, increased from £38 billion at the end of 1978 to £177 billion at the end of 1985.

15. Asset sales had realised £12 billion up to 1985. See Chapter 4.

16. For assessments of the Thatcher Government's economic record see C. F. Pratten, 'Mrs. Thatcher's Economic Legacy', in K. Minogue and M. Biddiss (eds) *Thatcherism: Personality and Politics* (London: Macmillan, 1987); Peter Riddell, *The Thatcher Government* (Oxford: Basil Blackwell, 1985); and Grahame Thompson, *The Conservatives' Economic Policy* (London: Croom Helm, 1986).

17. See Colin Leys, 'Thatcherism and Manufacturing', *New Left Review*, 151 (1985) pp. 5–25.

18. Perry Anderson, 'The figures of descent', *New Left Review*, 161 (1987), pp. 20–77.

19. Anderson, 'The figures of descent' p. 77.

20. Sir John Hoskyns as reported in the *Daily Telegraph*, 27 July 1986.

21. Patrick Dunleavy and Rod Rhodes, 'Government beyond Whitehall' in Drucker, *Developments in British Politics 2*.

22. Antonio Gramsci, *The Prison Notebooks* (London: Lawrence & Wishart, 1971) p. 161.

Further reading

Anderson, P., 'The Figures of Descent', *New Left Review*, 161 (1987) pp. 20–77.

Barry, N., *The New Right* (London: Croom Helm, 1987).

Behrens, R., *The Conservative Party from Heath to Thatcher* (London: Saxon House, 1980).

Bell, D. (ed.) *The Conservative Government 1979–84* (London: Croom Helm, 1985).

Blake, R., *The Conservative Party from Peel to Thatcher* (London: Fontana, 1985).

Bosanquet, N., *After the New Right* (London: HEB, 1983).

Brett, E., *The World Economy Since the War* (London: Macmillan, 1985).

Bruce-Gardyne, J., *Mrs. Thatcher's First Administration* (London: Macmillan, 1984).

Bulpitt, J., 'The discipline of the New Democracy: Mrs. Thatcher's Domestic Statecraft', *Political Studies*, 34:1 (1985) pp. 19–39.

Campbell, B., *Iron Ladies* (London: Virago, 1987).

Coates, D., *The Context of British Politics* (London: Hutchinson, 1984).

Cosgrave, P., *Margaret Thatcher: A Tory and her Party* (London: Hutchinson, 1978).

Cosgrave, P., *Thatcher: The First Term* (London: Bodley Head, 1985).

Cowling, M. (ed.) *Conservative Essays* (London: Cassell, 1978).

Dearlove, J. and P. Saunders, *Introduction to British Politics* (Cambridge: Polity, 1984).

Drucker, H. *et al.* (eds) *Developments in British Politics 2* (London: Macmillan, 1986).

Dunleavy, P. and C. Husbands, *British Democracy at the Crossroads* (London: George Allen & Unwin, 1985).

Fine, B. and L. Harris, *Peculiarities of the British Economy* (London: Lawrence & Wishart, 1985).

Gilmour, I., *Inside Right* (London: Hutchinson, 1970).

Gilmour, I., *Britain Can Work* (Oxford: Martin Robertson, 1983).

Glyn, A. and J. Harrison, *The British Economic Disaster* (London: Pluto, 1980).

Greenleaf, W. H., *The British Political Tradition Vol I: The Rise of Collectivism, Vol II: The Ideological Heritage* (London: Methuen, 1983).

Hall, S. *et al.*, *Policing the Crisis* (London: Macmillan, 1978).

Hall, S. and M. Jacques (eds) *The Politics of Thatcherism* (London: Lawrence & Wishart, 1983).

Holmes, M., *The First Thatcher Government* (London: Wheatsheaf, 1985).

Ingham, G., *Capitalism Divided* (London: Macmillan, 1984).

Jenkins, P., *Mrs. Thatcher's Revolution* (London: Cape, 1987).

Jessop, B. *et al.*, 'Authoritarian Populism, Two Nations, and Thatcherism', *New Left Review*, 147 (1984) pp. 32–60.

Johnson, R., *The Politics of Recession* (London: Macmillan, 1985).

Joseph, K., *Stranded on the Middle Ground* (London: CPS, 1976).

Kavanagh, D., *Thatcherism and British Politics* (Oxford: Clarendon Press, 1987).

Keegan, W., *Mrs. Thatcher's Economic Experiment* (London: Allen Lane, 1984).

King, A., 'Margaret Thatcher: the style of a Prime Minister', in A. King (ed.) *The British Prime Minister* (London: Macmillan, 1985).

Krieger, J., *Reagan, Thatcher, and the Politics of Decline* (Cambridge: Polity, 1986).

Langan, M. and B. Schwarz (eds) *Crises in the British State* (London: Hutchinson, 1985).

Layton-Henry, Z. (ed.) *Conservative Party Politics* (London: Macmillan, 1980).

Levitas, R. (ed.) *The Ideology of the New Right* (Cambridge: Polity, 1986).

Leys, C., *Politics in Britain* (London: Heinemann, 1983).

Leys, C., 'Thatcherism and British Manufacturing', *New Left Review*, 151 (1985) pp. 5–25.

Nairn, T., *The Breakup of Britain* (London: Verso, 1981).

Norton, P. and A. Aughey, *Conservatives and Conservatism* (London: Temple Smith, 1981).

Overbeek, H., *Global Capitalism and Britain's Decline* (University of Amsterdam, 1988).

Owen, G. (ed.) *The Thatcher Years* (London: Financial Times, 1987).

Powell, E., *Freedom and Reality* (Kingswood: Elliott Rightway Books, 1969).

Riddell, P., *The Thatcher Government* (Oxford: Blackwell, 1985).

Ross, J., *Thatcher and Friends* (London: Pluto, 1983).

Seldon, A. (ed.) 'The Thatcher Years', *Contemporary Record*, 1:3 (1987) pp. 2–31.

Thompson, G., *The Conservatives' Economic Policy* (London: Croom Helm, 1986).

Wapshott, N. and G. Brock, *Thatcher* (London: Futura, 1983).

Index

260